Advance Acclaim for
A Spirituality of Resistance...

"Roger Gottlieb's eloquent plea for more spirituality in a world of constant upheavals will touch the reader's heart and move it to moral commitment."
— ELIE WIESEL

"This book is a brilliant and important challenge to those who have developed an inner spiritual life while giving up on social change, on the one hand, as well as to people who think spirituality has little to offer to the movements for social justice and peace, on the other hand. In a profound and engaging way Gottlieb pushes us forward to confront a central question for the new millennium: how to move spirituality into practical world-transformation. This book should be in the hands of everyone in this society looking for spiritual guidance or a way to rescue politics from its current doldrums."
— RABBI MICHAEL LERNER, editor, *Tikkun;* author of *The Politics of Meaning*

"Gottlieb understands the reality of ecocide and the complicity of all of us in it, and he offers us a spirituality that unblinkingly faces the real evil that surrounds and pervades us — and resists. This book is a true spiritual guide for our day."
— JOHN COBB, Claremont College, author of *For the Common Good*

"In contrast to more passive brands of spirituality, Gottlieb invokes the power of anger, using it like a burning sword to cut through the numbness of denial. The power of this book lies in the author's depth of anguish and confirmation of resistance as a spiritual path. No one else before has been bold enough to link the moral horrors of the Holocaust with the devastating losses of the Ecological Slaughter. Disturbing and engaging, the book insists that spirituality can and should inform political activism. Gottlieb's own personal struggle with these questions is authentic and expressed with heart. Against the easy social preference for romantic nature, Gottlieb offers a spirituality that is more palpable, meaningful and ultimately more effective in protecting the planet we call home."
— STEPHANIE KAZA, author of *Encounters with Trees*, University of Vermont

"Fascinating and compelling... Beyond acknowledging denial and avoidance is the challenge to seek adequate answers amidst enormous human suffering and environmental destruction. This is a remarkable book that wrestles with compelling honesty with these key questions for our era."
— MARY EVELYN TUCKER, editor, *Buddhism and Ecology*, Bucknell University

A
SPIRITUALITY
of
RESISTANCE

Other books by Roger S. Gottlieb

History and Subjectivity: The Transformation of Marxist Theory

Marxism 1844–1990: Origins, Betrayal, Rebirth

Joining Hands: Politics and Religion Together for Social Change

Books edited by Roger S. Gottlieb

An Anthology of Western Marxism: From Lukacs and Gramsci to
Socialist-Feminism

Thinking the Unthinkable: Meanings of the Holocaust

A New Creation: America's Contemporary Spiritual Voices

Radical Philosophy: Tradition, Countertradition, Politics

This Sacred Earth: Religion, Nature, Environment

The Ecological Community: Environmental Challenges for Philosophy, Politics,
and Morality

Deep Ecology and World Religions: New Essays on Common Ground
(with David L. Barnhill)

Liberating Faith: Religious Voices for Justice, Peace, and Ecological Wisdom

ROGER S. GOTTLIEB

A
SPIRITUALITY
of
RESISTANCE

*Finding a Peaceful Heart and
Protecting the Earth*

ROWMAN & LITTLEFIELD PUBLISHERS, INC.
Lanham • Boulder • New York • Oxford

ROWMAN & LITTLEFIELD PUBLISHERS, INC.

Published in the United States of America
by Rowman & Littlefield Publishers, Inc.
A wholly owned subsidary of The Rowman & Littlefield Publishing Group, Inc.
4501 Forbes Boulevard, Suite 200, Lanham, Maryland 20706
www.rowmanlittlefield.com

PO Box 317
Oxford
OX2 9RU, UK

Copyright © 2003 by The Rowman & Littlefield Publishing Group, Inc.
Originally published in 1999 by The Crossroad Publishing Company

British Library Cataloguing in Publication Information Available

The cloth edition of this book was previously catalogued by the Library of
Congress as follows:

Gottlieb, Roger S.
    Spirituality and resistance: finding a peaceful heart and protecting the
earth / Roger S. Gottlieb.
        p. cm.
    Includes bibliographical references.
    ISBN 0-7425-3283-6 (pbk.: alk. paper)
    1. Spirituality. 2. Human ecology—religious aspects. 3. Religion and
justice. 4. Holocaust, Jewish (1939–1945). I. Title.

BL624.G67 1998
291.2—dc21   98–41350

Printed in the United States of America
⊖™ The paper used in this publication meets the minimum requirements of American
National Standard for Information Sciences—Permanence of Paper for Printed Library
Materials, ANSI/NISO Z39.48-1992.

To Miriam

for her fierce wisdom,
her brilliant tenderness,
and her radiant heart

Contents

Acknowledgments

One of the central ideas of this book is that what is most precious about our own lives is bound up with the fate of others. Whatever its implications for the rest of the world, that idea certainly holds true for the making of *A Spirituality of Resistance*. I have received inspiration, instruction, aid, and comfort from many people.

To begin with, I must acknowledge three voices that have shaped my basic ideas about spirituality, social life, and how the two connect. Søren Kierkegaard and Elie Wiesel are mentioned often here, Karl Marx not at all; but all three are present in virtually everything that I have written.

My effort to comprehend the environmental crisis was initially shaped by the writings of Bill McKibben and Joanna Macy. I owe a great debt to their courage and intelligence.

Many years ago, working with other members of the Boston Committee to Challenge Anti-Semitism, I first began to understand how focusing on the reality of resistance could change our sense of the moral and spiritual meaning of the Holocaust. I am grateful to them for the work we did together.

This book has been through many different stages and forms. Cecelia Cancellero helped me see that it was — or could be — a book about spirituality.

Many colleagues, friends, and strangers were kind enough to look over earlier drafts and give me valuable feedback: Lisa Lebduska, Stephanie Kaza, John Zeugner, Bettina Bergo, Raphael Sassower, Peter Canavo, Marianne Janack, Klaus Fischer, and Gary Cohen. David Barnhill, Michael Lerner, Richard Schmitt, and Mark Wallace went over the entire manuscript in the last stages, making comments that vastly improved the whole thing.

David Abram, Bill McKibben, Mary Evelyn Tucker, Arthur Waskow, Stephanie Kaza, and Michael Lerner graciously wrote letters of support to publishers.

Worcester Polytechnic provided a half-year sabbatical that gave me some clear time to think and read; and during that time the Boston

University School of Theology gave me a room (and a library card) of my own.

Audiences at the American Academy of Religion, the Boston Theological Institute, the University of Colorado, Swarthmore College, Yale University, the University of Maine, Norwich University, and the Alabama Sierra Club heard drafts of chapters 3 and 4 and told me what they thought of them.

An earlier version of chapter 2 appeared in Roger S. Gottlieb, ed., *The Ecological Community* (Routledge, 1997).

Elaine Markson was a wonderfully supportive agent, and Mike Leach of Crossroad an enthusiastic editor. Every author treasures the kind of encouragement they offered.

The moral inspiration for this book comes from two sources. The natural world, with its flowers and rain, birdcalls and mountain streams, is my home — the earth on which I would live with a peaceful heart. Those people who against all odds have resisted the Holocaust, the environmental crisis, and all the other forms of needless suffering teach me what it might mean to do so.

Finally, I owe a debt of intellectual comradeship, spiritual guidance, nurturing love, patient tolerance, and a smack in the head when it's called for to my wife, Miriam Greenspan. Miriam's passion for the fate of the earth helped inspire my own. She went over every page of this book, toning down my overstatements, challenging my confusions, pruning my prose, and deepening every insight that's here. While I am enormously grateful to her for help in those ways, what is most precious to me is that in our understanding of life and death, spirituality and social life, grief and joy, we have over the years moved closer and closer together. Insofar as any book represents a life and not just a mind, this one is hers as well as my own.

INTRODUCTION

A Peaceful Heart,
an Angry Prayer

The sun that glints through the dusty windows of my tiny writing room lights up the dust motes floating in the air — the dust that is partly harmless dirt and partly the residue of air pollution. Sounds of cars, a cold November breeze working its way past cracks in the insulation of this solid old house, and, beyond the porch, the bare branches of tall trees framed by a light blue sky. The morning newspaper tells me that a coalition of industry leaders is mounting fierce opposition to EPA calls for stricter controls on emissions of the tiny particulates that lodge in people's lungs. I wonder how the outcome of the battle will affect my daughter's asthma: my younger daughter, the one whose mysterious congenital disabilities may themselves be an effect of chemical pollution.

This is, quite simply, the world in which I live. It is my earth, which I share with people and dolphins, squirrels and earthworms. I love it; and I fear for its future. I love it; and I mourn, over and over, for the pain of past and present.

I will live here, between birth and death, on what seems to me to be our only home. And on it I would find a way to love and be loved, to care for trees and owls and friends and strangers. I would, if I could, do so in a way that connects me — morally and spiritually — to both the human and more-than-human beings who surround me. And I would make that connection with a peaceful heart: entrusting my life to an essential goodness that is not dependent on my possessions and ac-complishments, confident that ultimately all I care for is protected by a Spirit of Love. In that trust and confidence I could let go of some of my more petty insanities: the endless pursuit of recognition, the childish dependence on pleasure, the attachment to trivial animosities. My fear for my children's future, along with my grief for the multitude of sorrows suffered on this planet, could be assuaged.

1

Like many others, I believe that spirituality is the way to that peaceful heart — to a better and happier existence for myself and for all whose lives I touch. But the prospect of peace — of trust in myself and confidence in a benign universe — is darkened by the shadows of humanity's collective crimes: the Holocaust, countless other nationalist wars and ethnic atrocities, the lethal grind of daily social injustice. And now there is the specter of ecocide: the endless killing of the trees, the pesticide residues in mother's milk, the poisonous lead levels of the air in Manila. Our modernized world system has decimated "primitive" tribes and cultures simply by altering their environment; and the undeveloped and developed alike face fundamental changes in the atmosphere, increased danger from sunlight, the bleak prospect of a strangely warmer (and much less diverse) planet.

Facing and responding to these perils is part of what it means to live on *this* earth. What we make of them, and how we respond, are an essential part of the vision of spirituality contained in this book. I am writing about the struggle to find a spiritual heart in a dark time: a path whose authentic essence is the honest recognition of — and opposition to — the brutal and sacrilegious desecration of the earth and all who dwell upon it. It is about the attempt to bring into being a personal identity that takes past and present forms of social evil seriously and knows that it is living on an earth scarred by unjustified and irrevocable loss. As other spiritual paths may center on love of God or systematic prayer, on meditation or revelation, this one is bound by responsibility to protect the earth. In this path, spirituality and resistance to the destruction of life — human and nonhuman alike — are inextricably connected. It is, we might say, a spirituality of resistance.

My own religious background was a watered-down version of Reform Judaism. I reached adulthood untouched by most of traditional Jewish liturgy, theology, or spirituality. For a long time Jewish observance meant little to me, as I explored the lonely paradoxes of Kierkegaard, Buddhist meditation, and how the physical postures of yoga could loosen a stiff body and calm a jumpy mind. I spent years trying to figure out what kind of Jew I wanted to be and what kind of Judaism might fit my particular blend of New Age and New Left sensibilities. In my thirties I discovered the long tradition of Jewish socialism, studied the Holocaust, and found services where the rabbi went barefoot and played the guitar, a place where the other Jews were more like me than in the glitzy suburban synagogue of my youth. Once again, at least during the High Holy days, I began to attend services.

And so, some years ago, praying at Yom Kippur services, I encountered "Neshmat," one of the traditional prayers of Judaism. Read on the mornings of Sabbath and major holidays, it begins "The soul of every living thing shall bless your name, Adonai, our God, and the spirit of all flesh shall glorify, and exalt you...."

That particular Yom Kippur morning was not so very long after I had buried my son, born with severe brain damage and dead following sixty-five days on the neurology floor of Boston's Children's Hospital. It was not so long after a time of intense study of the Holocaust. My mind suddenly flooded with images of Aaron's seizures, of his choking on my wife's breast milk that he couldn't take in even through a tube in his nose, of his final days gasping for air. I thought of piled bodies in the concentration camps, of the Jewish resisters facing tanks with ancient pistols in their hands, of Jews who escaped to the forests only to be murdered by the Polish underground. Years of studying oppression and injustice offered countless other images: victims of rape and terror, of bureaucratic tyranny and laboratory experiments, of ecocide and ethnic cleansing. And as my mouth mumbled the words (in English, for my Hebrew has always been primitive at best) my mind screamed out: "*Every* living thing praises you God? Aaron, too weak to cough, the oxygen mist trying to ease his breathing, praises you? The dead of Treblinka praise you? All the tortured bodies, how do they glorify your name?" I sobbed, with grief for my losses, for all our losses. Along with the grief there was an enormous, helpless rage: at the killers, at a universe in which all this could happen, at God — at the very thought that "every living thing" could praise such a God.

Yet it was a time in my life when I had turned back to Judaism to find some solace for my pain, and when I sought to pray. Exactly to what I wasn't sure. Not, clearly, to a masculine creator God. Perhaps only to awaken my better self, or because I hoped the practice of prayer could arouse a gratitude, a moral seriousness, and an awe for the mystery of life that might take me out of my fears and insecurities. Perhaps because I felt that just possibly there was some kind of Power that could heal my heart. Whatever the reasons, and I am still not sure of them all, I wanted to pray. And this prayer had touched me deeply. My whole body shook as I said the words. But it did nothing so much as fill me with rage.

For weeks afterward I wrestled with the experience, trying to make sense of it. Then a simple thought occurred to me: just as some prayers are sung, and in a sense the traditional melodies through which they are expressed are essential to the prayers themselves, so a prayer might arouse emotions which are also part of it.

In this case my anger at God was not something I had to uproot before I could say the prayer. It was, quite simply, part of the prayer itself. Numbness, a false humility I didn't really feel, a forced truce with the Power-That-Be — these things couldn't have been part of what I was doing. But a simple, direct anger, a response that took God seriously enough to take Him to task for the suffering and loss I didn't understand and didn't accept, these had, I realized, a place in any spiritual life that was going to take place on this particular planet. And they would have a place whether that spiritual life centered on a particular God or on the pursuit of an Inner Truth or a Cosmic Energy. The emotional dynamic, and the spiritual dilemma, remain the same.

How are we to have a peaceful heart when our prayers include our anger? When along with love and joy the world fills us with rage, grief, and fear? When the looming specter of environmental damage makes us all want to hide our heads? *A Spirituality of Resistance* emerges from the struggle to answer these questions.

This spiritual path is also meant to resolve some distressing tensions between different sides of my own temperament: between the part of me that searches for peace — and the part that rages at injustice; between the part that would cultivate a forgiving heart — and the part that doesn't know how to let go of my anger at all the evil that has been done; between the part that tries to accept the world as it is — and the part that cannot affirm a world which contains so much unjustified pain.

A spirituality of resistance can also help bridge the gap between two frequently, but perhaps unnecessarily, opposed groups in the larger society: between the political fighters, animated by the struggle against oppression — and the spiritual seekers, who know you have to change yourself before you can change the world; between those who believe that any talk of spiritual values is just a mask for personal gratification or escapism — and those who look at all the revolutions that have sunk into brutal tyrannies and believe that such is the fate of every "politically correct" social movement. *A Spirituality of Resistance* speaks for both sides of these divisions: the search for peace — and the courage to rage; the task of changing ourselves — and the struggle to heal the world; learning how to let go of our own pain — and how not to shut out the pain of others.

But these larger issues really come later. We begin with a simpler, more basic, more familiar question that often seems to animate spiritual seekers and teachers alike: how can I live with less pain and more happiness?

This kind of spiritual perspective focuses on our daily pains, frustrations, disappointments, griefs, and longings and confidently assures us that these distressing states of mind are not essential to who we are. We can leave them behind as easily as taking our hands from in front of our eyes, if only we will. In a spiritual life we need no longer make ourselves miserable, no longer create our own depression or succumb to pointless anxiety, no longer turn our back on the preciousness of each moment that has been given to us.

The psychological truth of these teachings is, for many of us, immediately appealing (even if actually following the advice of these teachers proves not so easy!). Consider the notion of gratitude, or of being satisfied with what one has, alluded to by both the Talmud and Steindl-Rast. We find, for instance, that in traditional Judaism the first thing one does, before even stepping out of bed, is to say a simple prayer of thanks for living through the night. ("Thank you God ... for returning my soul to my body.") In other words, even if your back hurts, or you have to face the dentist or the I.R.S. right after breakfast, or you had a terrible fight with your husband last night, or you are in prison or a hospital, at least you are alive.

Isn't it the sad truth that we rarely wake up with words of gratitude on our lips? Yet isn't it obvious that if we did we'd be much happier? So much of the time there is, it seems, so much that we can find to be ungrateful for: the unwashed dishes from last night's dinner, the mess in the kids' room, fears for our aging parents, the arrogant boss at the office, the asthmatic cough echoing from my daughter's bedroom. With no effort at all, we can focus on how unsatisfactory all these are. But where will all this displeasure lead? If it is our habit of mind to focus on what we want but don't have, how long will satisfaction last when we actually get something we want? The very real relief that comes when my daughter's temperature, after four days of fever, finally gets down to 98.8 lasts until the next round of coughing. The pleasure of graduating from law school, after three years of drudgery in the library, gives way to anxiety over getting hired or making partner. The enjoyable prospect of a long weekend in the country will be swallowed up by the subsequent resentment at the boring workweek ahead.

Wouldn't we be happier if we simply felt grateful for what we had, if we took the same powers of concentration which rivet us on the disappointing and switched the focus to all the goodness that we do possess: that we are alive, that our bodies (to some extent at least!) work, that there are people and animals and trees in the world, that this new day may hold a surprise, a wondrous mystery that will illuminate the meaning of our lives?

In the message of gratitude we see something of the essence of spiritual teachings. Its simple and profound message is that by acts of mind and will we can deeply alter our lives. We are, the teachings go on, mistaken to think that the quality of those lives depends nearly so much on what happens to us, or on what we own, possess, achieve, or drive; on our bank account, marriage status, kids' grades, or the size of our waistlines. What is really important is the attitude we take to all these things. If we want, as we so often say we do, to be happy, to experience a little peace, to feel at one with ourselves, then we must undertake an inner journey: toward gratitude and acceptance; toward opening our eyes to miracles instead of closing them to everything but our own desires, attachments, and resentments; toward compassion for others instead of jealousy, contempt, competition, or fear.

Of course this message will mean little to people who are fundamentally satisfied with their lives the way they are. If our basic approach to existence is spontaneous pleasure, simple enjoyment, and (semi-) constant delight, we need make no changes. Alternatively, if we believe that today's temporary displeasure (which, we must admit, does seem to keep recurring) will be assuaged by the next love affair, raise, book contract, vacation, or new dress, then the spiritual message is not for us.

We are called by spiritual teachings only if we have begun to feel that in fact there is something basically wrong with how we have been thinking about our lives, about what makes for contentment and about where we have been looking for happiness. In response to a spiritual call, we may reflect on our experience and determine that the times we felt most authentically, vibrantly, alive had little to do with narrow forms of control, clinging attachments to personal relationships or buying stuff. Images of spirituality seem to offer a kind of freedom from needless pain, a spacious vista in which we need not be constrained by the bars of a psychic cage we ourselves have made.

Once we respond to those teachings, we start to see our lives — at least in part — as unfolding along a spiritual path. This path, it turns out, is complex and often confusing. Movement along it is neither simple nor direct. Its pattern is often two steps forward and one back — or one forward and two back.

For instance, we find that a certain meditation practice focuses our energies and calms our mind. We are able to relax after a day's work, feel less pressure during exam week, take a break from the screaming kids, or even find a bit of calm during a family illness. We buy the proper meditation cushion, set up a special place in the house to practice, or join a local group. We wonder how we ever could have survived without it. Yet then gradually, bit by bit, it starts to slip away. One night we go to a late movie, another we have friends over and drink a bit too much wine, the third we are "just too upset" to meditate. Before long we notice, to our surprise, that while things piled up at the office and at home we haven't meditated for weeks. "We ought to meditate more," I've often said to my wife, wondering how I'd let the impulse melt away.

Perhaps we begin to take the practices of a particular religion seriously. We go to religious services, find a priest or rabbi we admire, pore through holy texts. For a time these feel vital and significant. But then, sadly, they begin to empty of content. We keep on with them but notice that our pattern of being impatient with the kids or harsh with subordinates at work still exists. Religion isn't making us very different in our ordinary lives. We continue to go to church or synagogue, but what we are doing doesn't seem to open our hearts. The initial sense of excitement has worn off. Our religious observance becomes regular, familiar, ordinary . . . insignificant.

We may have some deeply mystical experience: of God's love, or bliss, or understanding our own perfect place in the cosmos. Afterward we promise ourselves that we will never again succumb to petty jealousy or foolish irritation. At last we see. We understand. We realize. And *this* time, we will remember. (The philosopher Pascal, it is said, sewed the image of a star into his clothes to remind himself of such an experience.) And then we find that gradually, almost imperceptibly, we return to our ordinary mind, with its familiar cares, preoccupations, and periods of selfishness or self-indulgence.

So the round continues. Spiritual teachers emphasize that this is a task for our whole lives, not one that will be over in a day or a year. While a few rare souls may become "enlightened" and never again fall prey to the habits of mind that obscure the wonders of the world, most of us go in circles. And even if those circles take the form of ever-higher spirals, we may still oscillate closer to and further away from what we seek. We still gain and lose our hold on gratitude, peacefulness, acceptance, and a loving heart. Yet as long as we remain on a spiritual journey, we hold on to its basic insight. We have come to believe, at least part of the time, that building our lives around material possessions, social status, physical appearance, or sensual gratification will bring (at best) only fleeting, often quasi-addictive, pleasure; at worst, they create disappointment and loss. Anything like lasting contentment cannot be found in them. Even personal relationships, unless we approach them with a sense of genuine serenity, will eventually lead to deep frustration; for we will end up fruitlessly seeking from others what must come from ourselves. It is in our spiritual identity that we seek to develop that which must be rooted within ourselves: a basic acceptance of who we are and an essential appreciation and embrace of the world. This embrace may center on God or Goddess, on a particularly exalted teacher or simply on the earth itself. In any case, it leads us back to gratitude and wonder for the daily miracles of creation.

Thus far, a spirituality of resistance can travel with other, more familiar, approaches. But then their paths diverge.

For in response to our ignorance and self-imposed discomfort, spiritual perspectives may err by directing us exclusively or mainly toward a purely interior self-examination, an inner transformation, a personal peace. We may be asked to accept the world as it is, without wondering how it can be made better; counseled to make our peace with things that in fact should not be lived with, but resisted and overturned. We may be asked to worship God, but not to wonder how God might respond to questions about suffering and injustice. Instead of helping us open to the world, such attitudes shut us off to whatever is unpleasant or threatening.

A spirituality of resistance, while recognizing the importance of working on ourselves, also directs us toward outer examination, outer transformation, and the pursuit of justice in the world. For a spirituality of resistance, the costs of living a purely "inner," purely "personal," spiritual life are too high: too much denial and avoidance of social realities, too much blindness to our own roles in those realities. These costs cripple any attempt to make spiritual progress. To find a peaceful heart, I will suggest, we need to live on *this* earth: fully conscious of what is happening on it, actively resisting that which we know to be evil or destructively ignorant.

If there is a central problem to the essentially private form of spiritual life, it might be summed up by a term used by the Christian existentialist philosopher Søren Kierkegaard. Kierkegaard is perhaps best-known for introducing the phrase "leap of faith," but his use of the term "aesthetic" to define a host of serious problems that can arise in spiritual life is particularly illuminating here. For Kierkegaard experiences, values, or ways of living are "aesthetic" when we believe that what is most important about them is the way they make us feel. An aesthetic experience is one evaluated purely in terms of how pleasurable or painful, interesting or boring it is. An aesthetic person is one who focuses on pleasing experiences as the goal of life and seeks above all to avoid displeasing ones. When adolescents say they hate school because it bores them, or middle-aged men dread the tedium of opera because the music leaves them cold, they are concerned with the aesthetic.

Now of course it makes sense to be aesthetically concerned with a concert: if the music doesn't move us, why bother? But it is another matter, warned Kierkegaard, when religion is thought of or pursued in aesthetic terms. For the life of the spirit is essentially a passionate, personal transformation, a commitment to a certain kind of truth about what we believe is most important in life. It is not, essentially, about how we feel. In other words, since spirituality speaks to our pain, loneliness, and frustration, the danger is that we will come to see the goal of spirituality as simply making us feel better. Our spiritual lives then become focused on the pursuit of the pleasant, a pursuit that will never be lastingly successful.

Examples of aesthetic spirituality are not hard to come by. The loveliness of religious music, for instance, can transport us to an ethereal reverie. As we listen, our communion with God is sweet, and we are soothed by thoughts of divine love. Of course there is nothing wrong with feeling good for a few minutes, but a difficulty arises when such feelings are equated with spirituality. What then happens when reality does not feel so good, when some task or dilemma raises its ugly head and confronts us? Will we retreat to that dreamy melody that brought us to God? When things are no longer agreeable will we feel that God is absent? To keep in touch with God, will we learn to avoid what is unpleasant?

A meditation class is held outside on a warm spring day. Our breathing slows and evens out. The soft chirping of birds, the gentle breeze rustling newly budded trees, perhaps even the distant sound of a brook tumbling over small stones — all these support our efforts to quiet and focus the mind. And in this setting the mind does become more serene.

The aesthetic move — the aesthetic mistake — is to think that these feelings of peacefulness are the heart of meditation, and that if we can only find the time, and similar calm, unpolluted places, then our journey toward meditative peace and spiritual development will be well under-way. So meditation centers are built in beautiful settings, far from traffic, poverty, toxic wastes, or anything else that will break the spell of the "pleasant." We learn a mantra or to focus on our breath, but rarely are we instructed to concentrate on an image of people starving or of chil-dren drinking polluted water. Few think to build meditation centers — as Joanna Macy suggests — at radioactive waste sites. As a consequence, it is not openness to life that we learn, but another version of the pur-suit of pleasure. Meditation becomes a relaxation technique and not a source of real spiritual development. Unfortunately, while of course all of us need some time to retreat from a painful world, no meditation practice can be ultimately "successful" if it screens out the unpleasant things of life.

We read spiritual literature. The stories entrance us. They show us how, with the proper attitudes of detachment and acceptance, things work out for the best. Consider, for instance, the following, told by a widely read and respected contemporary Buddhist teacher:

> I read somewhere about a family who had only one son. They were very poor. This son was extremely precious to them, and the only thing that mattered to his family was that he bring them some financial support and prestige. Then he was thrown from a horse and crippled. It seemed like the end of their lives. Two weeks after that, the army came into the village and took away all the healthy, strong men to fight in the war, and this young man was allowed to stay behind and take care of his family.
>
> Life is like that. We don't know anything. We call something bad; we call it good. But really we just don't know.

There is much truth here. Things often do have a different meaning than we suppose. But is this particular outcome supposed to be thought of as "good"? Is the dominant meaning of the tale that one family had a good experience? Or is it the sadness of men conscripted to fight in wars? The problem is not that this teacher is trying to get us to learn to acknowledge our ultimate ignorance of the meaning of what hap-pens to us. The problem is that the social reality of armies and violent conflict is taken as a background, a setting, for the unfolding of a spiritual message about our personal spiritual path. The essence of this story seems to be its focus on being happy with what you have or at least suspending judgment on the vicissitudes of life — when it is perhaps some kind of judgment about armies and wars that is called for. We know full well that there is something wrong with armies made up of conscripted peasants being sent off to fight the emperor's wars of conquest. We do not have to suspend judgment on that. (Would the author, reassuring us that we "really don't know" what is bad or good, want to apply that lesson to the Holocaust?) The tale is ultimately aesthetic because it isolates our lives and the judgments we make from the wider reality in which they unfold, because it makes our individual happiness or disappointment the center of things.

The paradox is this: our initial attraction to spirituality may be motivated by our experience of pain in ordinary life and by the growing belief that we cannot find fulfillment or satisfaction without some kind of spiritual transformation. Yet if what we are after is the avoidance of personal pain and the achievement of a kind of "spiritual" pleasure — one not subject to normal disappointments and let-downs — then (sadly) failure is guaranteed.

For a start, aesthetic life, including and especially the spiritual kind we are looking at here, inevitably leads to boredom. If pleasing experiences are really what we are after (no matter what we call them), then after a while we will find that any meditation practice, beautiful Gregorian chant, or soothing prayer will wear a little thin. They were pleasant; they have become tedious. We will be forced to move on, searching for new and perhaps ever more exotic spiritual experiences. If we got it from Buddhism last year, perhaps next year we will try Shamanism or the Black Goddess.

I am no stranger to the aesthetic mode of spiritual life. (I doubt that many of us are. It is a permanent temptation, especially in a country as wealthy as ours.) There were times when my ordinary mind — consumed with the drive to succeed at my profession, baffled with difficulties in my love life, deeply hurt by parents who didn't seem to love me — was so downright miserable that I used the trappings of spirituality as a kind of nonpharmaceutical tranquilizer. Visualization tapes helped soothe my constant anxiety over the struggle to find a decent job and my despair over all the rejection letters I got from publishers.

Quiet music and sweet incense helped me be a little more accepting of frustrations in my personal life. Mantra meditation before a lovely altar graced by candles and crystals worked better than having four drinks every night.

Worked better, yes. But the problem was that the goal was really the same thing: to distract, soothe, tranquilize. I was not confronting the deepest personal sources of my pain — which stemmed from a childhood in which I was given the message that I would not be loved for my soul, but only for what I accomplished and achieved. Nor was I able to see that the even deeper problem was that much of this spiritual activity was really about making myself feel better, and that the way I was using the trappings of spiritual life was not all that different from covering over my insecurity with career success or sedating myself with alcohol.

As long as I was after feeling good, I was doomed to disappointment. For real happiness, as Aristotle long ago pointed out, is not itself a substantial condition, but a quality of other activities: an adverb, not a noun. Happiness arises when we are at one with what we doing: when our chosen path in life seems worthy of respect, the way to it both possible and interesting, and we ourselves seem deserving of satisfaction. The more our sole goal is our own pleasure, peace of mind, and equanimity, the more they escape us. It is only when we turn our attention elsewhere that they appear. Because pleasant feelings are fleeting, addictive, and tend toward boredom, they never satisfy us for very long. Not surprisingly, then, after a while I got fed up with the soppy New Age music, neglected the soothing visualization tapes, and fell again (for a time) into the familiar compulsive search for a "success" that would validate the emptiness I felt inside.

Strangely, the aesthetic form of spiritual life can also take an opposite form: a desperate clinging to a particular set of religious beliefs, doctrines, or rituals. In this kind of aesthetic fundamentalism, the purpose of our spiritual life is, once again, to make us feel better. Only this time we do it by knowing that we (unlike anyone different from us and our friends) have found the one "right" way to do things. Our single-minded attachment to our beliefs makes us increasingly narrow-minded, arrogant, and (actually) insecure. As the New Age music soothes one kind of aesthetic urge, so a rigid attachment to a parochial truth soothes another. In both cases, the ultimate goal — acknowledged or not — is to satisfy and comfort our conventional ego.

Another problem with aesthetic spirituality is that it involves, it requires, denial and avoidance. These pitfalls will be discussed in detail later on, so I will say only a few words about them here.

At first glance, certain spiritual teachings seem very much opposed to denial and avoidance. Buddhist authors in particular stress the importance of an unrestricted and unguarded openness to whatever exists and the need to face the full reality of life. The problem, however, is that "full reality of life" is often described in very limited ways. The examples chosen repeatedly concentrate on essentially personal disappointments, comparatively mild irritations and frustrations. They tend to leave out the more perplexing and threatening issues of collective social evil, shared pain, or global threats to nonhuman and human alike.

For instance, when contemporary Buddhist teacher Sharon Salzberg wants to explain the proper Buddhist understanding of anger, she chooses as an example her irritation at a recalcitrant computer and her further vexations when she discovers that the resident computer expert could not be reached for help. We do not get what we want, the example tells us, and then we get angry. Instead, we need to "be" with whatever turns up, accept the essentially uncontrollable nature of life, become familiar with our tendency to think we can regulate that which is beyond our powers, and learn to surrender to the naturally frustrating qualities of normal life. This is good advice. Who among us hasn't lost it over the common frustrations of existence? traffic jams, erased computer files, the whole range of spilt milk over which crying — or raging — does so little good?

But while these essentially personal, in-the-long-run unimportant frustrations are (unfortunately) an essential part of our lives, surely they do not tell the whole story. What about, for instance, the anger of the woman who was forced to have oral sex with her father from age seven to age twelve, while being assured that if she told her mother her father would kill them both? What kind of anger might arise from cancer patients among South Pacific islanders, who were returned to their homes by the government after atomic tests despite the fact that the level of radiation was far higher than officials would have found acceptable for mainland, white Americans? Few books on how spirituality is conducive to a peaceful heart mention these kinds of situations. Fewer still examine them at any length. For a spirituality of resistance, however, such situations are the core of spiritual life.

In short, I believe that certain versions of spirituality succumb to the danger of making spiritual life appear too easy. The siren song of the aesthetic lulls us all (including myself at times) into a dreamy state in which the bitter realities of existence dare not intrude. This ease, I suspect, is both appealing and dangerous.

Kierkegaard had an analogous concern, which he recounts in this memory of the advice he gave himself while trying to figure out what to do with his life:

> " . . . wherever you look about you, in literature and life, you see the celebrated names and figures, the precious and much heralded men who are coming into prominence and are much talked about, the many benefactors of the age who know how to benefit mankind by making life easier and easier, some by railways, others by omnibuses and steamboats, others by the telegraph, others by easily apprehended compendiums and short recitals of everything worth knowing, and finally the true benefactors of the age who make spiritual existence in virtue of thought easier and easier. . . . You must do something, but inasmuch as with your limited capacities it will be impossible to make anything easier than it has become, you must, with the same humanitarian enthusiasm as the others, undertake to make something harder." . . . Out of love for mankind . . . and moved by a genuine interest in those who make everything easy, I conceived it as my task to create difficulties everywhere.

It is hard enough to be peaceful when we must struggle to overcome our natural attachment to simply getting what we want. Just working on our own tendencies to be dissatisfied when we might be grateful is a life-long effort. Things become even harder if we are going to be spiritually serene while we respond to unjust suffering, social evil, and the environmental crisis. Yet if spiritual life does not include that response, it becomes (paradoxically) too easy to be possible.

For most of us, death is one of the great barriers to a peaceful mind. The question of the spiritual approach to death is therefore a good place to reveal some of the limitations of the aesthetic approach to spiritual life.

The specter of the end of consciousness and the termination of our personal identity provokes a kind of dread that can darken everything. The philosopher Camus argued that one of the reasons life is absurd is while we are constantly "looking forward" (to our next vacation, to when we will have more money, to when we will fall in love), all such movements forward lead us closer to death. Other thinkers, from Ernest Becker to Ken Wilber, have stressed how much of our civilization is built on the denial of death. Collective aggression, the control of nature, the creation of personal fortunes, political empires, and great art can all be traced, they claim, back to our desire to bring into being some lasting aspect of ourselves that will escape the finitude of our mortal bodies.

By contrast, spiritual perspectives have always counseled us not to fear death. Whether in the traditional Jewish or Christian claim that our souls outlive our bodies or in the Buddhist notion that we have no enduring self to lose in any case, we have been taught that the proper response to mortality is to look it in the face and accept it.

Some contemporary spiritual voices have been particularly important in this regard. Elisabeth Kübler-Ross introduced the simple but (sadly) at the time unheard of practice of counseling terminal cancer patients in hospitals by talking directly to them about the fact that they were facing death. Remembering Tolstoy's character Ivan Ilyich, who reflected that the most painful part of his ever worsening illness was how the people around him kept pretending that he was not dying, we can appreciate how enormous Kübler-Ross's contribution was. Her gift was to encourage people to face the imminent end of their lives, to directly experience the fear and rage that the end was provoking, to finish whatever they could in the time remaining, and, thus, to be able to achieve some kind of clarity and peace as the end approached.

Stephen Levine adapted Kübler-Ross's work to a Buddhist framework. He counseled the dying and those around them to seek openness to whatever the present moment contains, including the realities of pain and imminent loss, and to allow the bounds of separate identity and ego involvement to fade in the process:

> You relate to one who is ill the same way you relate to any being. With openness. With an honoring of the truth we all share. Work to dissolve the separateness that keeps one lost in duality. Become one with the other. . . . See the conditioned illusion of separateness. . . . Allow both of you to die. . . . Not trying to change things. Not trying to make something or someone other than it is.

The lessons offered by Kübler-Ross and Levine are very important. I can still remember my own grief and fear when, eight years old, I fully realized that someday I would die. My mother's attempt to soothe me —

"Don't worry, that won't happen for a long time" — communicated her caring but missed the point. Now, well past the mathematical middle of my life, having been present at the deaths of both my son and my father, the prospect of that final change is no longer so overwhelming. However, at times I can still feel the shiver of fear that comes with the thought of how temporary everything is.

But while I agree that the prospect of death can be an opportunity for individual spiritual growth, I believe that this approach neglects something of critical significance. In this light we may recall one of Elie Wiesel's early essays, in which he describes how hard it was for him to honor his father's memory. It was some years after the war and the anniversary — in Hebrew the "Yartzeit" or memory time — of the day his father had died in Buchenwald concentration camp: "stretched out on a plank of wood amid a multitude of blood-covered corpses, fear frozen in his eyes, a mask of suffering on the bearded stricken mask that was his face." To commemorate a Yartzeit, Jews are enjoined to go to a synagogue and take part in a special reading of the Kaddish prayer, one reserved for mourners of the newly dead and those observing the Yartzeit of long-deceased family members. But Wiesel feels that he cannot say Kaddish for his father, a prayer which, by the way, makes no explicit mention of death but only extols the greatness of God and asks for peace. It would have been easy to say Kaddish, Wiesel tells us, if his father had died of old age, or sickness, or despair.

> But such is not the case. His death did not even belong to him. I do not know to what cause to attribute it, in what book to inscribe it. No link between it and the life he had led. His death, lost among all the rest, had nothing to do with the person he had been. It could just as easily have brushed him in passing and spared him. It took him inadvertently, absent-mindedly, by mistake. Without knowing that it was he; he was robbed of his death.

In other words, death is not always the same. There is the natural fact of our limited presence on earth: our mortality, the growth, flourishing, and eventual withering of our flesh. And then there is the unnatural, the wrong way in which some of us die. To be killed by the Nazis was not, Wiesel tells us, his father's "own" death, because it came from a destiny unchosen by him and unacceptable for anyone. We should not praise God for his death, accept it, or meet it — as in the closing words of the Kaddish — with peace.

This idea can be transferred with little effort to precisely the people whose illnesses and deaths are chronicled by Levine. We may wonder if the cancer patients with whom he deals are in fact enduring "their own" deaths or, like Wiesel's father, are having something unfit and misplaced imposed on them. It is a poorly kept secret, after all, that somewhere in the range of 60–80 percent of cancer stems from environmental causes. The chromosomal changes which lead to tumors and metastases come in the main from incremental stresses on our bodies. Bit by bit, we are transformed. These stressors are often substances people have put into the air, water, ground, and food. Our bodies are assaulted by tens of thousands of artificial chemicals, many of which are known carcinogens, and only about 2 percent of which have ever been studied. It is people who produce, transport, buy, and perhaps make a lot of money out of the substances that lead to an ever-rising cancer rate.

Levine counsels us, over and over, to be open to death, not to resist the pain, to accept the reality of our inevitable loss and the inevitability that some of us will fall to illness, that "there is no fault in this" and "no blame." Yet he seems to simply ignore the dimension of death of which Wiesel speaks. For instance, Levine thinks of what he would like to say to Alonzo, sixty-one years old and dying of stomach cancer: "...it's O.K. to die. It's fine. It's the appropriate thing at the appropriate moment.... Let go of the pain of not being able to protect everyone from everything.... It's all O.K." These thoughts are comforting. They soothe. And God knows people dying can use some comfort.

But what of the unasked questions, the ones that are not so soothing? Could Alonzo have gotten stomach cancer because his body is a little more susceptible to the nitrosomines that are used to preserve meats? Or could it be that Alonzo worked in dry cleaning and was affected by the carcinogenic Benzene used in the process? Could it have been the formaldehyde used in particleboard — present in virtually all houses built since World War II? Is it really "O.K." that these things are in our environment and that we are dying from them? What could "O.K." mean in this case?

Stephen Levine is a wise and good man. For years he selflessly offered himself as a counselor to cancer victims; and his own wife suffered from it. He writes that "resistance to the pain about us causes the heart to wither. Allowing that pain to enter into us tears our heart open and leaves us exposed to the truth." And he is offering us a great lesson.

But....

The truth is also that some of our deaths are, in Wiesel's sense, not our own. They may have been caused by the senseless dumping of poisons into the environment, from which a particular group of people made a good deal of money, and which others defended and lied about and kept on with even when they knew about the consequences of their acts. How can we make spiritual sense of what these people have done? How do we make our personal peace with them? What is the "proper" spiritual reaction not simply to death, but to a kind of impersonal murder? And how are we to face our own possible complicity when as consumers, producers, or passive bystanders most of us play some part in the unfolding disaster? Is our role in all this "O.K."? Can we be open to the truth, as writers like Levine constantly counsel us, without making some kind of judgment about what we see?

In a similar vein, it is important to see how one-sided is Levine's constantly repeated assertion — one he shares with many other spiritual voices — that "we are one." He tells us:

> Work to dissolve the separateness that keeps one lost in duality. Become one with the other. . . . For, in truth, there is no "other." There is just being, experienced from different focal points. When you are fully present, you see there is no such thing as "another person." There are just two perceptions of the one existence.

From the spiritual standpoint embodied in this book, I respond: what might it mean for Wiesel's father to see the Nazis as people to "become one with"? How about the woman whose daughter died from leukemia brought on by drinking polluted water? Should she "dissolve" the separateness between herself, her daughter, and the factory owner who surreptitiously dumped the chemicals that killed her daughter? How could she do this? Who are we to say she should? What does talk of the illusion of separateness mean when some people's actions are instrumental in spreading the substances that cause cancer in others? Does dissolving the "illusion of separation" mean that we suffer the same fate as the victims? If we "dissolve the separateness" between ourselves and the tribes made homeless by rainforest destruction, does that mean we join them, penniless and starving on the edge of the new settlements that have destroyed their village? Or that we invite them into our homes?

This book is an attempt to make sense of questions like these. They are questions that must be faced when our attempt to find a peaceful heart unfolds in this dark time, and I believe that they have answers. I do think that we can achieve spiritual peace even in the face of the kinds of social evils that afflicted Wiesel and amid today's socially caused cancers and environmental illnesses. I don't think that these afflictions make spiritual peace impossible or that we need to be in unrelieved anguish over the world's sorrow. Perhaps it is even possible to achieve some psychic empathy with those who are committing the crimes. But these dilemmas have been examined too infrequently and ignored too often in contemporary spiritual thought. Unless we confront them with the same energy and attention that we give to dealing with personal disappointments and individual fears or greed, our wisdom will be thin indeed.

Answers to these dilemmas may come from surprising sources — from the energy and passion of resistance to evil as much or more than from more familiar forms of spiritual acceptance and feelings of oneness. Consider Rachel Carson. Her *Silent Spring*, a study of the dangers of industrial chemicals and pesticides, helped create the modern environmental movement. She brought to her work not only scientific training and literary skill, but also an intensely spiritual view of the natural world. In her very last book, a simple evocation of the value of nature for children, she celebrated the infinite healing powers of the "beauties and mysteries of life," a power derived from the "recognition of something beyond the boundaries of human existence." In an earlier book, she offered an inspiringly nontheistic model of our place in the cosmos:

> Every living thing of the ocean, plant and animal alike, returns to the water at the end of its own life span the materials which had been temporarily assembled to form its body. Thus, individual elements are lost to view, only to reappear again and again in different incarnation in a kind of material immortality.

Carson's emotional identification with nature included a deep sense of moral responsibility to it. While writing *Silent Spring* she endured a host of acute illnesses, including a persistent and eventually fatal breast cancer. Part of her motivation to finish the book, she said, came from a feeling that if she had not done all she could in defense of both nature and human beings, she "could never again listen happily to a thrush song." In other words, she could find spiritual peace, which for her meant connecting deeply to the natural world, only if she simultaneously did her best to defend it. Her celebration could be authentic only if it existed alongside resistance.

In some respects, the idea of a spirituality of resistance is very old, and this book is part of a religious conversation that has been going on for thousands of years. One side of this conversation has typically stressed the need to develop the kind of spiritual virtues I described at the beginning of the chapter: listening to inner voices, renouncing attachments, being grateful for all we have, surrendering to the will of God. On the other side have been the rousing calls to serve God by feeding the poor, removing the arrogant from the seat of power — or at least extending a helping hand to your neighbor. There are those who center their energies on the search for personal peace, and those who see resistance to evil as essential to the spiritual path. There has been the "horizontal" dimension of concern for social justice and collective well-being. And there has been the "vertical" dimension of a personal relationship to God or spiritual development. The crucial, and often quite difficult, task is to join both dimensions. And, for our time, to do so in the face of global environmental catastrophe.

During the third century B.C.E., Buddhism split into the Mahayana and the Theravada schools precisely on this question of how the individual spiritual seeker relates to other people's suffering. The original system (Theravada, or "wisdom of the elders") was criticized by the newer voices of the Mahayana (who called themselves the "greater vehicle") for focusing too much on an essentially personal enlightenment. While the Mahayana agreed that attachments to self or objects of desire brought pain, they thought the initial teachings contained a somewhat distorted view of how to end that pain. Charging the Theravada with a hidden but persistent selfishness, the Mahayana sages asked: If you pursue your own escape from pain, what will become of those left behind? Of what possible service is your enlightenment to others? Are you still driven by fear of pain? Is your own sense of self, which needs to wither to attain enlightenment, still very strong? You need, they counseled, to develop a disinterested concern in the liberation of every being, and not just a passion to save yourself.

The Theravadan response was that in fact the individual Buddhist sage could be of immense service to those around him: just by demonstrating that escape from earthly pain was possible. To the Theravada, people are trapped by ignorance of how attachments cause unhappiness. In our ordinary lives we are like people stranded on a riverbank, desperately wanting to cross over a river but not knowing the way. The spiritual sage, then, is a person who fashions a canoe with his own hands and paddles to the opposite shore. His help for others consists in showing that ending attachment and a consequent spiritual liberation are indeed possible. Witnessing his success at overcoming attachments and desires, the rest of us will see that we can do the same.

The Mahayana teachers found this view sorely lacking. They changed the orientation of Buddhist teaching: away from a focus on ending personal pain and toward an impersonal, universal compassion extending far beyond the boundaries of one's own individual situation. To them a true religious hero had to do more than simply provide an example. They told a different story of what makes a person spiritually developed. It is as if, an early Mahayana dialogue explains, a young prince is accompanying his large, extended family on a long and dangerous journey through the forest. There are wild beasts and robbers, and the way is long and difficult. Soon the family is lost, left with little food and no sense of the way home. The babies cry, the aged grandfather bows his head in resignation, the two pregnant nieces are struck dumb with fear. Does the prince — a powerful and healthy youth, a warrior, a forest explorer — go off to save himself? No, he stays with his family. He will not leave the forest without them.

In other words, any fear for one's own condition gets submerged in concern for others. The Mahayana taught that this concern, properly tempered by patience, sensitive intelligence, and awareness of human frailty, is the heart of the very liberation from pain that animated Buddhism to begin with. The paradox is that only if we can stop being so concerned with just our own pain can we ever free ourselves from that pain. Spiritual development for ourselves cannot be achieved directly, but only in the roundabout way of forgetting who we are, and why we consider ourselves so important.

In a very different setting, some of Judaism's greatest prophets made comparable claims against the religious establishment of their day. Time after time they rejected the notion that empty rituals would satisfy God's demands. Time after time they "spoke truth to power" — and sometimes ended up getting hunted by the king's soldiers for their pains! The point is that for these prophets a spiritual form of life had to include responsiveness to the hunger or anguish of those around us, as well as seeing and resisting the authority of the arrogant and privileged who controlled the kingdom. As in the Mahayana perspective on enlightenment (though in a very different religious idiom), the prophets made it clear that acts of religious devotion had no merit if they were motivated by self-interest, or — most important here — if they depended on ignoring the desperate plight of other people, especially those toward the bottom of a hierarchical social structure.

It is interesting that on Yom Kippur, a day occupied by extended prayer, complicated rituals, and fasting, one of the major readings from the Bible is a prophetic passage castigating the ancient Jews for self-serving and hypocritical observance — in precisely their celebration of Yom Kippur! Speaking for God, Isaiah warns the people:

> They ask: Why do you not see when we fast; we afflict our souls and you do not notice? For on your fast day you seek business and oppress your laborers. You fast for strife and contention; to smite with a fist of wickedness. You do not fast this day to make your voices heard on high. Can this then be the fast that I have chosen — a day when man afflicts his soul, to bow down his head like a reed, to sit in sackcloth and ashes? Is this what you call a fast, an acceptable day to Adonai? Behold this is the fast that I have chosen — loosening the bonds of wickedness, undoing the straps of the yoke, sending the oppressed free and breaking every yoke of tyranny. Break your bread with the hungry, and bring the impoverished into your home; clothe the naked when you see them.... If you remove from your midst the yokes, the stretching out of a finger and wrongful speech. If you reach out to the hungry and satisfy the afflicted soul, then your light shall shine forth in the darkness (Isa. 57, 58)

This wonderful passage carries a simple but powerful message: doing the will of God necessarily includes a response to what is going on around us. That we comply with religious rules is not enough. The general idea is often expressed by the notion that God asks us to engage in "Tikkun Olam," the "repair of the world." The cosmos, on this view, is unfinished and imperfect. God left its defects for us to remedy. If we fail to do so, our spiritual destinies are incomplete.

In this century liberation theology, religious civil disobedience as taught by Martin Luther King, Jr., and Gandhi, and representatives of feminism and the environmental movement have modeled a spirituality of resistance. They have all affirmed that spiritual virtues involve much more than overcoming nagging anxieties or frustrations in our personal lives. As King put it, we are bound up in an "inescapable network of mutuality"; and thus our personal spiritual development leads us necessarily toward concern for others. If none of us can be truly free while others are enslaved, so none of us can be truly enlightened or at peace if the fate of others is absent from our awareness. Responding to the environmental crisis, many thinkers have passionately extended that sense of mutuality and moral concern to our relations with the natural world. They have helped bring the depth of our pain for the environmental devastation to consciousness and told us that helping to heal that devastation is an essential part of our spiritual work.

All these perspectives advise us that if spiritual contentment is what we are after, we cannot achieve it by ignoring the injustice to which we, or others, are subject. From Elie Wiesel to Gandhi, from Joanna Macy to Abraham Joshua Heschel, from Dorothy Day to Cesar Chavez, the message has been clear. This book continues their efforts.

The particular historical background that animates my version of a spirituality of resistance is that of unprecedented crimes by — and threats against — humanity. It is the uniquely frightening specters of genocide and ecocide, the prospect of mass death for entire communities, species, and ecosystems. I will concentrate first and foremost on how environmental concerns challenge spiritual life. To illuminate that challenge and tap the lessons of an event which exemplifies nearly limitless evil, I will make constant reference to the Holocaust. I know that this comparison will be shocking to some and obscure to others; and therefore subsequent chapters will explain why I think the Holocaust carries a weight of warning far beyond the boundaries of the communities actually involved. I will develop two main ideas. First, I believe that what Nazis did to their victims can serve as a kind of warning about the potential consequences of our own ecological madness. Second, Jewish resistance to the Nazis can serve as a model and inspiration for the courage we need to confront the environmental crisis.

If spiritual life is not to sink into the merely "pleasant," mass murder and unprecedented threats to the future of life on our planet must be a spiritual seeker's daily bread. A spirituality of resistance exists in the shadows of Auschwitz and leaking toxic waste dumps. In striking new ways these matters test the conventional spiritual virtues of open-minded awareness, acceptance of life, compassionate forgiveness, and concern for others. They ask us to think about things we would much rather not think about, to learn lessons we'd rather not know, and to engage in a difficult and detailed examination of our own place in the social realm.

Further, in my particular vision spirituality is meant to guide us to a life of peace on *this* earth. Unlike certain conventional forms of Judaism, Christianity, or Hinduism, or indeed some of the comforting types of New Age thought, I am unable to place my trust in some other reality, some Force from Afar guaranteeing that things will all come out right in the end. My terms of reference are the earth and all that dwell therein — and nothing else. That is why I believe that if a spirituality of resistance is to succeed, it must not lead us away from what we face here and now, but ever deeper into it. Indeed, I do not believe there is anywhere else to go.

What then is new about our situation, so novel that earlier attempts to connect spiritual values to social life are not fully adequate to it?

To begin with, the magnitude of the environmental crisis is more threatening than anything we have ever seen in the past.* That is why the danger of denial is part of this spiritual setting in a way that is not typical of other forms of social suffering. Victims of rape or colonialism, for instance, do not usually need to be reminded of what they are enduring. The difficulty in facing the reality at hand is not usually part of the spiritual response to war or racism. But the prospect of the "end of nature," in Bill McKibben's chilling phrase about the consequences of humanity's alteration of the earth's atmosphere and climate, is so vast and yet so diffuse that it is extremely hard to hold it in our minds. Taking in the truth of what we are doing is very difficult. There is some analogy here to the way many of Europe's Jews simply could not believe the full scope of the Nazi plan for them and rejected the truth when they heard it. Similarly, most of us, most of the time, cannot begin to fathom what we have done to the Earth — or ourselves.

Further, the very extremity of our situation means that once we get

---

*I include here as part of that crisis the threat of nuclear war, which itself would be the ultimate environmental disaster.

beyond denial, it is very hard not to lose heart entirely. As Joanna Macy observes,

> We are barraged by data that render questionable the survival of our culture, our species, and even our planet as a viable home for conscious life. Despair, in this context...is the loss of the assumption that the species will inevitably pull through.

Hope for the future, confidence in the moral standing of our civilization, a sense that there is a place where we really can belong with grace or harmony, such things become increasingly difficult to come by. How are we to find a peaceful heart while facing the full — and bitter — truth? In a sense, that is the single question this book attempts to answer.

Finally, it is not just the extreme consequences of what is taking place that is so antithetical to the openness and peace which spirituality promises, but just how much of global society would have to change for things to be different. The extent of the environmental crisis, and its deep roots in virtually all facets of contemporary civilization, make the present task of resistance uniquely daunting. To resist the environmental crisis is to seek an essential change in how we produce, distribute, and consume. A real solution will require that we alter our most basic ideas about what is important and what we want for our children. I do not believe any kindred spiritual orientations faced a task of such magnitude. The teachings of Gandhi and King, for instance, as immensely valuable as they are, concern national independence or the extension of civil rights to a racial minority. These goals, while formidable, are not comparable to what must be done to respond to global warming or the worldwide proliferation of toxic materials into all life forms. A contemporary spirituality of resistance thus proceeds not so much from national outrage or group struggle, but from a kind of global despair.

Besides the environmental crisis and the severity of our emotional responses to it, my contemporary version of a spirituality of resistance has a very specific cultural background. Worldwide, there has been a vibrant and surprising growth in religious concern, and in the West, a very singular form of spirituality has emerged.

These developments have arisen partly because of a fundamental weakening of the social authority of science. We have seen technological competence used to build gas chambers and, inadvertently, damage the ozone layer. There is widespread distrust in unceasing technological innovation, detached professionals, unlimited scientific research, and stiff, unfeeling doctors who practice medicine as if patients were collections of body parts. These "accomplishments" cast a very long shadow over the supposed bright light of a purely scientific and technological understanding of society, knowledge, and selfhood. A good many people now doubt that in and of itself the endless growth of science will create a happier and more just world.

Similarly, a life based on secular values of consumption no longer commands the kind of automatic respect it did forty years ago. Sophisticated production and mass consumption of gadgets can coexist, we have come to realize, with drug abuse, casual violence, and deep veins of unhappiness. Many of us have so many "things" — yet are, much of the time, harried, frustrated, or depressed. Instead of calm enjoyment and appreciation, we are gripped by ever-increasing desires that are only temporarily satiated by new acquisitions. The Christmastime orgies of consumption leave a lingering sense of emptiness. Obsessions with career success and wealth never seem to be placated. As we get older, we begin to wonder if all these possessions and accomplishments can really bring us anything but the most fleeting of pleasures.

Challenges to science and consumerism have helped prompt a resurgence of interest in spiritual values and religious worldviews. "Spirituality is the new religion," proclaims *Mother Jones* magazine, polls report that an awful lot of people believe in angels, and *Self* magazine asks why it's so hip to be a Buddhist. However, in the developed world many versions of that interest have taken a particularly — and unfortunately — self-indulgent and narcissistic turn. Aesthetic values command much of what passes for spiritual teaching. That is why there is a distinct importance in stressing the role of resistance in spiritual life now, when it is all too easy to turn spirituality into an extension of feel-good psychotherapy; or when spiritual "experiences," in the most trivial and self-interested sense of the word, are too often presented as the heart of spiritual life.

At the same time, contemporary spirituality contains a historically unprecedented eclecticism. Many people are willing to take heart wherever they can find it, believing that the crux of spirituality is similar in all the major traditions. The perspective developed here is both compatible with and an extension of this new capacity to celebrate insights from widely different sources. The movements led by King and Gandhi, by contrast, emerged from and were couched in the idioms of Christianity and Vedantic Hinduism respectively. Further, a spirituality of resistance is able to express the spiritual aspirations of people who have no traditional religious beliefs whatsoever. It can flourish for unbelievers as well as believers and requires no relation to Jesus, Buddha, Krishna, or any particular holy book or institution.

Despite the work of King, Gandhi, and countless religious feminist and peace activists, the historic antagonism between spirituality and politics, between those who want to "get their heads together" and those who want to change the world, still continues. I would like to soften that antagonism. I reject the all-too-common belief that a religious temperament and a political one must be at odds. And, while most of my energy here is directed to bringing awareness of the importance of political resistance to spiritual life, I will also describe some of the distinct ways in which spirituality can and should inform political activism.

Finally, the view I am presenting here contains, I believe, an original understanding of the spiritual role of resistance to social evil. In my view the liberating practice of resistance is itself the moment of spiritual fulfillment. For it is only in the act of resistance, when we embrace that which is most disturbing not by accepting but by seeking to overcome it, that we can know ourselves as fully one with all of reality. It is only in resistance that acceptance is actual, and not a mask for denial. And thus it is in resistance that we encounter the face of God, awaken to the call of the Goddess, and realize our deepest connections to the mysteries of human life. The precious moments in which we face the truth and resist evil are the culmination of our spiritual journey.

That journey begins with the problem of denial.

CHAPTER TWO

No Place to Hide:
Spirituality, Avoidance,
and Denial

Spiritual teachings offer us peace in place of pain. Or at least they offer us a way to accept the inevitable distress that comes from being alive. Yet if we choose to follow those teachings, we face a dilemma. On the one hand, awareness of the generalized suffering which afflicts people in the world — and of environmental or political threats to my own life — makes me feel decidedly *unpeaceful*. I'd rather not be aware of them. Various forms of escape are so attractive, and seem so natural, in a world like ours. On the other hand, spiritual growth cannot be accomplished while I'm screening out the pains and dangers around me. This response will thwart my spiritual aspirations and leave me no better off than when I began.

What am I to do?

People respond to this dilemma in different ways. I will focus here on avoidance and denial. These forms of escape are important because they permeate not only our personal lives but society as a whole. Sadly (but not surprisingly) it is not just our individual minds that want to look the other way. Many of our most prestigious and influential institutions are built on doing just that. The spiritual task that faces us as individuals is therefore made especially difficult by the fact that it would be so easy simply to conform to the escapist style of our surroundings.

Any painful or threatening reality — from unnecessary poverty to the abuse of women, from AIDS to breast cancer — may give rise to the desire to escape. However, this desire is especially likely to surface in response to the environmental crisis. This is so because the scope of the environmental crisis dwarfs other social problems, no matter how important they may be.* What is at stake is of such immense value that the prospect of its ruin is very hard to take in. Even in our technologically overburdened times, we have a special relation to the "more-than-human." The complex and often disappointing world of human relationships is for many of us offset by the simple delight and comfort that we get from ocean or forest, birdsong or sunset. When we think of species made extinct, or particular places altered (for the worse!) forever, we find ourselves overcome by feelings of helplessness and hopelessness. The prospect that nature's powers to heal and comfort might be eroded or eliminated is just too painful to bear.

Also, our own well-being is so tied up with the environment that its deterioration threatens us directly. It is not easy to really acknowledge all the dangers lurking in the food, the water, and the air. Unlike wars or poverty, environmental threats can be silent and hidden. Often created by technical powers of which the average person has little understanding, they are pervasive and long-lasting. We often don't know how and why they begin, or — from the lead in our backyard gardens to the pesticides leeching into our drinking water — if they are still around us.

Perhaps most frustratingly, there commonly seems to be so little we can do about these far-reaching problems. Unless by profession we are environmental lawyers or Sierra Club staffers, it appears virtually impossible to make a real difference in what is going on. We can recycle, drive less, and eat organic foods. But while these responses are good, they have limited effects on the major sources of environmental destruction. So it may be hard to accept that our individual actions are so inadequate to the real scope of the problem. Alternatively, it might appear that the only way to do anything is to overturn society, renounce everything we have, and sever all ties. When we fail to take such steps, our own sense of inadequacy and guilt grows. We realize that we are behaving just like everyone else, and that there is nothing to be done. If this is indeed true, we may again move toward various forms of escape. After all, why should we pay attention if we can't change anything?

Usually, such motivations to escape thinking and feeling about the environmental crisis exist well below the level of conscious awareness. To acknowledge that these feelings exist would in fact be to begin the process of overcoming our tendency to run away. It is our unconscious

---

*With the possible exception of war — which in our time always includes a strong element of environmental destruction.

drive not to know or feel the truth that prompts us to try to escape in the first place!

Yet no matter what short-term composure we gain from our flight, we lose much more. Psychic and institutional retreats cast a shadow over any attempt to really be happy with one's own life. We cannot feel at home on this earth if we are not ready to take in what it is. In the end, we will be stifled both morally and spiritually.

Many years ago, I was part of a small group that researched, wrote, and produced a theatrical presentation on Jewish resistance during the Holocaust. In the early months of working together we shared the results of our initial inquiries. Each of us volunteered to study a different area, for example, causes of the Holocaust, resistance in the ghettos, life and death in the concentration camps. At each meeting we were to report to the group on what we'd found, as part of a preliminary process toward writing a script for the final presentation.

Several times people who had committed themselves to doing a particular piece of research would show up empty-handed, having failed even to do the reading. Later my wife, who was also part of the group, heard me fume: "I just don't understand. How can they promise to do the reading and then not do it?" "What do you expect," she would reply, "Reading about the Holocaust raises all kinds of painful feelings. These are so hard to deal with that it's easy to forget or avoid the whole thing."

At that time I really couldn't understand. After all, I never missed an assignment, never failed to study one site of mass death or another; and I had little patience for the people who couldn't handle the material. They didn't do what they said they would. I did. They were avoiding. I wasn't.

It was only years later, as I began to concentrate on humanity's relation to nature, that I became aware that in regard to environmental issues I had done exactly the same thing for years.

It was a simple process, really. In an almost physical way, I would simply move over or around what I didn't want to know. For instance, I would be reading the newspaper, going through stories on congressional activity, Middle East violence, welfare mothers, drug policy. Then a small story would catch my eye: "Rash of Wild Frogs Born with Abnormalities, Environmental Causes Suspected," or "Long Island Beaches Closed for Seventh Day, Runoff from Area Sewage Plants Blamed."

Now the trick is that in the very moment of seeing the headline, I would turn away. My seeing was a kind of purposeful, yet barely conscious, not seeing. There would be a scarcely perceptible tightening of my face, a surreptitious pulling back in my chest, a split-second unconscious decision that this was not what I wanted to read about. My avoidance was a jerky psychic movement, the mental equivalent of a small animal who finds himself on a hot surface: a series of jumps and sideways shuffles until it escapes the threat.

During those years I was a graduate student or college teacher: a scholar, a professional intellectual. I wrote on the history of the Middle East conflict, compared different theories of the transition from feudalism to capitalism, and plowed through text and commentary of dense works by Marx and Hegel. I was at home with vast library resources, professional journals, obscure and detailed accounts of all sorts of things. I was, in short, no stranger to doing research and informing myself about how things stood.

Yet for those years of my adult intellectual life, from my late twenties through my early forties, I had read only one short book on environmental issues: and I had never consulted a single specialty magazine or journal — not even the glossy ones aimed at general readers. What I knew came from odd bits of information overheard on radio news, from casual glances at the headlines, and from the material that events like Earth Day pumped into the general culture. Of course, as a card-carrying member of the sixties generation, I had no trouble believing that large corporations and militaristic governments could trash the environment to further their short-term ends. I could easily imagine that things were bad — and I didn't want to know any of the details.

If I had been asked, "Why don't you find out what is going on?" I might have answered, "Well, it's not really my area" or "I don't have time" or "Later." But no one did ask. If I'd actually had to offer such answers, I now realize, I might have sensed how ridiculous they were. In just this way, my own avoidance was buttressed by that of just about everyone I knew. (And we were all politically correct types who constantly discussed sexism, corporate abuse, and racism.) We all managed not to ask each other: "Why aren't you finding out?" In retrospect, I can see that I — we — were simply avoiding. On a rational level, of course, this made no sense. After all, if air and water and toxic poisoning are not everyone's concern, part of every group's "special interests," part of every academic's "field," what is? (Years later, when I appealed directly to some colleagues to include environmental issues in their courses, courses into which the material would have fit easily, I got precisely that response. "It's great that you are doing this, Roger, but it's not my field.")

The simple fact of the matter was that I was afraid to find out more than the bare minimum. I didn't want to have anything like an adequate awareness of what was really going on. Because I was scared to know more, I managed to be content with the little I knew.

There were many reasons for my fear. From a young age I had been in love with the natural world and the threat to it frightened me deeply. The house in which I grew up had a large backyard, with many trees and a muddy little brook. Beyond our wire mesh fence there were — before being developed into another suburban enclave — a few acres of woods. And at the foot of my dead-end street there was a whole little forest, with rock outcroppings to climb over and little hollows in which I would make small fires on cold November afternoons. These were the places I went when my childhood loneliness grew especially painful. The trees, muddy brooks, and rich breezes of late autumn or early spring made me feel I had a place where I belonged. They soothed me, in a way no person I knew would. The pseudo-wildness of my suburban youth — and as an adult the really wild settings of Wyoming national forests or the Himalayas — gave me an emotional support I couldn't get anywhere else. At the times when I felt most at one with everything that breathed or grew or shone in the sunlight, the natural world seemed like part of my true family, as connected to me and the people I loved as any favorite aunt or good-humored cousin. So for years the thought that this family was being poisoned was more than I had the courage to endure.

What does this story of my own personal avoidance, which I believe might be representative of many people's experience, have to do with spiritual life?

To begin with, consider that it is impossible to avoid something without, in some sense or other, knowing what it is you are avoiding. If I hadn't "known" or "sensed" or "believed" that the environment was in bad shape, I wouldn't have had to exert that spontaneous little movement to avoid the threatening news stories. With the same peculiar combination of stoicism and eagerness with which I studied sexism and the Holocaust, I would have examined what pesticides were doing to migrant workers or what clear-cuts were doing to forest ecosystems. I didn't pursue the matter in all its gory details because I was scared: of the truth, and of how the truth would make me feel. But to the extent that I had to know — to sense, to intuit — the truth in order to avoid it, I was having the emotional response already. Buried in the back of my mind, under the floorboards of a consciousness ever so occupied with other things, was a barely discernible anguish over what was going on. The emotions were there; I just wasn't willing to face them. I was closed to a part of my own reality as well as to a part of the world. There was what I somewhere "knew" and didn't acknowledge; and there was the limited reality that I tried to pass off as all I needed to think and talk about. Psychologically and spiritually, I was split.

Such a split mind is a profound barrier to spiritual development. Emotions hidden are not really gone. Whether or not we realize it they have pernicious effects on our lives. Unacknowledged anger becomes hostility directed inward or outward. A grief suppressed becomes a quiet depression, numbness of spirit. It can lead to what Kierkegaard called "a disorder of feelings, the disorder consisting in not having any." If spiritual life means a quiet enjoyment of what we have, a spontaneous gratitude for what God has given us, an open-hearted empathy for both the joy and the suffering that exists around us, then spirituality will be diminished if I give my energy over to avoiding the world and choking off my reactions to it.

Are our prayers of spiritual appreciation to read something like: "Thank you God, for the beauties of my life (and please let me not think about the high cancer rate in the next town, or what might happen to me if I don't use a #45 sun block)"? Am I to "do unto my neighbor as I would have him do unto me" without thinking about what I am actually doing? (For instance, that the smoke from my factory is killing his forests?) Can I manifest authentic gratitude for what I have if I'm also spending a lot of energy avoiding looking at what other people (or species) are going through? The comparable point can be made, without too much trouble, for other spiritual virtues. Compassion, humility, integrity, equanimity, and all the rest require as a bare beginning that we be able to confront the truth.

In avoidance we approach and, quickly, run away. We avert our eyes, as we sometimes do when we glimpse someone with a crippling disease or a facial deformity. And the hidden message to ourselves in all this is that we are too frail to live with the facts. By avoiding we are acting as if we must absolutely have something that doesn't exist: in this case, a world without an environmental crisis. We thus commit ourselves to being the kind of person who is incapable of taking in what is going on. Like the family member from whom some horrible secret must be hidden ("Don't tell dad, you know he just couldn't handle it"), we require protection. Our consciousness becomes a defensive window and we experience the world as through a glass darkly.

Such a stance diminishes our capacity for either spontaneous joy or confidence that we really can be at home in this world. Ultimately, it is an aesthetic message. It suggests that we must have a restricted realm of experiences in order to live well. And if the world doesn't have the properly limited range, we'll limit it ourselves by avoiding what threatens our precarious grip on happiness and well being.

The first day of my environmental philosophy course I tell students of my own fear, grief, and rage about the ecological crisis. I admit to years of avoiding information about just how bad things are, share my helpless anger over the threats to my daughter's health, acknowledge a temptation to despair for the wilderness forever lost.

I then ask them to speak in turn about what they feel. They respond slowly and hesitantly, emboldened by my example but still somewhat unsure that a university classroom is the proper place for emotions. As the hour progresses, however, their statements become increasingly more revealing.

"I'm pissed off," one will say, "because the field where I used to hunt for grasshoppers was turned into a parking lot for a mall, and they hardly even use it. What a waste."

"I'm scared," a young woman admits. "Every time I go out in the sun in the summer I think about skin cancer. My aunt died from it."

Several young men tell me they don't see much use in thinking about all these problems. I ask one: "What would happen if you did think about it?"

"I don't know," he replies. "I'm not sure I could go on with what I'm supposed to do in this life. If I started to cry, I might never stop."

People's spiritual lives do not unfold in a vacuum. The surrounding culture shapes our tastes in music, food, and clothes, our beliefs about history and the physical world, our expectations concerning romantic love or friendship. In exactly the same way, we are spiritually affected by the way the major institutions of our time confront — or avoid — the most serious and threatening aspects of the environmental crisis. To a significant extent these institutions offer models for how to deal with what is going on in the world.

Government, media, and schools do not really talk about environmental issues very much; and when they are talked about, the conversation is often superficial. This chapter is not the place to try to prove this assertion — which might strike the reader as yet another overblown claim by another hysterical tree hugger! To test it, however, you might try the following simple experiment. Put this book down, go to any bookstore or library, and get a copy of any one of several solid, but hardly technical or arcane, environmental magazines: *E Magazine, Sierra Club, Audubon, WorldWatch, The Ecologist, Garbage,* and *Buzzworm* are all good. Read the magazine from cover to cover: every story, news byte, ad, and letter to the editor. Then ask yourself: "Did I know about much of this? Did I have any idea how serious it was in the [pick one or more] forests, third world coastlines, fishing industry, use of chemicals in agriculture, environmental effects of militarism, other?" And, presuming that you are a reasonably educated, reasonably aware person, you might ask yourself: "I listen to public radio, I watch the news, I read a newspaper, I subscribe to [pick all that apply] *Time, Newsweek, Ms., The Nation, The New Republic, New Age Journal, Yoga Journal, Sports Illustrated, Mother Jones, Cosmopolitan,* other, . . . yet how little I knew about all this. Why is that?"

This exercise is the first reading I have students perform in my environmental philosophy class. Having made it into one of the top engineering colleges in the U.S., these students are scientifically and technically gifted. They typically score above 650 on their Math SATs, they are not afraid of science, and they have all been educated decades after the first Earth Day — decades into a period in which public schools are (supposedly) including environmental issues as part of the curriculum. After doing the reading, many of them end up in a state of semi-shock.

For a number of reasons, environmental issues do not get the attention they deserve. For one thing, some of the richest, most powerful institutions in the world both cause a lot of the damage and also own a good deal of the media. Yet there is also the fact that particular reporters and editors are, like the rest of us, scared. For too many of us, too often, the facts are emotionally overwhelming, and responding to them would require basic changes in how all of us live. And so avoidance wins the day.

The second dimension of institutional denial is in some ways even more pernicious. It occurs at those times when the environment becomes yet another part of the ever-changing spectacle of our media-saturated times. We have the "year of the environment," pop stars for the rainforest, TV specials for clean air, Disney movies highlighted by songs which reject putting a price tag on nature, and pious declamations from politicians, corporations, and anyone else who has access to advertising, a microphone, or a web site. Our own personal concerns are reflected back to us through media images of public concern. These images seem to promise action to redress wrongs, solve problems, and restore public safety. Experts galore provide analysis and devise programs. We start to believe that the authorities are willing and able to handle the problem.

Often, however, no really significant action is taken. To begin with, much of corporate action in these areas takes the form of "greenwashing." Corporations mount large-scale public relations campaigns to obscure what they've actually done or take credit for improvements mandated by laws against which they themselves vigorously lobbied! Perception of change, not change itself, is often what they are after most. Further, by the time the commissions of inquiry and studies of the problem are concluded, our attention is focused somewhere else. The environment will have had its fifteen minutes of fame, until of course we get another really, really hot summer, or the beaches are once again littered with dirty syringes. The rainforest in Brazil had, I just read, two of its most destructive years in 1995–97 — and this after how many conferences, stories, rainforest benefit CDs, and boxes of rainforest crunch sold at health food stores? We thought something would change, yet an entire country (world?) afflicted with Attention Deficit Disorder is just not capable of focusing long and hard enough to keep one problem before our eyes. We look, we look hard, one might even say with a touch of hysteria — and then we look away again.

Some years ago, my avoidance of environmental issues began to break down. There were a number of reasons, including a little more emotional maturity on my part and the examples of people like Joanna Macy, Miriam Greenspan, and Bill McKibben, who were willing to face the facts and the emotions that went along with them. In person or through their writing they asked me: "Well, why *don't* you think about it?"

I immersed myself in all the material I had avoided: studies of toxic waste dumps causing raised leukemia rates, descriptions of the burning, chemical-filled rivers of Poland, and long dispassionate lists of lost species. I wept bitterly as the facts were paraded before my eyes, and started carrying around both a deep anger at those in power and a nagging guilt over my own years of complicity, complacency, and ignorance.

But there was something else: something powerful, liberating, and astonishingly joyful. The energy I had poured into avoidance was freeing up. I could cover my desk with books like *Toxic Nation* and *Who'll Save the Forests?* and know that I'd read them soon. I was no longer (subconsciously) telling myself: "Watch out, here comes something you can't handle." I was no longer acting as if what was happening was so bad that I couldn't even think about it! I was no longer crippled by fear. Like Rachel Carson, my joy in the natural world was renewed just because I was no longer hiding from what was happening to it. Instead, I felt determined to find out and respond. While I had always believed that spiritual development required some engagement with the world, I finally developed the courage to apply this insight to environmental issues.

Perhaps most important, happiness in my own (actually very limited) ability to do something about these problems was fueled by admiration for those strong souls who were fighting back against the devastation. As in the case of my earlier study of the Holocaust, the bravery of resisters altered the spiritual meaning of the situation. My sense of horror remained, but that sense was now accompanied by a kind of wonder at what people could face and do under the most difficult of circumstances. As the Holocaust was not only a time when people were murdered, but also a time when they resisted, so the environmental crisis comprised not only the destruction of the earth but also its protection.

The change I underwent when I put my avoidance away was, and can only be described as, a kind of spiritual awakening. There was a lightness in my step and a new twinkle in my eye. The world, with all its pains and problems, seemed fresh and vibrant. I was "reborn" as someone who no longer had to live in fear of finding out what the truth was, as downright scary as that truth might be. I felt, in a way I hadn't in years, truly at home.

When reality threatens us directly, when the little movements of avoidance don't suffice, we may turn to denial. The difference between avoidance and denial is the difference between passivity and activity, or between the tacit and the overt. While avoidance takes those little hops and jumps away from what frightens us, in denial we look it right in the face and say it isn't there. And then that thought guides how we live.

At bottom, the many forms of denial have a simple message in common: "It's not that bad." "It's not that bad" can mean, for instance, that there is a place to go where we can get away. It's too bad about the cities, we might think, but there is always the country. Or: it's too bad about the U.S., but there is the rainforest (the mountains of Canada, at least the Arctic?). Or: it's too bad about what's happening somewhere else, but here (in this suburb with green lawns and big trees, or nature reserve, or national forest) we are safe.

In reality, of course, there is no safe place and no place left unchanged. In the most general terms, as Bill McKibben devastatingly argued in *The End of Nature*, now that we've altered the climate and thinned the ozone layer, all of the earth has been affected by human actions. If we think of "nature" as something which functions without our intervention, we must acknowledge that nature is lost forever.

Less abstractly, there is also the painful truth that pollution is everywhere. Arctic seals have PCBs in their fat cells, Antarctic air carries toxins, litter can be found at the bottom of the ocean and on the tops of mountains. (And if it's a *famous* mountain, there are liable to be huge mounds of trash left from the glossy, high-tech expeditions that come to climb them, right alongside the ever-increasing telecommunications towers that make the cell phones work.)

Consider my friend Jack, who moved from metropolitan Boston to a peninsula on the coast of Maine. He and his wife let their income drop by 50 percent in order to live a more rural life and to establish a small spiritual community with some friends. The tiny town they settled in had a population of five hundred; the nearest "city," with a population of twelve hundred, was fourteen miles away. The only local industry was small-boat fishing, seafood processing, and a summer ferry to a small offshore island. Jack was two hundred miles from Boston, a hundred from Portland.

Yet there is a strange confluence of winds in Tenants Harbor, Maine, an unpredictable pattern that can cause different kinds of air pollution to collect along the coast. This barren, rocky, and beautifully evocative place, graced by seabirds and lobster beds, can have bouts of terrible air quality. When Jack went jogging, pains in his chest made him wonder if he was developing heart problems or lung disease. "No," said his doctor, "your heart and lungs are fine." While reading a story in the local paper about other people experiencing trouble breathing, especially while exercising, he discovered that it was something else. As the local air quality monitoring station revealed, his tiny village often had more ground level ozone than Boston. Ground level ozone is a prime component of classic smog. And here it was, miles from nowhere.

This story is less about Jack than it is about all of us. Green with envy, I and his other friends saw him as someone who had left pollution behind. While each of us had our own reasons to stay tied to the city or the suburban sprawl, he (we thought) had gotten out. And if he had gotten out, then it was at least possible that we could too. Yet the sad truth, the one we were all denying, is that there is no more "out."

Another form of denial rests on the idea that scientific and technical wizardry will take care of these problems. Sadly, however, we can no more place uncritical trust in scientists and engineers than we can expect to find a totally pristine seacoast. Just like the rest of us, those with highly specialized knowledge can get caught up in an institutional temptation to put what is ugly or threatening out of the way.

As an example, consider the history of CFCs (chlorofluorocarbons). Most of us have learned that these chemicals, so useful to modern refrigeration and auto air conditioning, do something destructive to the atmosphere. As they escape in the process of production or in worn-out units, they release chlorine molecules that make their way inexorably up to the ozone layer, a band of special oxygen molecules at eighty thousand feet above the earth's surface. Once they reach the ozone, the chlorine molecules begin to break it down, with each chlorine molecule able to destroy tens of thousands of ozone molecules. The result is less protection from the sun's ultraviolet radiation. The consequence of decreased protection is, at least, higher incidence of skin cancer and cataracts. This we are sure of. Less certain, but perhaps even more frightening, is the possibility that increased UV radiation will weaken the phytoplankton, the basis of the ocean's food chain, or that it might have unforeseen effects on animal (and, therefore, human) reproduction. There is some suspicion that a worldwide decrease in various species of frogs, especially ones whose eggs sit in sunlight, is a result of increases in UV radiation.

My focus here is not principally on the factual details of such environmental disasters, but on their spiritual meaning — and especially on how we deny them. What is striking about the disaster of CFC production — a production that continues as of this moment, aimed at distribution in the third world rather than in Europe and the U.S. — are two remarkable examples of denial that mark its history.

The first example comes from the times when the potentially damaging effects of CFCs were first under serious study. Two chemists, whose work was shadowed by fears of the professional ostracism that often attends scientists who challenge large corporations on matters of public safety, began to be convinced that CFCs would impair the ozone layer. They offered an elegant theoretical model of how this could be occurring. The ozone producers replied that these claims were simply speculative science that could not be taken seriously without some confirmation in the real world. Years passed, during which the lead scientist of the pair, Sherry Rowland, found his career under a cloud for having gone public in a "policy" matter instead of staying in the realm of "pure science." Despite his status as a nationally recognized senior chemist, invitations to present his research to business and academia dwindled to the vanishing point. (Ironically, twenty years after he asked the simple question of what happens when CFCs get released at ground level, Rowland got a Nobel Prize for this work; by then, however, the damage to our world had been done.)

In fact, however, the confirmation the chemical companies said they were waiting for was already in existence. For some years data from British Antarctic Survey instruments had been registering a thinning of the ozone layer. But this information had been so shocking that it had been disbelieved, written off as a failure of the satellite's instruments rather than as an indication that the ozone was really being depleted. The evidence directly in front of the researchers' eyes was denied. They thought: this just can't be happening. Yet it was.

In this particular instance the chemist Rowland was the professional victim of a generalized form of institutional denial: the notion that science is (or should be) detached from the rest of society, that it is a perfectly neutral source of knowledge and technical expertise. Unlike politics, commerce, or personal interests, we are sometimes told, science will give us the direct, unvarnished truth. This idea ignores how the vast majority of contemporary scientific research is funded by corporations or the government. It is therefore governmental or corporate interests that determine the direction and content of research. The truths that are known are those that are sought after by researchers who must conceive of problems in the way that is congenial to those paying the bills. Of course many times this works to everyone's advantage. The knowledge that is gained is equally relevant and valuable for us all. In other cases, however, the results are partial, biased, or damaging. Research on energy is conducted on sources of power that can be centrally owned by large utilities; health research focuses on finding expensive drugs rather than on low-cost prevention. In such cases (and many more could be described), it is not that the scientific or technical claims are necessarily false. It is that someone had to choose what would be investigated — which questions would be raised and answered. In other words, all science has to fit into somebody's image of what is important or good, for it is always somebody other than the scientist who is paying for it. Any suggestion that scientists should leave policy issues alone presupposes that other policy makers are not already influencing it. Unfortunately, this is not the case.

The second example of denial in the history of CFCs goes back to its origins. The Dupont chemists who developed the stuff had tried to be reasonably cautious. In theoretical models and lab tests they sought to find out what would happen when CFCs entered the atmosphere. There is only one problem with their studies: they stopped at a level of forty thousand feet. The ozone layer, however, is at eighty thousand feet. What did they think would happen after the stuff hit forty thousand? How could they have ignored what would happen next?

We live in a civilization permeated by this kind of denial — of our vulnerability, of the limited scope of our knowledge, of how badly things can turn out. The fruits of such denial can be found in many other cases: the "miracle" pesticides which ten years later are made illegal, the anti-miscarriage drugs which cause birth defects, the economic development that poisons those whose lives it is supposed to enrich.

This kind of denial continues in the illusion that we can have anything money can buy. What CFCs are about, after all, is refrigerated foods and cars that are cool in 95-degree weather. To have used the chemicals as we did requires that we believe that these things can be had without some corresponding loss. In this and comparable cases, sub-stances are developed, produced, and distributed while their potential real cost has been denied. For example, the vast majority of man-made chemicals which we inject into our surroundings have never been tested for their carcinogenic effects. They are innocent until proven guilty, that is, until it can be proven that they are harming people. And al-most none of these chemicals are examined for what they will do to us in combination — which is, after all, how they are experienced by our bodies. When they are regulated, the corporations who make them exercise frightening control over how the regulations are observed (or eluded). They authorize biased research, bribe regulators, pay off legis-lators, or end up getting asked to write the regulations themselves. Is it any wonder that despite the great orchestrated public denial embodied in trumpeted claims about the powers of medical research and high-tech treatment, in many if not most areas we are losing the "war on cancer"? Is it any wonder that in the 1990s the rates of breast, colo-rectal, brain, testicle, and kidney cancer continued to rise? Or that we can now expect that between one-third and two-fifths of us will get cancer in our lifetimes? What the frequent public campaigns of medical self-congratulations offer is the denial of our frailty, our vulnerability, our imperfection. They deny the simple truth that we will not win the war on cancer unless we change the way we live.

As I write this chapter, the movie *Titanic* is enjoying great success. The film tells the story of the ship that was supposed to be invulner-able, which had no use for lifeboats — and which sank on its maiden voyage. As I watched the film I sensed that the whole tale is a disquiet-ing metaphor for much of our own time. In the self-confident folly that said the sea had been mastered, a folly so clearly based in a denial of who we really are, was inscribed the deaths of fifteen hundred people. Our shortcomings of knowledge, competence, and foresight — and of the actual complexity of the world — were denied. Does this remind us of anything that has happened and continues to happen in the realm of the environment?

In fact, countless other examples can be found of a mistaken, irra-tional confidence that our actions won't have negative effects. What occurs, time after time, is a kind of willful refusal to see what we are doing. Not so much an avoidance — which, as I understand it, is a movement away from, a skipping over, a leaving out — as an active act of exclusion. To deny is simultaneously to confront, to reject, and to obscure. To deny is to look the truth in the face and say: "this isn't so." And then, if we can, to hide that truth out of sight. World Bank "development" projects which devastated the rainforest and poisoned the natives would sometimes plant a line of trees around the local helicopter landing spot, so visiting dignitaries would not witness the ruin that had taken place. The favored response to oil spills is often to apply a chemical that simply makes the oil sink out of sight. The damaging effects of the oil continue, but on the bottom of the sea, where they can't be easily seen. Environmental offensives against native peoples typically take place away from TV cameras or adequate news coverage. Consequently, some of the most terrible assaults never get reported. This invisibility of the environmental victims, especially if they are not white, is itself taken for granted by some of the major players. When Exxon sought to locate a new mine in Indian territory in Minnesota, for instance, it had to prepare an environmental impact statement. It did so, but managed to omit any mention of possible effects on Indians living immediately downstream from where the mine would be located.

Under the regime of denial, when the truth does surface, people attempt to hide it. Thus we have countless examples of companies or the government authorizing studies of products or procedures, and then asking (or telling) the authors to rewrite their documents. For instance, a mining company hired a scientist to evaluate workers' complaints that widespread ulcers were related to handling radium. After the research confirmed the workers' claims, the company barred the researcher from publishing his results and lied to the government about the findings. Pesticide manufacturers, who also threatened to sue her publisher, called Rachel Carson, now hailed as the saint of modern environmentalism, a communist. While Carson's attackers proved too weak to accomplish much, thirteen states now have laws holding people liable for damages if they make (vaguely defined) "false" statements about agricultural products. The goal of these "food disparagement laws" is to create a psychic climate of fear and a public atmosphere of blanket denial over the dangers of and lack of reassuring research about hi-tech food processes like irradiation and genetic engineering. These laws may in fact be unconstitutional, but they nevertheless have made people wary of facing major corporate food producers in a lawsuit. (Oprah won her case against the beef industry, but how many of us have her clout?) In another situation, a time- and money-consuming freedom of information lawsuit by a pesticide manufacturer has harassed a leading researcher studying the presence and effects of the pesticide toxaphene in the Great Lakes. The goal is to warn her and other researchers that if they speak too directly about the effects of chemicals in the environment, every scrap of paper they ever used in their work can be subpoenaed.

Of course, it is not hard to see why people might want to protect their jobs, their corporations, their income — and lie to do so. What is critical here from the spiritual point of view is that at this time in history all of us are implicated in denial. When avoidance fails, we all, at one time or another, use denial in its stead. The corporate defenders of CFCs were in denial about their — and their children's — vulnerability to UV rays; as if people of wealth don't live in the sun's neighborhood. The defenders of questionable food processing forget that they too eat, and that if exposing meat to radioactive waste isn't the safest of all ways to sterilize food, they too will suffer as a result. When those of us who are not corporate spokesmen or well-defended bureaucrats simply continue with business as usual, we too are part of our culture's denial. At times even the most environmentally conscious, bogged down in the demands of daily life, turn away from what is right in front of their faces. I remember making light of an asbestos-wrapped pipe in my house, refusing for a while to acknowledge how much the dust it was shedding could be harming my family. "Don't worry about it so much," I told my wife. "Half the houses in our town have pipes wrapped like that." "So," she asked, "why should that reassure me?"

And of course there was no reason for her to be reassured. I was just whistling in the wind, hiding my real fear under a false confidence.

What is the spiritual problem with denial? It is, I think, the pain, confusion, and sense of unreality that arises when we both know the truth and refuse to acknowledge it. It is another kind of "double consciousness," one which takes an enormous amount of effort to live in. Our minds have to grapple with a reality split between what actually exists and what we would like to exist. We cannot fully engage with what is, because we are constantly picking and choosing between the parts of reality we will accept and those we will deny. Spiritual development, however, requires that we engage with reality. And that we be able to see it for what it is. As avoidance leads to the repression of energy, denial cuts us off from the truth, makes us doubt our own sense of how things are, keeps us from listening to others or the world and from changing the way things are.

After the Holocaust, a Polish worker who kept track of the number of people entering Treblinka concentration camp said: "Of course, one had no conception of what 'extermination camp' really meant. I mean, it was beyond — not just experience, but imagination, wasn't it?" This man saw, and kept a record of what he saw. He allowed himself to be changed, to develop a new "imagination." In denial, by contrast, we reject what we are seeing and refuse to extend ourselves.

Or, in our effort to hide away that which is true, we simply foist it off on others. So the toxic incinerators are concentrated in poor and black communities; the uranium mines are on Native American property. As a result the cancer rates in both communities far exceed the national average. Or, in a different setting, we find that many inner-city kids in Los Angeles have stunted lung growth due to air pollution. These Others carry the stuff that those of us who are richer and luckier don't want to see or breathe, that which we deny in our minds and our social policies. The truth of our society's collective denial is written in their bodies.

If avoidance leads to a kind of sickness of the self, a diminished sense of who we are, denial corrodes our ability to stand for something. It sucks the integrity right out of us. We say things that somewhere in our minds we suspect are untrue. Harboring a lurking fear that what has been repressed will return to haunt us, we try to banish the offending realities. The sad truth is that to the extent that we live in denial our lives are a little empty, just because (as with avoidance) somewhere we sense what we are doing. And thus we sense that at any time something can come along and bust right through the denial that has been (we think) sustaining us. We are haunted by suppressed anxiety and dishonesty, and our ability to live in spiritual truth is diminished.

Alternatively, denial represents a kind of frantic childish fantasy of omnipotence. "I will close my eyes," we seem to be saying, "and it will disappear." If we just continue on as if the wolf is not at the door, if we don't pay too much attention to the millions of pounds of toxins in the air and water, if we put the destructive effects of chemical agriculture out of our minds, if we continue to say "this can't be changed, don't be an alarmist, let's be practical" — if all these things are done, then, in fact, there is no crisis.

Finally, if all else fails, we can pass the whole thing off as a problem faced by separate individuals. "Isn't it too bad," we say, "that his wife died of breast cancer. So young, so vibrant, so special. What bad luck (karma, fate, God's will...)." And then we don't have to think about all those chemicals stressing the DNA in our own breast cells, or those of our mothers or wives or daughters. We don't have to think about how breast cancer is a collective problem, not some huge collection of individual hard luck stories. That, in fact, we've brought a lot of it on ourselves.

In a culture shaped by denial and avoidance, spiritual truth will often arise from strange sources: dreams, madmen, shrill political groups making all sorts of proclamations about the end of the world. The more our dominant institutions avoid and deny, and so many of us manifest the same response in our personal lives, the more a real awareness of the truth will necessarily often exist only on the margin. Part of the spiritual task of facing the truth about the world in which we live, part of living on *this* earth (and not one sanitized by the attempt to escape from the pain) is to begin to be aware of these sources of the truth — both within ourselves and from others.

Consider Elie Wiesel's classic memoir *Night*, in which he tells of Moche, the janitor from his little town's synagogue. While Wiesel and his neighbors remained in the town, Moche had been expelled back to Poland and had miraculously escaped when the Nazis had murdered his companions. He returned and tried to tell the townspeople what he had seen. The janitor had always been a strange man, poor and unassuming. Now, in the confusion and despair of wartime, people in the town wrote off his strange and frightening story. "What an imagination he has," people said. Or: "Poor fellow, he's gone mad." Perhaps what he had seen had driven him a little out of his mind. Nevertheless, he alone knew the truth.

Or consider the story told by Terry Tempest Williams, in her haunting essay "The Clan of One-Breasted Women" — so named because of the epidemic of breast cancer that runs through her extended family. For years she had a strange, frequently recurring dream. She is in the Utah desert not far from her childhood home. Each time she is there she witnesses a strange flash of light against the night sky. After years of having this dream seared into her consciousness she mentioned it to her father. His answer shocked her:

> "You did see it.... The bomb. The cloud. We were driving home. ...It was an hour or so before dawn, when this explosion went off. We not only heard it, but felt it.... We pulled over and suddenly, rising from the desert floor, we saw it, clearly, this golden-stemmed cloud, the mushroom. The sky seemed to vibrate with an eerie pink glow. Within a few minutes, a light ash was raining on the car.... I thought you knew that... it was a common occurrence in the fifties."

It was at this moment that I realized the deceit I had been living under. Children growing up in the American Southwest, drinking contaminated milk from contaminated cows, even from the contaminated breasts of their mothers — members, years later, of the Clan of One-Breasted Women.

Of course it is not as if there aren't a lot of respected and respectable voices, from the Audubon Society to Al Gore, who claim to speak to the environmental crisis. Too often these voices are drowned out by the collective forces of avoidance and denial, but they do exist.

Perhaps more dangerously, at times the dominant powers in our society create the illusion that they are heeding the call of environmental sanity. Attention is being paid, we think, and it seems that those of us who do not control the economy or the courts or the EPA can leave it to others. "After all," we might be saying to ourselves, "wasn't there just a huge international conference in Kyoto about global warming? Surely, they'll take care of the problem. And didn't a bunch of countries meet years ago in Montreal to take care of the threat to the ozone layer? They had foreign ministers and top scientists and all the rest. Surely they'll know what to do, now that they are thinking about it!"

Sadly, this too can be a kind of denial. For as much as we would like to believe that all the headlines and TV stories and loud speeches mean that things have been taken care of, if we look very carefully we will see that this is often not the case. Indeed, the Kyoto agreement was a step forward. Yet even if abided by, it would only roll back the emissions of greenhouse gases to what they were in the mid-1980s. But those levels were already sufficiently high to warm the earth. What was needed at Kyoto, most responsible observers said, was a fundamental commitment to decrease dependence on fossil fuels, the only step that might really reduce the warming trend. Such a step would require a full public acknowledgment of just how significant the threat is. In fact, we would have to admit that it is so significant that in transportation, energy production, agriculture, and housing (to name a few) we cannot go on with business as usual. To avoid this conclusion is to perpetuate the denial, if even in a slightly reduced form. Even worse, I discover as I finish this chapter that many members of Congress are so opposed to reducing our greenhouse gases that they are trying to eliminate funding for even the discussion of climate change, education about global warming, or preparation for the passage of the Kyoto treaty. If successful, denial-as-enforced-silence would be imposed on the administration, on the EPA, and on other government agencies.

Further, to find an account of Kyoto that reveals these truths, we have to look beyond the most accessible sources of information and dig deeper: to the environmental journals and news services and on-line information sources. Just as Wiesel's town should have listened to its mad janitor, and Williams needed to find the truth in her dreams, so spiritual seekers who want to overcome denial in an age of ecocide need to pursue information and analysis that is not quite so readily accessible as the TV news or the local newspaper. But this search, I am suggesting, is as much a part of our spiritual journey as the more traditional examination of our personal moral failings. Without it, we will never really be part of the world in which we live.

At the same time, we need to listen to our own doubts and fears, our own intuitions and common sense. Even without graduate degrees in environmental science or an exhaustive knowledge of global warming, we may well have access to some of the critical truths we need to know.

The notion of an inner truth is basic to spiritual traditions. It is frequently suggested that we can find the most important of truths within ourselves, if only we devote sufficient devotion to prayer, meditation, and honest introspection. Consider, for example, the "Arhat," the sage of Theravada Buddhism. In his religious practices the Arhat seeks an end to the confinement imposed by an identification with a self bound to desires that inevitably cause suffering. The question that arises for such a person is, of course, whether it is possible to be alive as a human being and not identify with such a self. Spiritual wisdom arises when the student directly experiences a state of mind in which identification with self dissipates. As one early practitioner is reputed to have said, when questioned by a fellow seeker: "During my meditation I reached a point where I had no thought that 'I am this; this is mine; this is my self.'"

Or consider the prophet Elijah. Fleeing for his life from Jezebel's wrath after he put to death the prophets of Baal, he encounters God not in a mighty wind, an earthquake, or a fire, but in a "still, small voice."

Consider how the poet William Blake saw Christ suspended in air, dancing outside his window. Or the states of ecstatic no-self produced by Sufi dancing or tribal chanting; or the transformations of consciousness which come on a Native American Vision Quest, prepared for by days of fasting and isolation.

In all these, examples, and in the many more which could be discussed, spiritual teachings tell us that wisdom can be found within ourselves, if only we open ourselves to it. This wisdom provides an alternative to the ego's twisted identification with permanent dissatisfaction, greed, or violence. In it, we find truths that are usually inaccessible to a mind bound by the conventional social order.

And it is just this wisdom which can be sought, and followed, in regard to what is around us as well as what is within us, in regard to social conditions as well as to our own personal spiritual condition. Our senses, our intelligence, and our emotional wisdom can instruct us about the wider relationships in which we live. The truth of these intuitions is not guaranteed (any more than they are certain to be true when they concern our inner life.) But like Williams's dream or the stories of Moche the beadle, they deserve our attention.

When the urban summer air is called "unhealthy" for the seventh straight day, and once again nothing is being done to reduce car traffic in favor of public transportation or bikes, doesn't some part of ourselves sense that our political and industrial leaders are making a huge mistake? When we find researchers making the exact same plea — first in 1955 and then, after forty years of near silence, in 1995 — for an investigation into the relation between cancer and chemicals in the environment, isn't there some part of us that knows that our scientists, for all their brilliance, are simply not doing what so terribly needs to be done? In instances such as these we sense that things aren't right. Our inner voices prompt us to awareness. And it is part of our spiritual discipline to pay attention to these feelings, to use them as we might use the information from an environmental magazine or the revelation that our drinking water is not as safe as we thought.

For spiritual development to take place, we cannot ignore our own inner knowledge. When we sense that something is wrong — in our-selves, in the world — we must respond. If we do not, then the prayer and meditation, the listening to the voice of God and exploring our own hearts, will count for little. The point of those practices is to find, and heed, the most basic truths. If we are going to listen and search, we had better take seriously what turns up, no matter how scary it is. We need to attend to the truths known by others, no matter how shrill and marginalized they may be, and to the truth as we know it ourselves, even when it is fragmented, confused, and unfinished.

How are we to live with the truth? When we do move beyond avoid-ance and denial, how are we to retain any sense of joy in life? How can we keep from succumbing to dread or despair?

In essence, I believe that only if we become increasingly aware of the resistance of others and resist ourselves can we regain the sense of peace that necessarily leaves us when we end our own flight from reality. While a more developed answer to this question will be offered later, a few thoughts are relevant here.

First of all, from the point of view of a spirituality of resistance, it is necessary that we not be afraid of the depths of our feelings about the environmental crisis. While these feelings are painful, they also re-veal the depth of our connections to the rest of the world. As sources of precious information and measures of our love, they deserve to be honored. They teach us that despite everything we can still care for the world and mourn the many deaths around us. In directly experiencing our feelings about these matters, our souls may recover some strength and vitality: qualities that are very much essential to any real spiritual growth and that have been eroded by avoidance and denial.

To realize these qualities anew we may need to go through a period, which in fact may recur, of focusing on the desperate, terrifying truth.

I remember, for instance, what happened to me when I was doing the detailed research for the Holocaust presentation I mentioned earlier. Immersed in historical material about deportations and mass killings, I began to see boxcars carrying Jews when I took the subway, and to think of SS vans when I heard sirens in the night. I had entered another world. Similarly, when years later I focused my attention on the environmental crisis, I would bore people at parties and give my wife nightmares, compulsively sharing the latest ecological horror story just before bedtime. Walking among beautiful birch trees, I thought of what the ravages of acid rain were doing to the forests of New England. A trip to the beach reminded me of the tumor-afflicted whales in the Bay of Newfoundland. I was shot through with grief and anger.

At this point I, and perhaps anyone else who goes through this process, faced, paradoxically, two more temptations to slip into denial.

The first temptation is that of despair. So much has been lost forever: so many people and animals poisoned, so many beautiful places turned barren. Once the denial and avoidance recede, a tide of hopeless gloom naturally starts to inch forward. While a temptation to conscious despair is inevitable at this point, it can be resisted. For what despair obscures is that the matter at hand is not closed, not finished. It is, in fact, still in doubt. The attraction of despair is that we no longer have to make the effort of hope, an effort which could give rise to further pain and disappointment. In despair, after all, we need care no longer because everything has been settled. As deeply as such despair might be felt, it too is a kind of denial. For while the environment has suffered greatly, there is still much to treasure and protect. Grief can legitimately become despair only when there is no hope left: nothing, that is, which is still worth saving.

A spirituality of resistance can build here on the countless spiritual teachings from a variety of traditions which have told us quite simply: there is no grief which cannot be endured, no loss that need become the sole meaning of our lives, no emotional pain that will not heal if it is entered into fully. We can feel the fear and grief and still do what needs to be done. Despite our losses, we can still resist — if, that is, we do not succumb to the rejection of hope which is the hidden message of despair.

From a spiritual point of view the steadfastness of hope is essential, just because it expresses our capacity to think beyond the pain we ourselves are experiencing in any particular moment and to delight in the prospect that someone, somewhere, can still find some happiness. The Italian Marxist Antonio Gramsci coined the telling phrase "pessimism of the intellect, optimism of the will." He meant by it that we must seek to know the bitterest of truths but can embody in our actions our continuing commitment to create new, and different, realities. If we can still mourn, then we can still act. And while there is the capacity for action, there is the possibility that what we do will bring some happiness to some of our fellow beings. The persistence of this thought is the essence of hope, even in the darkest of times. We do not have to believe in some power greater than ourselves that is overseeing what is going on. To have hope we need not have faith. All we need is to admit that despite all the pains of the present, the future is still in doubt. That ignorance may be our greatest source of hope.

The second temptation is a kind of suppression of the self. We adopt a purely factual, business-like, pseudo-rational approach to the crisis. We accept the facts but start to deny the emotional pain by pouring everything we have into information, information, information and action, action, action. We focus on facts and figures, policies and procedures. We make a lot happen and fight the good fight. For a while this type of denial is quite useful. It helps us Get a Lot Done, wins us a lot of (well-deserved) admiration, and seems to keep the demons at bay.

But how long will it be until we become shrill and a little crazy, burn out, or lose any sense of joy? How long can we ignore the feelings that got us here in the first place? The simple truth of the matter is that we are human, and human beings have feelings about their lives: about their families and friends and about the world in which they live. We cannot separate the facts of the matter from what we feel about them. Quite simply, the feelings we have are part of the facts: that we feel this much grief and fear about what is happening is something which needs to be attended to, just as much as the DDT level in the Arctic snow or the decline in water quality. We need to share our sadness and rage, to get some solace so that what we know doesn't eat away at our souls. Once we face the truth of what humanity has done to the world, we carry a permanent grief. This grief will not cripple us if we honor it, but it will poison our hearts if we pretend it is not there.

My times of being overwhelmed by the environmental crisis passed. I survived, none the worse for wear and in fact basically happier, more alive, and more in touch with the world and my feelings about it. If we open up a dam of feelings, is it surprising that a great rush comes forth? Rather than avoid this rush and keep the best parts of ourselves suppressed, we can ride it — knowing that a much healthier balance will surely follow. In this balance we will not forget about what acid rain is doing to forests, but will find a newly fresh joy in the trees around us. We will savor the birds before our eyes, even as we grieve for the ones dying because their meadows have been turned into parking lots. We will feel, and this may be the greatest blessing, a new and profound connection to nonhuman nature in all its brilliant diversity, and to our comrades and partners in the struggle to turn things around. Putting aside our own denial and avoidance, we can sense much more clearly the greatness of those who — from the Brazilian rainforest to the Afro-American factory towns to the California redwoods — have fought back to protect themselves and this earth on which we all must live.

CHAPTER THREE

Working Ourselves to Death

The usual approach to happiness is about fulfilling the demands of the normal ego. Based on how much we can possess, control, and own, it promises more than it can deliver. As an alternative, a spiritual perspective offers gratitude instead of grasping, simple joy instead of compulsive consumption, openness to life instead of a driven (and fruitless) attempt to control everything. These priceless gifts, however, do not come cheap. In order to receive them, thoughtlessness needs to give way to awareness, arrogance to compassion, addiction to balanced calm. The more we are willing to transform our lives in these directions, the more the spiritual promises of increased peacefulness and connection to the miracles of life will come true for us.

Paradoxically, however, we won't get very far if all we do is transfer our compulsive style of desire into the spiritual realm. If this occurs, the "spiritual" will turn into another form of the "pleasant," and the promises of spirituality will become just as empty as those of conventional life.

A further concern arises if we sense that in our attempt to live spiritually what we do matters as much as what we feel, and how we affect others is as essential as our own state of mind. In particular, along with our sources of satisfaction and our awareness of what is taking place around us, we need to think deeply about how and why we work. Work is especially important because many of us are so emotionally tied to it. It is not just a paycheck at the end of the month, but provides a fundamental source of meaning and recognition and helps determine who we are. If we identify with work too much and in the wrong way, we may feel lost without it and desperate when it is threatened.

In an age when the most ordinary occupations can contribute to ecological disasters, our attachment to work is particularly dangerous. To keep our work, who knows what we might do, whose orders we might take, and where we might stay when, in our hearts, we know we should leave?

I can make this point more concrete by talking first about my own life. (I would not use myself as an example so much, if, as Thoreau said, there were anyone else I knew so well.)

One thing I do know well, and from the inside, is how necessary it can feel to be recognized and acknowledged. As I pursued an adult career in academia, I continued a drive that had animated me since grade school: to "succeed" and do well, whether this meant getting As, making the varsity wrestling team, winning the local music contest, besting my friends' college board scores, or getting into Swarthmore. I desperately needed to feel recognized, to belong to something that told me (which I clearly didn't believe) that I was important, of value, special. And for the most part I managed to do all this. Once past graduate school, however, I ran into trouble: years of part-time or temporary teaching jobs, piles of rejection letters from publishers. The sense of myself as a brilliant kid who would always get the public recognition he craved started to dry up. I felt more than a little lost, and deeply frightened — as if something dreadful and hidden were slowly coming to light. For most of my life I had counted on public recognition, felt that no matter what else I might do or what might happen to me, I could be assured that in the public space I would be a "winner." And now that ground of my identity was dissolving under my feet.

This period was at its worst for seven difficult years. What kept me sane (to the extent that I stayed sane at all) was the sense that I was something other than my professional life, my CV, my list of accomplishments.

For during that time I also had an identity in the institutions and activities of left politics, and that, at least, gave me some other place to hang my hat besides the world of professional philosophy. I was, my friends and my wife told me, a good person, a good comrade, a decent man trying in a rather overly serious New Leftish kind of way to make the world a better place. These aspects of myself gave life a meaning other than what I was failing to achieve in the realm of my public career.

While that career barely survived, this alternative location saved my soul. As a form of identity it was surprisingly spiritual. By that I mean it was a place where I really did submerge my personal ego, did not seek power or control or to be the top of the heap. I wasn't involved in politics to be a "success"; just doing my part was enough. I would write the manifestos if need be, or I would simply lick envelopes and sweep up. I felt that the love I gave and the love I received were all that I needed. I was "somebody" just by being part of a movement that (despite the naiveté or arrogance we shared) was trying to make a real difference.

In a spiritual sense, politics brought out the best in me. Without calling it such, I was guided by the spiritual value of giving without hope of personal reward. This attitude was fundamentally different from much of what went on in professional life. That setting was shaped by competition, desperate striving for recognition, wanting to stand out and stand above. Politics meant cooperation, supporting others, being concerned pretty much only with the fate of the movement as a whole.

Thus when I speak in this chapter about the perils of a public identity, I don't mean that spiritual life should drive us into a purely private existence. My political commitments led me, after all, straight into the heart of the community. I am not saying it is wrong to be involved in one's work, to want to have an effect in the world, to be emotionally connected to a wider reality than one's personal existence. It is even true that I had a powerful and authentic bond to philosophy as a calling that involved using the mind to discern the meaning of life and the sources of human happiness. The problem came when that "calling" to do philosophy got connected to an ego-bound desire for recognition, when satisfaction with my work in the world became dependent on career success, when satisfaction with what I was doing was turned over to judgments by "the profession." Thus the perils of conventional public identity, as we shall see, center not on the simple fact of being public, but on what happens when our approach to public life aims to fill — as it did in the case of my ego-driven relation to my profession — a deep inner emptiness. All too often in such cases, our work in the world is driven by fear of failure, being average, or not belonging, by the compulsive need for success, recognition, or power. In order to fill our internal void we accept whatever work comes along — and this may lead us to take on work that is, quite simply, toxic.

I had other sources of support besides the political dimension. Psychedelic chemicals had exposed me to states of mind very different from my typically driven attempt to achieve. These experiences taught me the possibility of letting go. From them I caught a glimpse of the idea that I didn't have to work so desperately hard to earn acceptance or love. They were just there. These encounters led toward the practice of meditation, which in soberer ways taught me a similar message of self-acceptance.

I also found some relief in the writings of Kierkegaard. What I particularly appreciated was his repeated idea that the spiritual and moral task was not to be a great success, but to make of oneself a person worthy of relating to God. Striving to Make History (to "be somebody") only presumed to a control of life that no individuals possess. Also, and worse: it reflected a view of reality in which only a few people's lives could be important. Out of the mass of men and women, how many, after all, manage to become famous, powerful, or extraordinarily successful? But, said Kierkegaard, if the task is to devote oneself to being worthy of a relation with God, then each person's life is of infinite importance! In this task, he pointed out, no one's success comes at the price of anyone's else's insignificance, no one can do the job for another, and the task itself carries on for a lifetime. Of course, I didn't have to accept Kierkegaard's rather tortured overall account of God and religion to get the point. The important thing was that I realized I faced a choice in the way I would make meaning of my life. I could devote myself to being a decent person and embodying a spirit of love, an enterprise which I had to work at just as long and hard as anyone else, for my whole life and with no time off as a reward for doing really well last week. Alternatively, I could try to satisfy my endless craving for recognition, a craving which, in all probability, would never be satisfied no matter what happened. (A friend of mine once said that all he wanted was to have a few thousand people cheering for him each morning when he got out of bed.)

Political life, psychedelic experiences, meditation, and Kierkegaard did not completely eliminate my desire for conventional success in the public world. I still wanted a successful "career." I was still depressed over my professional hard times and still occasionally blamed myself for them. But I did have some supports against the assault my sense of self took in the conventional public realm. These supports gave me some rest from my driven pursuit of a public recognition that (in my folly) I thought would make me feel valuable and loved. They helped me see that my work in the world did not have to be keyed to conventional public recognition and that there was an alternative way to understand what was important and valuable about who I was.

Without those supports, what would I have given to "make it"? What would I have ignored? What might I have been willing to do? To what twisted enterprise might I have lent my energies just to make sure I had some place in the world?

A good deal of the behavior involved in technological and bureaucratic mass violence is committed by people who have too little sense of self outside of the way they serve the dominant — and damaging — social institutions. Because they are overidentified with "careers," desperate for external recognition to compensate for an internal void, their ability to take a critical view of what they are doing in the world gets paralyzed. That is why the environmental crisis is not only frightening to us personally; it also raises profound questions about how and why we participate in the public arena. In our time of big government, big corporations, big military machines, and daunting technical expertise, we risk finding that our work, which may seem essential to our sense of identity, has appalling consequences.

In other words: how we construct our personal identity, our most familiar feelings about who we are, helps lead to global catastrophe. How does this happen? What is the connection?

If we ask ourselves, "Who am I?" it is not hard to find an answer. We need only think of what occupies our minds when we wake up in the morning; what we worry about before we drop off to sleep; where we put our best energies. We can discover "who we are" by discerning our passions and anxieties, realizing that we weave our identity out of our activities and preoccupations. Whatever these may be — building a career or caring for children, writing a best-selling book or getting through a boring work week to bring home a family paycheck, trying to get teenagers off drugs or trying to make money as a crack dealer — they are our lifeline to a day-to-day understanding of who we are. These sources of meaning structure our days and months and years. They organize the moment-to-moment happenings into a pattern of effort, success or failure, connecting all the details of our experience into a life that makes some sense.

There is a wide range of activities that offer us meaning. My concern here is principally with work. I will examine overconsumption and family life only briefly — and as instances not of pleasure seeking or private gratification but of attempts to prove that one's personal life has some public validity. For many of us work is the core of our attempt to feel that we are significant, that we count or matter. Through our work we establish ourselves, become "somebody," get recognized. We are special, important, of note. Through work we both connect to society and also are able to stand out from the crowd. Whether as a success or just one of the gang, we feel a sense of belonging. The price of all this is that we ally ourselves with the dominant institutions of society. Thrown into a social world we have not chosen, we are dependent on it for a sense of identity and validation. We join the destructive dance of modern life, not for its own sake, but because we can see no other way to feel real.*

It is liberating, but also frightening and difficult, that in our time people are supposed to find the meaning of their lives by themselves: to sift through a nearly limitless range of occupational, relational, ideological, and even geographic options and say with confidence: "This is what I stand for, what I identify with, what I will work and sacrifice for to know that my life means something." Our parents, the supportive ones at least, tell us: "You can be anything you choose to be." And they usually have no idea how frightening that statement is. For one implication is that if we don't choose to be something, we won't be anything. Our being something depends on our choosing and on our continuing to substantiate that choice over and over again.

At the same time, while we may choose as individuals, the range of options before us is determined by powers far beyond anyone's personal control. We can choose to work, but cannot determine the basic economic relations of our society. We can choose to live wherever we want, but have little say in what these places will be like. We can pick from an array of goods and services, but don't seem to be able to slow down the economic and industrial growth that poisons the land and fills the malls with "stuff." Confronted by an abundance of variations on a very limited theme, in a setting shaped by distant and impersonal forces, we have to choose our own source of meaning.

It is perhaps the greatest tragedy of a very painful century that at this time many of the available choices of personal meaning will cause

---

*Some readers may be wondering if I'm talking only about men here. I'm not, but I'll explain why a little later on.

global environmental destruction. This is why a book on the most intimate aspects of spiritual life must simultaneously discuss the details of our social existence. As the more familiar versions of spiritual life stress how ordinary ways of thinking cause us pain, so a spirituality of resistance helps us realize their social consequences. In the beginning, we see that narrow self-interest keeps us from experiencing the miracles of life. Now we may realize how in our efforts to create meaningful lives — as producers and consumers, professionals and bureaucrats, workers and members of families — we too often become agents of ecological devastation. If we do not find another source of meaning, some other peg on which to hang our identity, who we are will be defined by activities that ravish much of what we hold dear. With our very sense of selfhood tied to participation in destructive institutions and cultural values, there seems to be no alternative. At its best, identification with spiritual truth can alter our sense of self and thus provide an alternative to this abyss of socially destructive behavior.

Our need for a source of meaning is not just one desire among others (as if we could list them: make money, have a good sex life, buy a new car, establish the meaning of our lives) but sits at the center of who we think we are. If it is not satisfied, nothing else will make us feel comfortable with ourselves or at home in the world.

We live in a large and complex society that structures the effects of our actions and that is now bending those actions toward environmental ruin. That is why we must find some form of identity separate from the dominant social order: some way of understanding who we are that enables us to feel our worth even if we do not achieve conventional public recognition or have a place in powerful public institutions. We must find a way to be ourselves without being dependent on what is conventionally called a successful life. If we don't have some other resource, we may just take what is offered. The result can be catastrophic. A spiritual identity, I believe, can serve this purpose. It can help us find, we might say, a moral stance in an immoral society.

Of course the acts that pollute the world are motivated by the pursuit of money, political authority, or military power, as well as by people seeking to find an identity in public work. Corporate greed, governmental hypocrisy, and simple self-interest have important roles. My concern here, however, is with the part played by those of us who are not terribly rich or terribly powerful. Further, in many cases money or power are themselves pursued to a great extent because they serve as measures of self-worth. While they have their own appeal, no doubt, the intensity with which we seek them often indicates a kind of desperation, not just the simple desire for more cash or a larger office. They serve as a kind of desperately needed psychic reassurance, especially for the type of people who are not forced to labor to stave off poverty, homelessness, or starvation. And it is precisely this group of administrators, engineers, intellectuals, managers, bureaucrats, researchers, and professionals that designs and administers the major tragedies of our time.

How do these tragedies unfold?

Consider: engineers, marketing consultants, government administrators, military analysts, chemists, pesticide salesmen, geologists hunting for uranium, real estate developers, and intellectuals — all get caught up in institutional and bureaucratic structures of corporate life, government service, and career. They find meaning in what they do. They possess reasonable ambitions and want to support their families. They pride themselves on having a place, on being hard workers, on being "experts" at something. This all sounds innocuous enough. Sadly, however, too often their need for this work will take precedence over closely examining what they are doing to the rest of the world.

Consider: in the "normal" course of life a young person may graduate from the engineering college where I teach. Burdened by educational loans, he finds employment, monetary rewards, a chance at independence from parents and all the pleasures of young adulthood. Typically, little thought will be given to the ultimate environmental consequences of his professional activities. Often, he will be working on complicated projects the ultimate goals or effects of which are not his immediate concerns. What he does know is that his years of study have paid off; that he is acknowledged as competent by a large organization; that he is able to use the skills it has taken him years to acquire; that every morning he has someplace to go — a place were he is welcomed by older, smarter, and more powerful people as part of the team. He has proved himself, or is in the process of doing so. He is making his mark, even if he is not so sure what that mark is or what it will do to others. Of course he is not emotionally identified with the destruction of the planet. How could he be? But neither is he a soulless automaton. He cares about what he does, but for him what he is doing centers on creating a substantial identity by participating in the public world. To achieve this identity, he must join in with the dominant institutions over which he has little individual control.

He certainly does not seek to damage the environment. Bit by bit, however, he becomes an accomplice to it. There is (in a phrase we shall see again) a "gradual, almost imperceptible, descent" to a point of no return.

A young man in Austria, whose name was Franz, had a father who died young. Franz's mother remarried, and Franz, though generally well treated by his stepfather, always felt that he was less important than the new father's birth children. His stepfather had a uniform, which Franz says that he hated, but which, it seems, he also envied and coveted. Franz was not without talents, becoming a master weaver at a remarkably young age, and certainly not without ambition, for when he came to believe that weaving held little room for advancement, he became a policeman. He had his own uniform now; he had (what he had missed in his childhood) a sense of being special. He could make things happen in the world, could make his mark. He was Franz-the-policeman: solid, dependable, honest, effective. He even received a special commendation for breaking up a ring of the then illegal Nazi party in Austria.

Then in 1938, when Germany took over Austria, Franz — still in uniform, still wedded to the desire to makes things happen, to be effective in the world — became caught up in the Holocaust. For our Franz is Franz Stangl, weaver turned policeman, who became an integral part of the Final Solution.

Not too long after the SS gained control of the Austrian police, Franz was assigned to the police staff at the Nazi Euthanasia Institute in Hartheim. His job was to help provide "order" for the systematic killing of chronically ill and retarded "patients," whose families were generally told that they had died of natural causes. Later, along with about four hundred others from the euthanasia program, Stangl moved "up" to the death and concentration camps. He directed the construction and was the first head of Sobibor, and then ran Treblinka. During his time, these camps slaughtered approximately eight hundred thousand Jews.

Later, much later, he said that he hated what had happened in the camps, but that he couldn't leave. He said he would never have wanted to do it, yet he did. He had his place. He made his mark in the world.

Stangl said:

> I never intentionally hurt anyone, myself.... But I was there.... So
> yes... in reality I share the guilt.... Because my guilt... is that I
> am still here. That is my guilt.... I should have died. That was my
> guilt... I should have killed myself in 1938.

As it was in the Holocaust, so it is in the environmental crisis: people
desperate for a sense of personal identity can take part in public work
that brings ruin to the world. Our drive to have the kind of work that
makes us feel important is thus as spiritually significant, and perhaps
much more dangerous, than the familiar problems of personal greed or
attachment.

Thus I have brought up Stangl because contained in the Holocaust,
in terrifying boldface, are some of the distinctive perils of our age. It
is not that the Holocaust is the "worst" that has been done to people
(though it may well be). But the Holocaust is, I believe, the signal event
of our time. Like a signpost in the gloom, it can help us find our way
toward the light; but only if we read it with the greatest of care.

When we discover the myriad of radiation experiments done on un-
knowing subjects and communities in support of the Cold War, do we
remember the medicalized torture of children in Auschwitz?

When our communities face pesticide-spraying airplanes, dioxin-
spewing industrial chimneys, chemical food contaminants, and leaking
landfills, do we remember the Zyklon B flowing into the gas chambers?

When we listen to our children cough, and wonder why so many
have asthma, and continue a way of life that creates the air pollution
that weakens their lungs, do we remember how well-meaning, passive
bystanders helped make the Holocaust possible? When we hear about
the countless indigenous peoples with monstrous cancer rates because
of uranium mining on their land, or victims of cultural genocide because their forest homes were turned into so many board feet of lumber,
their villages dispossessed in the name of some mindless "development"
scheme, do we remember how the world (most of the Allied governments, the Catholic Church, the spokespeople for great and noble
causes) managed to ignore what was happening to the Jews?

When we see the full force of our own denial of the ecological dangers surrounding us, do we remember that it was thought impossible — especially by the victims! — that a modern, industrialized state could systematically slaughter millions of unarmed civilians?

When we see how the assault on the rainforest eliminates dozens of species of trees that have been evaluated as having potential for cancer treatment (even for the cancers that may afflict those who direct the assault), do we remember how the German government made transporting the Jews to the death camps their first priority, even when that priority interfered with their own military goals?

When we hear of some corporation lying to the public to protect some toxic chemical, or paying off a legislator to get some environmental regulations weakened, do we remember how the Nazi elite got rich off Jewish slave labor?

While the Holocaust involved the centralized, strategically planned annihilation of a particular group, ecocide stems from a myriad of sources and is not anyone's self-proclaimed goal. It happens because corporations pursue profit, governments develop military power, ordinary citizens seek a "better lifestyle," and peasants deforest hillsides so they can cook dinner. From these varying strategies for profit, power, pleasure, or simple survival come the ruin of the world. Yet what the Holocaust does reveal, and part of what connects the two events, is just how devastating modern states, bureaucracies, and technologies can be, and thus how carefully we "ordinary men and women" must examine our participation in them. This lesson carries into the present, teaching us that while environmentalists' direst predictions must always be evaluated in detail, they cannot be dismissed out of hand due to a mistaken confidence that governments and corporations would not commit mass murder, or that intelligent citizens might not just sit back and let it all happen. After Auschwitz, such confidence makes little sense. In a way, the Holocaust "prepares" us to take in the fact of ecocide, teaching that there is virtually no limit to human folly, lust for power, and bureaucratic complicity in mass murder. The slaughter of six million Jews and five million other victims, carried out coldly and "rationally" by civil servants and professionals as well as politicians and soldiers, by a "legitimate" government and with the sanction or passive acceptance of much of the rest of the world, is an omen for the environmental ruin we are creating now. This time, however, the catastrophe may spread far beyond the borders of any particular community, nation, or region.

Some years ago, Holocaust survivor Elie Wiesel commented on the television mini-series *The Day After*, which focused on the consequences of the potentially final ecological catastrophe of nuclear war. Seeing images of the few tattered, starving survivors of the conflict, he said: "I think I have seen these pictures before; only then it was my people. Now it seems that the whole world has become Jewish."

Wiesel was not saying that a nuclear war would have been just like the Holocaust. And neither is the environmental crisis "just like it." Despite the obvious differences, however, the Holocaust can serve as a warning. This is so because there are several important analogies between the two events. The Holocaust and ecocide both depend on highly developed technology and large, impersonal bureaucracies; and both demonstrate how irrational these modern ways of life can be. They reveal a profound inability to empathize with other people and other forms of life, expressing a vision of human relationships keyed to domination and exploitation. That is why the Holocaust and ecocide call into question many of the basic premises of the way we live. Our religious traditions, family structure, notions of personal identity, and distribution of economic and political power are all called into question when humanity's way of life undermines its own survival.

Also, both events depend on a complex structure of aggressors, victims, and bystanders. Thus both raise particularly complicated moral questions about good and evil, guilt and innocence, responsibility and forgiveness.

Finally, in both settings people facing overwhelming odds have fought back. The presence of this resistance can help change the way we think about the Holocaust and the environmental crisis, transforming them from examples of unrelieved horror to settings in which, despite everything, people managed to resist. Indeed, resistance is a way to have an identity that gives meaning without being a slave to the institutional identities that pollute and destroy. In the reality of resistance we may find some hope for both past and future, some way to find a peaceful heart in a dark time.

Zyklon B was the gas used on Jews in the death camps. It came to the attention of a young SS officer as Auschwitz was just being put into operation. Remembering how a Hamburg pesticide firm had fumigated the insect-laden Polish army barracks that the SS had taken over, Hauptsturmführer Fritsch decided to try the pesticide on people. It worked well enough. The next move — from killing insects and rodents with a powerful chemical to killing millions of Jews the same way — was not very difficult. The Nazi leadership believed, after all, that Jews were vermin, and that the "health" of Germany required that the Jews be exterminated.

Ironically, while the Nazi machine has long been defeated, the use of chemical pesticides still threatens human beings; and the notion that "vermin" can simply be exterminated without any ill effects on those of us left alive has led to widespread poisoning of life forms — including our own. In agricultural communities throughout the world, for instance, water supplies are tainted by pesticide runoffs. In some areas so much has accumulated in women's bodies that breast milk is legally considered too dangerous to feed infants. And breast-fed babies have, reveals one recent study, more than three times the amount of the toxic chemical PCBs in their bloodstream as bottle-fed infants.

Of all the parallels between the Nazi genocide and the environmental crisis there is, for the purposes of this chapter, one that strikes closest to home. What is crucial about the Holocaust in this respect is that it was partly executed by bureaucratic and technological personnel who obeyed — but were not necessarily in ideological agreement with — the dominant authorities. The tragedy was that too many of these Germans could not imagine a meaningful life outside the institutions of the Third Reich, for they were too emotionally identified with their membership in its professional, corporate, and governmental enterprises. Such people did have deep emotional connections to the social institutions responsible for genocide, but these were not predominantly the connections of shared belief. Rather, they often stemmed from a desperate need to be a person in the public realm, to buttress oneself with a job, a function, a title, and a position.

For instance, a fanatical hatred of Jews was at times minimal among actual executioners or their immediate superiors; and throughout German society there were various forms of mild dissension from Nazi policies. Historian Christopher Browning's studies of "middle managers" (such as administrators of large ghettos) indicate that for a number of these it was not a limitless desire to kill but conventional anti-Semitism, support of authority, and careerism that led to a "gradual, almost imperceptible, descent past the point of no return." These men were brought to genocide, Browning shows, not solely or at times even mainly because they sought it. Rather, they were attuned to a bureaucratic structure that dispensed salaries, career advancements, and approval. Raoul Hilberg echoes this view when he distinguishes the "hard core" of men like Auschwitz commandant Rudolf Hoess, who enthusiastically embraced concentration camp life, from the many who "took their assignments indifferently or even apathetically." In an essay about the onset of the Final Solution, Browning comments, "careerism could be exploited to harness ordinary people in the service of mass murder." Could there be a more apt description of how ordinary people get caught up in environmental catastrophe?

These cooperating careerists, however, should not be written off as passionless bureaucrats. At times they would express deep satisfaction in how much they had accomplished, cheering themselves on for a job well done. At others they would acknowledge how terribly hard it was to kill defenseless people, or to (in Himmler's words) "remain hard" and resist their natural tendencies to save their "favorite Jews." Ironically, the death camps themselves were developed because Himmler — struck by how a mass shooting had affected the killers — sought "more humane" forms of murder. Underneath the business-as-usual masks, there were other motivations.

What was happening for many, I believe, is that while they tried to appear cold, they were in fact desperately pursuing a sense of self-importance by joining in grandiose public enterprises. Adolf Eichmann, who organized the deportation of several hundred thousand Hungarian Jews to their deaths, put it clearly at his trial: the highest goal of his life was to serve his superiors. Some people hear these words and think of a man with no feelings. To me, however, the statement reveals a person possessed by a very real passion — one directed at establishing a place in the large and powerful enterprise he serves. This is not an absence of feeling, a "banality of evil" as it has been called. It is an unremitting effort to prove oneself no matter what the consequences. Thus when the Nazi functionaries wrote their heartless memos about how to improve gas chambers or calculate the rate of extermination, they were concealing something of great importance. With their personal identity tied to serving large social institutions, these ordinary citizens went "past the point of no return."

Is this really a problem of authority rather than a desire to get recognition or make a meaningful life? Is it that German society (like our own) was keyed to obedience? Actually, seeing the problem as one of too much obedience goes along quite well with what I have been suggesting. After all, you engender automatic obedience in people partly by making them feel that without the approval of those who control society their lives do not count. The fear of authority is the flip side of the desire to please it, the need for recognition and respect from the powers-that-be. In both cases, people are trained to lack a sense of their own value outside of the dominant authority. In both cases they lack an autonomous understanding of their own value. In both cases they are dependent on the dominant institutions for a sense of self-respect, validation, and meaning.

Did people go along out of a simple fear that they would be punished if they disobeyed? Did they think they would be shot or jailed if they didn't follow orders? Perhaps this is so, and certainly it is what some of the killers said later. However, historians have found very few examples of times when Germans who refused to cooperate with genocide were seriously punished. On the contrary, there are many examples of people avoiding extermination activities who were left alone, transferred, or given the mildest of administrative rebukes. It was love of authority, as much as fear, that drove many of the killers. It was dependence on their superiors for approval, as much as it was hatred of the Jews, which drove some of them.

Was a simple fear of being different, rather than of serious punishment, at work? German society, after all, was keyed to conformity more than most. Did the less ideologically motivated killers go along simply because they didn't want to stand out? Absolutely! Again, however, how compatible this point is with what I have been saying about constructing personal identity through overidentification with work. For what is conformity if it is not feeling that our lives have no value if we don't belong to some social structure, some "crowd"? As a child, this may simply mean the peer group of other kids. As an adult, however, we will bind ourselves to large institutions. In a modern society that has long left village life behind, we will conform to the government, the corporation, and the profession.

A number of writers have suggested that the killers simply hid from their public acts by placing their selfhood in their private lives. They could "write off" a day performing medical experiments on children or machine-gunning naked families by being tender to their wives and children, listening to Bach on portable phonographs, and playing with their dogs. What became important was a "private, still moral" self. I believe, however, that the killers continued to find meaning in their public activities. This public meaning triumphed even when the actual task was seen as repugnant, although alcoholism permeated the ranks of the executioners, and despite the fact that some Nazi leaders often found the direct viewing of genocide distasteful (Himmler himself once nearly fainted at an execution). Revulsion engendered by the murderous task was overshadowed by individuals' dependence on participation in the public realm for their very sense of self. Membership in the dominant institutions gave meaning, value, and a sense of personal security to people who had no other sources of purpose or importance in their lives.

The enormous cruelties, the attachment to authority, the celebration of their horrendous accomplishments, the way they turned blind eyes to what they were doing — do all these dismal realities mean that the Nazi executioners are totally different from you and me? I do not think so. People still close their eyes to the consequences of their acts in order to maintain their connection to a social order that gives them meaning. They still identify with institutions to get a sense of who they are. People still want to count, to belong, to be important. The motives that drove the less ideological, less "committed," less mad Nazi functionaries continue in the present. We are closer to them than we would like to admit.

Today's managers and engineers of the damaging pursuit of military power, industrial expansion, ever higher consumption, and destructive "development" are often neither cold bureaucrats of "growth" nor immensely rich and powerful. Rather, they may be going along with institutions over which they have little control and from which they benefit psychically as much as materially. While they may be repelled by the environmental consequences of their professional or personal lives, their emotional dependence keeps them from responding morally to what they themselves are doing. For them, the "system" seems inescapable.

One reason the system is so compelling is that our society makes it particularly hard to find a sense of meaning. We face ruptured communities, urbanization, impersonal mass media that replace traditional culture, geographical mobility, the decline of religion, and the spread of a frantic commodification that puts everything up for sale. In such a society, we cannot take for granted that we belong, that we have a place. Selfhood, at once so needed and so without constraints, cannot be assumed. Rather, it must be achieved. This demand is particularly true of those who have neither immense wealth nor the closer social ties of some lower economic groups. For the broad reach of the middle class, it is (paradoxically) in the worlds of technology, science, nationalism, the military, professionalism, and corporate power that a "haven in a heartless world" can be found. In these settings, at times as much or more than in the intimacy of private life, selfhood gains what appears to be some of its surest supports. Work becomes like a second home, our profession like a lover, our institutional setting like the little village we never had. Of course it is a rare work life that really answers to us as individuals, really meets our personal needs, really provides a "home." We may feel alienated from what we do and sense that whoever we work for cares little about us. We may be in danger of downsizing or be planning our own next career move. But for all the reasons sketched above — the need for recognition, the fear of authority, the desire to conform — we are unable to disobey or stand out. Even if we leave or are fired our best hope is to go to some other place not that different from this one. Few of us want to face not having work, no matter how alienating work may be. We all need some place to go in the morning, even if it is only to log on to the network from our home computer.

Some people, it is true, may find the public realm too impersonal and unrewarding. Instead, they try to be their own person, defining themselves by their sports utility vehicles, their in-line skates, their trips to Tuscany. This consumption, I believe, is not simply a matter of the pursuit of pleasure. The endless stream of commodities is actually a substitute for love, community connection, and really feeling at home in the world. In a sense, it is yet one more attempt to "prove oneself." As the hero of Flannery O'Connor's novel *Wise Blood* says: "No one who has a new car needs to justify himself." Consumption becomes another measure of public identity. It enables us to feel that, because of what we can buy or own, we belong. It may not be as ultimately satisfying as the feeling that one's acts, abilities, or accomplishments have done the trick. But it is something. Thus to ask us to buy and own less to preserve "nature" is to ask us to *be* less. And who among us would consent to that?

And so the circle is complete. There seems to be no way out. The damage to nature and humanity continues because changing our current way of life seems to threaten the institutional and personal structures that provide us with a sense of selfhood. We continue with business as usual. The corporation does "well," and the air and the water don't. Rather than directly assessing and acknowledging disastrous conditions in local settings, government bureaucracies seek to protect their own turf and status: too often focusing on preserving the status quo of environmental legitimacy or furthering a particular political party or office holder. They try, as hard as possible, not to lose their place in this or that office. In doing so they damage their surroundings and other people. Ultimately, of course, they also damage their own souls. Often, by the time they realize what they have done, it is too late.

What do all these generalities mean in particular situations? Consider the mentality of the government officials overseeing occupational health and safety in uranium mines in the 1950s and '60s. The general movement was to ignore critical environmental dangers to workers. Particular officials and scientists went along with the general organizational drift of the institutions that paid their salaries and defined "public interest." For example, scientists, following the policies of the Atomic Energy Commission and the Public Health Service, caved in and kept virtually silent about the effects of radioactivity on workers in mines long after the dangers were known:

> We did not want to rock the boat...we had to take the position that we were neutral scientists trying to find out what the facts were, that we were not going to make any public announcements until the results of our scientific study were completed.

The scientists were asked to watch what was happening, but not to inform those at risk. As a Public Health Service scientist admitted: "By the late 1940s there was no question in anybody's mind that radiation in the mines was a real problem.... But nobody in the AEC wanted to pay attention."

Need we suppose that the officials and technicians involved in this situation were unfeeling of the hurt they were causing? Can we not see that for at least some their deepest need was simply to belong to whatever gave them a social identity? Not to "rock the boat" so as to make sure that they would stay in it! Were they scared of losing their jobs? Tied to supporting their families? Of course. But is it just the loss of money that is at stake, or what the money means as well? If it were only money — measured solely as the ability to have more stuff — would people act so immorally? Does it not seem plausible that the money itself means more than the ability to buy? I believe the question is not only what we lose materially when we lose our job, but what we think such a loss means about who we are.

More recently, we see that at the present moment a coalition of coal and oil corporations are recruiting scientists to oppose the international global warming treaty of 1997. This coalition plans to spend five million dollars in two years to convince Congress, the media, and the general public that the facts about global warming are still seriously in doubt. Their strategy will unfold despite the enormous confirmation of global warming: measurable amounts of increase in average local air temperatures, ocean warming, shrinking glaciers, increased floods and rainfall, earlier arrivals of spring, and movement of plants and diseases consistent with higher temperatures. Coordinated by the public relations staff of the American Petroleum Institute, the campaign flies in the face of the overwhelming opinion of scientific expertise. Just as was the case with the scientists, doctors, and public officials, those defending coal and oil may not be vicious liars — even though it is clear that they are playing fast and loose with the truth. Rather, they may be so tied to their jobs, their corporations, their identity in the public realm, that they will do anything to keep these things going.

On a more mundane level, how many of us like to prove that we are somebody, have done something in the world, or have a viable public identity by an unending round of consumption? All of us drive, heat our homes, use chemicalized agricultural products, and consume in ways that are environmentally harmful.

Dominated by work or by private consumption directed to the same end, we each contribute to environmental problems in our own way. Of course even a commitment to a deeply spiritual life will not magically solve the problems at hand. We will still drive a car, plug in our toasters, and use our credit cards. But a spiritual sense of ourselves can help us see that, in critical times, there are other choices besides this particular job, level of consumption, or pursuit of recognition. Our commitment to the spiritual journey can be the basis for a solidarity with other beings, one that eludes conventional social life. If we do not have a spiritual alternative, that life is the only game in town.

It might be suggested that while there is some truth in what I am saying, it applies to men, not women; that while masculine identity is desperate to prove itself in the public world, women tend to be much more concerned with relationships. Women think of themselves less as makers of the world than as participants in a web of connections. They pour their energies into love, children, family, and friendship — seeking to connect, relate, communicate, and nourish. Unlike Franz Stangl, women do not feel this need to stand out and be "different from all the rest." Because women's identity is not tied to the public realm in the way that of men is, they are less tied to the institutions that are destroying the world.

We certainly should not forget that in our society the identities of men and women tend to be structured differently. The culturally female stress on connection, empathy, and communication can lead in very different directions from the male stress on accomplishment, autonomy, and separation. And it is men, after all, who tend to control and manage the institutions responsible for most environmental destruction. Corporate executives, engineering staffs, accountants, town planners, researchers, marketing experts, military officers — these are the people who exploit the wilderness, leave toxic wastes behind when they close military bases, spill radiation into the air when they test nuclear weapons, defend polluting factory farms, and guide dangerous pesticides past a flimsy regulatory process.

It is true that women have achieved enough social equality to at times be the ones performing these tasks. Yet these tend to be women who have come to think of themselves in male terms. We have seen enough women like this — from female heads of state (Thatcher) to the attractive, smiling, lying spokeswoman for Exxon after the *Exxon Valdez* oil tanker spilled twelve million gallons of crude oil off the Alaskan shoreline — to know that the norms of cultural masculinity are now available to women. In these cases it is not the biology of the perpetrators that is critical, but how they think of themselves. Women who think of themselves in male terms can be just as destructive as men.

Yet in a darker vein we can also ask: How many women measure the public meaning of their lives by their own or their family's level of private consumption, a seemingly private matter which is too often part of a public ecological catastrophe? How many approach consumption a little the way men approach work? Making the house beautiful, getting the latest clothes for their kids, cooking a splendid dinner are expressions of love and also, sadly, part of a compulsive need for a public proof of love, connection, and adequacy. What is really there between the woman and her family is not experienced as enough — any more than a man typically feels he is enough without some badge of productivity. This yearning for public identity through consumption is yet another source of our destruction of the environment.

During his years at Treblinka, Stangl said, he could sleep at night only if he had a large glass of brandy before going to sleep. He claimed, and in fact it might be true, that he hated the killings, tried to get out of what he was doing, sought a transfer. He stated that he joined the euthanasia brigade only to escape an unpleasant superior and that later he stayed on for fear of being punished if he refused.

Stangl's statements might have been exaggerated self-excuse or part of a real ambivalence about Nazi policy. In either case, some intriguing things do emerge from his story and from what others said about him. Most important, he does not appear to be much of an anti-Semite or a particularly violent or vicious person. One Jew who had dealings with him described Stangl as someone with whom one could talk more freely than with other officials of his department. Another man, a survivor of Sobibor, favorably contrasted Stangl to the vicious killers among the guards or other SS personnel. Stangl himself claims to have had enjoyable, "quite friendly relations" with some of the Jews who managed the camp.

What held him? He tells us: "Of course thoughts came. But I forced them away. I made myself concentrate on work, work, and again work." His assistant says: "I think what he really cared about was to have the place run like clockwork." And in Stangl's own words, the worst experience of all came when during his first camp assignment Sobibor prisoners revolted and caused the camp operations to shut down. Waiting to hear how his superiors would respond was, he remembered, his "hardest time." He took great self-satisfaction in the fact that he made sure the Jews' confiscated money and jewels went to the Nazi government, where it was "supposed" to go. Instead of amassing a personal fortune as some of his superiors did, he prided himself on his honor in not stealing — at the same time that he presided over an enormous death factory.

When he was asked why, besides the mass killing itself, there was so much extra, gratuitous cruelty in the camps, he replied: "It worked. And because it worked, it was irreversible."

What was that work? Well, in the end perhaps it didn't really matter what it was, as long as it worked. To do something, to make something happen, to distinguish oneself through a sense of one's effects on the world, this is what calls to us all.

One of Stangl's sons said of him:

> My father was . . . a joiner, neither very good, nor bad. . . . But I can remember when he got that black SS uniform: that's when he began to be "somebody." And then, in Treblinka — it is inconceivable, isn't it, what he suddenly was: the scope, the power, the uniqueness, the difference between himself and all those others.

And it is precisely here that Franz Stangl becomes terribly relevant. Stangl is, after all, not one of the men who set the policy, not part of the inner party circles that decided to try to kill every Jew in Europe. He had no mad passion for mass murder, and neither did he profit from it in some immense way. He was a medium-sized cog in a vast machine. If Stangl had been a rabid anti-Semite, a secret Nazi sympathizer, he would simply be a despicable man who means little to us. We could study him like a member of some horrible faraway tribe, a lesson on the dreadful possibilities of the human animal, but a possibility that is far removed from our own lives. He seems, however, to be more like us than we would like to admit. In the very beginning, he got drawn into the Holocaust because he wanted to "be somebody." As his son suggested, he deeply enjoyed the "difference between himself and all those others." He blotted out the consequences of his actions by making sure that "the work" got done efficiently and conscientiously. If these were his goals, does he not seem at least a little familiar, someone whose life can teach us something? Perhaps the most important lesson from his twisted life is that without something other than a conventional public identity to rely on, we too risk sinking into a pit of moral horror. Because a life without "work" may not seem worthwhile, we will end up staying "there," because we simply don't have any other place to go.

❖

Formaldehyde is just one of thousands of chemicals that permeate modern American life. It is best known for its use in the construction of wood products: subflooring to go under carpets or hardwood slats, particle board in furniture, plywood in walls and kitchen cabinets. Virtually every new or modified house built since World War II contains formaldehyde.

This common-as-dirt product is dangerous. Not only is it listed by the International Agency for Research in Cancer as a probable human carcinogen, but it can also gag, sicken, and weaken some people at even extremely low levels. At times, exposure to it can lead to debilitating environmental illness marked by nearly lethal asthmatic sensitivity to virtually all artificial chemicals.

My focus here is on efforts by the producers of formaldehyde to obscure its impact and limit government regulation. These efforts include high-intensity lobbying to restrict federal control and lower safety standards, donating millions to congressional campaigns to insure friendly legislatures, buying off victims of formaldehyde poisoning with secret cash settlements and scaring them with threats that lawsuits will involve a detailed examination of every aspect of their lives (much as the sexual history of rape victims can be used against them in court).

Of course, we are used to thinking of large corporations as somewhat dishonest, inordinately protective of profits despite the consequences, and unresponsive to criticism. It is not these familiar foibles that concern me here. Rather, I want to consider the psychology, the sense of identity, of the people who do the work of protecting corporations by currying legislators and attacking regulators, vocal victims, and whistle-blowing scientists.

What is it like to be such a person? Although we may be familiar with the clichés of the ruthless lawyer, the upwardly mobile graduate of a distinguished business school, the tunnel-visioned attempt to support a family by pleasing a superior, we still wonder how someone can do such things. First of all, it is hard to imagine that someone truly believes in formaldehyde. These corporate defenders may not love redwoods or spotted owls, and they may well trust that technology will magically solve all the problems it creates. These attitudes will often blind them to real environmental dangers. But in advocating formaldehyde they are doing something much more extreme: spending their professional lives defending something which they themselves know to be hurtful. Such work involves the careful spreading of untruths, planned campaigns to discredit opposition scientists, delaying tactics in which they self-consciously try to sell the lie that "we really are trying to find out the truth about formaldehyde."

Let us think of them going to work, writing memos, issuing statements to the press, quietly lobbying congressmen, attacking victims in court ("Why," a victim of formaldehyde poisoning was asked in court, "do you smoke? And our expert psychologist believes you have a neurotic tendency to blame other people for your problems.") Perhaps they face this distasteful task accidentally. Few people are explicitly hired, we may suppose, to defend toxins. It just sort of happens. Could it be that they continue because they feel they have no other choice? That they feel that without their job, they have nothing. Could it be that if they lose this position — the salary, the stationery, the place in the office, the business card, the special phone lines, the ability to say "Yes, I did this today...." — that if these are all gone, there will be nothing left?

Of course if people have a strong ideological motivation — if they believe deeply in formaldehyde — we don't have to wonder why they do the things they do. Like the fanatical Nazis who lived only to kill as many Jews as possible, such people do not have much to teach us about ourselves. But we are concerned here with more ordinary people, people not unlike us. How do any of us get into positions where we destroy so much even though that is not our intention?

For instance, how do you get someone to design and test nuclear weapons, work which has been responsible for a significant and dangerous increase in background radiation throughout the globe? A recruiter for Livermore Laboratories, one of the two major U.S. facilities responsible for this work during the 1980s, put it simply: they sought to "get candidates' interest in the physics to outweigh their natural repugnance at the task." Often young researchers would accept a position without really knowing what they would be doing. "We would just interview people in this big room with no windows and assure them they would be working on something interesting." In other words, it was the *work* that mattered: the prospect of doing something "interesting," being part of a large, well staffed, highly respected, influential institution. Doing what? Perhaps for many the details didn't matter all that much: as long as the task matched their training, gave them a place to work, and made them somebody.

None of this excuses what they do. But it does help us understand. That is why the question of why ordinary people end up doing deeply harmful work is of deep spiritual, as well as social, significance. Spirituality cannot be just a matter of soothing a troubled heart, breathing into the present moment for calm, finding joy in a sunset, or extending care to single individuals. It is essential to our spiritual journey that we are very clear about what is most important to us, and to see how spiritually and morally dangerous it is to find our personal meaning in our social position. It is up to us to find some other way to deal with our desires and attachments, some new way to form an identity.

Our complicity lies on a broad spectrum: few of us get paid to defend formaldehyde or conduct fall-out producing nuclear weapons tests. But a lot of us do focus on our work to the exclusion of other things because without work we wouldn't feel real. We ignore or forget the truth because we feel empty without engaging in just those things that are destroying the earth. We consume much more than we need because buying and owning is another way to prove ourselves. We are scared to lose what we have because what we have is what we are. Even if our particular work has minimal effect on the environment (and such work is increasingly rare), we don't want to take time away from that work to respond to what is going on. We rarely ask ourselves: "What would happen if I had to give up my job? How do I make myself feel that my life is important? How desperate would I feel if all this were threatened? What would I do to keep it?"

We are tied in, we are hooked up, and we don't know how to stop.

Someone might say that I have it all wrong here, that people actually put most of their identity into their private lives. Don't many of us, after all, seem to be living for romantic love or for our families? Don't a lot of folks just seem to be going through the motions at work, waiting for the evening or the weekend? Don't a lot of us spend our energies on our hobbies or vacations?

Private life, however important, doesn't escape the demand to accomplish, be effective, and make our mark. Ironically, the personal need to find meaning in public space is recreated in the arena of private life. Alongside the honest care and love we shower on our children, for example, is the desire to prove something — to the world, to ourselves — through them. We are often torn between the need to accept our kids for who they are, to love them on their own terms, and the fearful, at times desperate, desire to have our own ability and status as parents confirmed by what our children achieve. Waiting to see his report from school, or to watch her perform at a piano recital or soccer game, we feel a jitteriness in the stomach, a sense of immanent defeat or victory, a nervous sense of our own success or failure. Their accomplishments seem to confirm our worth. Our children can, in this sense, become another public badge of adequacy, another proof of our worth (or lack of it). Or, as someone wrote in my thirtieth college reunion yearbook: "My children are my greatest accomplishment."

Alternatively, think of our marriages and love affairs. There is a tendency to ask: is this a "good" marriage? a "good" relationship? And to perform the reckoning in terms that are publicly measurable. How many times, we might ask, have we had sex in the last month (or year)? Are we as hot with each other as the couples described in the latest bestseller, *The How to Have Passion in Your Marriage Workbook?* When we think of ourselves as a couple after twenty years, when we evaluate our home, how many friends we have, the measure of our combined incomes, do we ask how they measure up? Permeating our direct connections to each other, to our own lives, is something else: a gnawing sense that we are not right unless we are doing well, even in the marriage bed. "Be everything you can be," say a host of ads. And we want to know, in clear and measurable terms, just how much that is. In other words, we bring the same deep personal anxiety and the same need for measurable validation into the private realm that we bring to jobs and careers.

Many of the same tendencies exist in the seemingly even more private realm of "hobbies," "interests," or "leisure pastimes." Some years ago I was riding in a car with four other thirty-something, very male-ish academics. We all lectured, researched, wrote, and were married. And we were all runners. I was just recovering from a painful shin splint period and wondered aloud if I was the only one who had been injured recently. I was surprised to find that they all had. And they all had for the same reason as myself: trying to fulfill goals which we charted each day in our little running diaries; keeping a close eye on the read-outs from our expensive chronograph watches (with waterproof wrist bands, delivering performance times to the hundredth of a second); pursuing objectives we refused to modify until the pains in our shins (ankles, arches, knees, hips) grew unbearable. We wanted to feel effective in our running, to be masters of our (physical) fate, to know at the end of a workout that we not only had huffed and puffed and worked up a good sweat, but had — by God — done a good workout and had something to show for it. Something we could see on our watches, record in our training diaries, talk about to our wives (who usually didn't care anyway) and friends (who, if they were runners, would care). At the least we would know that, yes, we had done something worthwhile this day.

I remember once coming in, sweaty and satisfied, from jogging. "What a great run," I beamed at my wife. "I just did four miles and took two minutes off my time from a month ago." She looked at me with a combination of bemusement and honest befuddlement. "So you ran two minutes quicker, and you're very pleased. I don't get it. What's your hurry?"

But what about when private life is not quantified? Isn't there an alternative to the disastrous public realm in the heart-felt connections of real love, authentic family life, and enduring friendships?

The dilemma is that, for many of us — and especially for those people who staff the destructive institutions of modern society — private life is insufficient. Marriage, children, and family just don't seem deserved, trustworthy, or justified if one doesn't have a public presence. We might use as an example Willy Loman, the forlorn hero of *Death of a Salesman.* Willy never doubted that his wife loved him, and just before his suicide he realized that his long-estranged son, Biff, loved him too. That love, however, was not enough. Willy kills himself so that the $20,000 life insurance benefits will give Biff a stake in the business world. This final "productive" sacrifice, he believes, will earn Willy his family's love and respect. Without that accomplishment, his position in life is untenable; to achieve it, he is willing to die. For Willy love, like everything else, has to be earned. The arena in which this earning takes place is the realm of institutions, organizations, careers, money, and power. This is where we prove ourselves, and thus prove that we deserve to be loved. When we have a place here we can run the world, save the world, or at least belong to it. Once we belong we get an e-mail address and a business card. And even if we try to make our way as individuals — lone entrepreneurs, solo cowboys of business, art, science, or knowledge — we will end up measuring our success or failure by how the conventional public world judges us. The rebellion of the individual is all too often yet another attempt to win attention and approval.

Even if there were a simple way out, even if we could put all of our sense of self in our personal relationships, what would that do to them? Love and friendship, as important as they are, usually cannot sustain the weight of all the other connections we don't have. Love becomes desperation, marriage a hiding place or a prison, friendships too intense to last.

What is the drive behind our common need to accomplish, achieve, and prove ourselves? What pushes us?

For myself, the push for public recognition can be easily found in some of the details of my biography. My parents seemed to love me only if I accomplished something. They also seemed to feel that since I was accomplishing a lot I needed no other care. The school and the community rewarded my performances and cared little about my soul. Everyone was pleased as punch with my knowledge of American history or *Beowulf*, but expressed little concern about how much self-knowledge or compassion I had. I took in the message that I was, at bottom, what I accomplished. If I was to continue to be, I had better do well. What would happen if I stopped accomplishing? I didn't want to find out.

If this problem were mine alone, it would be only (at best) of passing interest to anyone else. But I don't think that I am particularly unique or unusual in having these feelings, for I see too much of my seemingly private neurosis (and spiritual malaise) manifest in the rest of society. There were, after all, those four other young professors in the car, all of whom were also trying to prove something to somebody, all of whom carried demons which made them run into a variety of injuries. There are all the other people I know (you may know them, as well) with overfull date books and too many meetings, burdened under a few more commitments, phone calls, and activities than they can handle. These are people who may be making enough money, who have done "well enough" in their careers, and who may even be blessed with healthy children and reasonably good marriages. Yet they seem perpetually on the edge of being overwhelmed, without flood, fire, or famine at the door. They do not feel adequate unless they are constantly proving that they can produce, achieve, and take on more. Any sense of satisfaction seems only temporary, always conditional on what was just done, always about to be displaced by a gnawing sense of self-doubt.

What are we all trying to prove? What is it that we are scared might be true, that haunts us through every success and failure, every effort and every exhaustion from too much effort?

We can call it a lack of self-esteem, a permanent sense of inferiority, an unsatisfiable drive to fill an unhealed fracture in our most private selves. We could chalk it up to the fact that the media confront us with an endless series of media images of adequacy that we can never live up to: impossibly beautiful people, strong people, rich people, smart people, successful people, thin people. We could, and often do, blame our parents for not loving us unconditionally. But even the most loving of parents can't make up for the fact that in the modern world a strong sense of community is missing and therefore we don't really feel at home anymore. Compared to past times, our connections to others are tenuous and thinned out. The cost of individual freedom — to choose our jobs, religion, geography, marriage partners, politics, diet and health club — is loneliness. Much of the time we feel, and we are, adrift, cut off, isolated. This void and the pain it causes are filled with drugs, alcohol, psychotherapy, consumption, violence, compulsive sex, depression, Prozac, and too much work. And we know that after a lifetime of those, and of seeking the connections that too rarely come, we will die being cared for by strangers.

It is no wonder that we might turn to work, to seeing that we've done something or been somebody in the public world, for solace.

It was work, Stangl said, that occupied him in the death camps. He had managed to stay "sane," to keep going, by trying to keep his camps running smoothly. He was especially interested in making sure that the stolen property went to his superiors instead of lining the pockets of thieving underlings. And once he had chosen to make sense of his situation by focusing on the "work" it involved, then whatever was necessary to keep the work intact would surely follow. The cruelty that went along with the mass murders and the exploitative labor — the needless tortures, the little degradations — was maintained, he tells us, simply "because it worked." It made things orderly, provided a proof that he himself was doing his job.

What is the meaning of work? This is a key question in an age when we use our "work" to fill the void left by a lack of community and when our work can produce gas chambers and holes in the ozone layer.

Marlow, the stolid, self-disciplined moral hero of Joseph Conrad's classic story *Heart of Darkness,* also depends on work in a dark time. And the place of work in this story, which is about the evils of colonialism, may reveal something about the meaning of work for us.

Marlow had been fascinated with Africa as a child. During a lull in his career as a seaman, he takes the job of piloting a steamboat into the interior, through colonial territory. His task is to help transport ivory and to find out what has happened to an initially successful, but now seemingly erratic, company operative named Kurtz. As Marlow gets deeper and deeper into the Belgian Congo of the 1870s, the brutality of the Europeans and the terrible treatment of the black natives forced into semi-slavery horrify him. He appreciates the mysterious beauty of the tribal people on the banks of the great river, as well as the loyalty of his native crewmen, who refrain from turning on the Europeans even though they have been left with nothing to eat but rotten hippo meat. Marlow is not seduced by the eloquent madness of Kurtz, who initially came to the wilderness with a mission of uplifting the natives and has now set himself up as a petty local deity, decorating his compound with the skulls of "rebels."

Kurtz had made himself the center of "unspeakable rites." For Conrad he stands as the moral opposite of Marlow. Marlow, it seems, manages to stay sane. He is not drawn into Kurtz's dementia of self-aggrandizing violence. Unlike the once philanthropically minded trader, Marlow resists the freeing up of all the dark forces within himself that lead a man to uncontrolled appetites and put an end to responsibility and discipline. The savage cries made by natives as his boat passes them by, though they tug fiercely at Marlow, are resisted. He does not give in.

What sustains him? What keeps him lucid and responsible? Work. It was, he explains, the task that kept him going: the need to pilot his boat up the treacherous river, past snags, shallow spots, and dangerous tribes who might attack. He had to cope with poorly trained native sailors, a temperamental engine, and weeks of waiting to get the rivets that would allow him to continue. Patiently or impatiently, he endured the conniving of the representatives of the trading company and then his own disappointment at Kurtz's descent into ferocity. He had hoped Kurtz would be a beacon in this darkness, not its very heart. And as Marlow faced all this, he had no one to rely on. He was alone. It was only his work that held the jungle at bay, that gave him a sense of who he was when the truisms of conventional morality were obscured by the tropical sun and the riot of vegetation that took him back "to the beginning of time."

But what was the work? What was the point of what he was doing? We are never quite sure. To pilot a steamboat for a bunch of thieving colonialists whom he despises? To find and bring back a man who used the razzle-dazzle of European technology to become a tin god to the natives? Marlow is never really clear on just how his "work" sustains him.

What we notice from his tale, however, is that only the task in front of him could keep him from succumbing to what surrounded him. And of course what surrounded him — the specter of uncontrolled passion, a riot of deeper, darker, impulses — was also within him. We must, the book implies, have something to hold on to — or else we are in danger of descending to the level of the traders, who will do anything to anyone to get what they want, or rise to the madness of Kurtz, who had nothing to keep himself from being swept away by the uncontrolled savagery of the jungle. "The mind of man is capable of anything, because everything is in it," Marlow tells us. Without some protection, something to ward off all the dire possibilities, a man is lost. Because he has his work, says Conrad, Marlow is not lost.

And so we see that work keeps the world at bay: both the inside world that threatens to engulf all restraints and the external world in which we might dissolve into insignificance. Without work we are not only "nobody" in the world; we lose ourselves to whatever comes along.

Although Conrad's tale reveals the evils of colonialism, it misses the point of the meaning of work. This mistake is very dangerous, for while our dedication to work may keep us sane, it also affects the rest of the world. It has consequences that call into question the seeming reasonableness or decency of the person performing it. Marlow cannot be a moral hero just because he wasn't as sloppy, undisciplined, bizarre, or cruel as the people around him (just as Stangl is not a moral model because he doesn't "steal" Jewish property from his superiors). In his work Marlow serves pretty much the same ends as the despicable Europeans and the pitiable Kurtz. Through his work he helps the traders, he brings Kurtz back and tries to save his life. In his dedication to work, in his deep need of it, he cannot stop doing what he is doing. He is as tied to work as the traders are tied to ivory, as Kurtz is tied to his mad grandiosity. Despite himself, then, Marlow is one of them. Whatever his intentions, he too descends past the point of no return.

Marlow might have said: "I refuse to work here. I'd rather be without work, without something significant to do in the world, than help these people." He might have seen where it was all heading and refused to go there. He could have chosen not to fulfill this particular "responsibility," or joined with the natives, or found some Europeans who were against the ivory trade (which killed about one-half of the Congo's population in ten years). Work kept the terrors of the wilderness at bay — the wilderness that confronted him from the riverbank, and the wilderness of his own psyche. In Marlow, we see a character who feels it is better to join in with a meaningless, even evil enterprise, than face the demons which rise up when we abandon work.

If we cannot trust to an essential worth that persists regardless of our measurable social accomplishments, if we cannot find a way to connect to others that does not depend on achievement, if we do not escape our slavery to an endless need for recognition, if we cannot rest in the sense that what we have done is enough, if we cannot see that trying to accomplish in the social world can be a very dangerous business, especially given the society we live in, if our actions in the public realm do not spring from a moral and spiritual center rather than a conventional ego of accomplishment, if we don't realize that society creates effects out of our actions that we ourselves don't choose — if all these things remain the way they are, then how can we not, even against our will, contribute to the damage around us?

As an object lesson in those dangers, let us now look in some detail at someone whose drive for recognition, search for success in the public world, and deep need to accomplish something had devastating consequences on human and nonhuman nature alike. Central to this man's life was a desperate attempt to use his participation in large social institutions to meet his own deep need to feel he was having an effect in the world, that he belonged to something important, that he himself was "somebody," that he could stand out from the crowd.

Robert was born in California in 1916, into a not untypical middle-class family. His mother was devoted; his father, not unlike Franz's, somewhat distant. But from his earliest years they both wanted great things for him, and he soon found out that the best way to get attention and love was to do well at school. He would be grilled by his parents if he got an A– rather than an A and was quite conscious of the competition between himself and the "Chinese, Japanese and Jewish classmates" who tried to beat him at school ("which they rarely did," he remembers with pride). At Berkeley and Harvard Business School he studied economics and the new mathematical forms of corporate management. He identified with numbers as a way to grasp reality and as a way to distinguish himself from his "ordinary" background. Like Franz's love of a uniform, Robert's attachment to numbers promised to make him somebody special in a demanding world filled with competitors. During those years he also manifested a continuing need to be praised by authorities, a need which would lead him to hide his actual beliefs in order to get approval from college presidents, graduate mentors, and senior members of his first workplace.

Something of a youthful idealist, Robert said early on that — unlike a friend who wanted to serve individual patients as a doctor — he himself sought to "help the largest number of people." And throughout his adult life he did try to use numbers, charts, graphs, and a host of other seemingly rational and effective techniques to make the world a better place. Yet when the numbers didn't actually say that he was helping people, he ignored them, lying about what they represented to people in authority (and to himself), in his relentless attempt to be someone "special." In the major works of his life his fanatical desire to succeed, to exceed, led to suffering and devastation on an enormous scale.

Our Robert is Robert McNamara, who careened from modernizing Ford Motor Co., to directing the expansion of the U.S. involvement in the Vietnam War, to being the head of the World Bank. While his role in the Vietnam War has been studied by himself and others, I am concerned with the World Bank years. Under McNamara's leadership the bank vastly increased in size and world influence, funding and directing massively destructive "development" projects throughout the world. The story of McNamara's work at the bank is a cautionary tale about how environmental destruction unfolds, and it provides important and personally challenging lessons about what happens when we take our sense of self-worth from an amoral sense of how much impact we have on the world.

Throughout his life McNamara sought public power and personal success, and he used complex sets of statistical data and projections to buttress his authority and to distance himself personally from the people with whom he worked. Yet he also passionately wanted to "do good" and never lost the dream of helping "the largest number of people." He was not a simple careerist, in the conventional sense of someone who wants only money or position. He was a believer. Soon after he took over the bank, he redefined its mission to focus on large-scale issues of development. This mission, he claimed, was a response to the sheer magnitude of world poverty. He could be eloquent on the subject, reminding audiences that the world's poor "are human beings. And they are dying, now: at this very moment; while we are speaking."

Part of what is so striking about McNamara is the way he combined a sincere concern for doing good in the world with a limitless personal and institutional ambition. When he first took over the World Bank, he saw it as underutilized, remarking that it was "an inefficient way to run a planet." By increasing its grants tenfold, he wanted to remedy that situation, to find an efficient way to run the planet and personally save the millions dying "even as we speak."

It is this passion that belies the typical characterization of McNamara (and others like him) as either an unfeeling bureaucrat or a simple man on the make. At times he could be very expressive. He wept at public speeches about poverty and hunger and once furiously scribbled notes over an entire restaurant tablecloth while discussing a new project. At the same time, however, he was generally frightened of emotions, because they might reveal that he himself was "ordinary." To be subject to feelings would be to become like everyone else. In fact, we may suspect that at the core of his desire to manage a world-controlling institution was an identity so weak it had to run a planet to feel real, and which therefore pretty clearly was always on the edge of feeling unreal!

McNamara's need to feel like a powerful presence in the world made him a servant of the institution he controlled. As the potential savior of the "largest number of people" he was going to find the one way to overcome world poverty and promote "development." Colleagues saw him pursuing "a standard approach so powerful and efficient that it could easily be transferred from one situation to others and between countries.... One couldn't help [but get] the impression that he had the belief that if we prototyped in a few places we could go off and put it onto the production line." He and his staff would find it, and in doing so he, Robert McNamara, would direct an institution to fulfill his dream. In this perspective — and out of this psychic need — the actual particularities of real, living communities got erased. As we will see later on, this kind of attempt to make the entire world the same is at the heart of much of ecocide. The need to erase differences also expresses a psychic insecurity that can be assuaged only in a world in which the self is endlessly repeated. Everything must be made similar, safe, controlled.

Sadly, the actual consequences of World Bank policies were very different from its stated intentions. While at times the bank made things better for ordinary people (in its campaign against black-fly-spread blindness in Africa, for example), most of the time the gigantic projects it helped initiate, design, fund, and oversee led to cultural upheaval, environmental degradation, and increased economic inequality. The "development" sought by the bank essentially replaced subsistence economies with export-oriented ones, turning the third world into a resource base for developed nations. This transformation brought in a great deal of technology and destroyed traditional — and often much more satisfying and prosperous — ways of life. Local resources were no longer available for local consumption; large loans were necessary to keep the new agriculture or industry going; millions of people who had survived by subsistence farming or local craft work were displaced. The result was the creation of a "fourth world" of refugees from development: driven out by the destruction or pollution of their native ecosystems and by a rending of their traditional social fabric.

For instance, the World Bank funded the industrial development of the Singrauli region in India. Enormous power stations and industrialized factories were built. Along with these supposed contributions to a modernized economy, Singrauli produced devastating accumulations of toxic wastes and high rates of environmental illnesses among workers and the surrounding population. A critic complained: "Planners and financiers... forgot two things: the people who lived there and the very existence of the land, air, and water except as abstract industrial inputs."

In a similar vein, the cultivation of eucalyptus plantations was imposed, with this fast-growing tree seen as the basis of a new lumber export business. This project was touted as "social forestry," supposedly aimed at raising the standard of living of the poorest peasants in the area. Yet in fact,

> International aid went principally to support commercial tree farm schemes managed by state forestry agencies and benefiting more

prosperous landowners. The large-scale monoculture of eucalyptus often left the land useless for other purposes, depleting soil fertility and draining water tables in arid regions.

The bank, supposedly a model of clear-thinking professionalism and solid rationality, often acted irrationally and even lied to obscure its failures. In one case it asked a scholar to evaluate the effects of a new road on land held by a collection of tribes in the Polonreaste section of Brazil. One of the world's leading academic experts on these tribes, he wrote a blistering condemnation of the dire consequences of continued "development." For example, he pointed out that part of this project was massive export logging, which had used a highly toxic defoliant that decimated the tribe. The bank ignored the report and continued on. The Nambiquara Indians declined to virtual extinction.

The long-term effects of bank development schemes often led to what has been called "export-led collapse." In this sequence, jungle settings and subsistence agriculture are swept away to make a place for cash export crops like coffee and cotton. The local people, much less self-sufficient, now depend on exports instead and are therefore subject to a world market over which they have no control. The increase in production leads to a glut on the world market, which causes a world price collapse and leaves local economies devastated.

In rare cases, even the bank's own self-assessment admitted its failings. For example, the bank had to admit that in one of its largest schemes — moving poor people from other regions to Brazil's Nordest region and developing export agriculture there — "few of the poor of the region benefited from the Bank's programs."

To bolster his own sense of efficacy in running the planet, McNamara committed bank funds to practically anything that gave the illusion that the bank was a leading force of change. For instance, he supported a massive transmigration scheme in Indonesia, which led to enormous rainforest destruction and cultural genocide. McNamara to some extent went into this project with his eyes open, knowing quite well that the author and ultimate director of the plan, Indonesia's corrupt dictator Suharto, was much more concerned with promoting his own power and wealth than in helping the poor. Yet as McNamara admitted, he couldn't turn down the chance to be part of the action. If there was something going on, he needed to be connected to it.

According to a colleague, McNamara hid from his own impotence and the bank's failures by using "numbers to suppress uncertainties." He was compelled to lie because his attachment to public status made real rationality, truth, and efficiency impossible. In the end, people cannot be truly "efficient" or "rational" if they so desperately need to be successful that they cannot face the truth. It was not that he didn't care. Rather, if he hadn't cared so much, he wouldn't have had to appear invulnerable, to keep forging bigger and bigger schemes of ever more doubtful value. Driven by a hidden desperation that wouldn't let him stop and see what he was actually doing, haunted by the fear of not being somebody important, special, different, he had to keep going no matter what the consequences. Ultimately, like Marlow's attachment to work or Stangl's to his uniform, attachment of this kind leads us to ignore the ultimate consequences of what we do.

Many writers have suggested that the root of the behavior which leads to the Holocaust or the casual disasters of the World Bank is a lack of feeling, empathy, or subjective self-awareness. For Susan Griffin, the McNamaras or Stangls are like "severed heads," so removed from the reality of their own embodied life that they cannot be responsive to the pain they cause in others. Others write of a "murderous objectivity" or a "banality of evil." The image is always of unfeeling semi-automata, nearly sleepwalking their way through policies of enormous brutality.

For reasons I have indicated already, I do not agree. Of course, the people in control of these institutions typically seek to *appear* uncontaminated by strong emotions. Since we live in a male-dominated culture that has associated emotionality with femininity, weakness, and irrationality, this is not surprising. However, we should be cautious about accepting the images men project of themselves. The fact that the institutions that run the world are coded to operate without acknowledging the feelings people have about what they are doing does not mean that these feelings do not exist. It just means that public discussion and personal awareness of those feelings have been banished from the public sphere.

While pretending to a kind of surface calm, the crucial figures often reveal themselves as driven. What they are passionate about, however, is whatever allows them to feel like subjects of a meaningful life. For Stangl, it was keeping order wherever he was assigned; for McNamara, it was building a bank to run the world. Stangl's main goal was not to

kill Jews, but to be, his son told us, "different from all those others." Mc-
Namara wanted to eradicate poverty, not devastate indigenous peoples
and pollute the environment. Yet he too, his biographer suggests, was
driven by a need not to seem "ordinary."

Those who serve in the dominant institutions are often passionate
about what they are doing precisely because they have nothing else by
which to establish themselves, nothing else about which to be passionate. Desperate to guarantee that the lost self of masculine modernity
will at last feel at home in the world, these men are not "machine-
like," "bureaucratic," "unfeeling," or invested only in their private lives.
Because, as Miriam Greenspan observes, we live in an emotion-fearing
culture, to be outwardly emotional would be to lose authority, to put
in jeopardy one's right to be part of these world-controlling enterprises.
When Adolf Eichmann talked, with evident sincerity, about how the
highest goal of his life was to "obey orders," he was not revealing himself as a man without passion. Rather, he was showing us just where
that passion was trained. And so the lives of Stangl, McNamara, the
defenders of formaldehyde, and countless others are lessons of what can
happen when ordinary people are so empty of a sense of meaning and
connection that they need "work," no matter how destructive, to feel
that they are worthwhile human beings.

And it is not just "them"; it is also "us." For we too may fear being
"ordinary" or be desperate to belong. We too may need to know that
we amount to something and therefore might be willing to grasp on to
some institution, movement, job, career, or social setting that seems to
promise that we will. We too may seek to do all of this through our
work. Even if it is boring and we hate it, where would we be without it?

Of course, the vast majority of us have a very different place in society than Stangl or McNamara and don't have the chance to do evil on
such a grand scale. We do not direct concentration camps or dispense
billion-dollar loans. We are trying to get by: to pay the mortgage, put
our kids through school, deal with a marriage partner's illness, find a
little help for our aging parents, save enough money for a better car or
a summer vacation. We'd like to do well at our jobs, be respected, and
have a place where we belong.

Our affinity to Stangl and McNamara lies not in the immensity of
what we do, but in the similarity of motivation, and the way our historical situation leads us, regardless of our *personal* beliefs and goals, to
be part of destructive institutions. The danger is that we too can de-

scend, bit by bit, past the point of no return. Like Stangl, we might be overattached to our work, because we don't have anything else to be attached to so intensely. Like McNamara, even if the numbers don't add up, we might want to be where the action is. We might tell ourselves little untruths to support the big lies that protect the institutions that give our lives meaning. If there is no alternative source of value, concern, and identity, what choice do we have?

Is what I have been describing here better, and more simply, understood as an *ethical* matter? Is the problem with the Stangls and McNamaras less that they have no independent sense of self than that they are immoral? Is what we need to live decently in the world not a spiritual sense of ourselves but enough ethical backbone to refuse to go along with an immoral society?

My first answer would be, "absolutely!" A spiritual life without moral commitments is, I believe, a contradiction in terms. Purely self-oriented spirituality will take us nowhere. It simply reproduces all the problems of attachment, the self-interested ego, and inevitable boredom or disappointment that haunts conventional life and leads us to spiritual teachings in the first place. Yet simply attributing the problems I have described to moral failings may not go deep enough, for we will still need to ask: what is going to sustain us in our morality? Give us the strength to carry through in our values when so much is at stake? Stangl seems to have been aware, after all, that what he was doing was wrong. But he had no alternative sense of himself to put against the lure of the uniform. McNamara was not a "bad" man and clearly had strong moral feelings. Yet he lied to protect his idea of the bank's worth, because without that idea, his own life might have turned senseless. At its best, by offering us a sense of meaning that does not conform to conventional images of adequacy and efficacy, a commitment to a spiritual identity can give us the strength to follow through with our moral values. Spirituality in this sense requires no particular theology, no precise belief in any particular religion. It does require that we find our greatest worth in places other than conventional social values. What we are ultimately here for, what is of ultimate value for us, must be separate from what the social world calls "success." The particular content of this identity may be described as a humble, compassionate sense of morality, as a genuine, selfless political solidarity, or as a pursuit of a spiritual Inner

Truth. How we describe it is not important. What counts is that this identity enables us to be free of the seductive, addictive need for the approval of a society that is capable of destroying the earth.

We can live out our values in a dark time only if we tell a new story about what it means to do well, accomplish things, and matter. Having the right beliefs about moral obligations is important, but in the end it will not be enough. For better or worse, what we do is going to flow from who we think we are. We need to be able to act without a desperate need for recognition, have a sense of our own worth separate from the dominant and dangerous institutions that control most of society. We might do so by identifying with the body of Christ or Buddha's teachings or the good of the community or the Jewish ideal of repairing the world. But in any case we have to have something else on which to rely, on which to base ourselves when we say: "This is who I am."

There is a story about a man during the frantic and frightening arms race of the 1980s. He worked in public relations, living the good life on the West Coast, cruising along with a six-figure salary. Somehow he got past the denial and avoidance that keep most of us going and really faced what a nuclear war would be like. He quit his cushy job and became a low-paid staffer for the peace lobby. His old friends were shocked at his change and asked him how he could leave his successful life and be content with making $20,000 a year for some little political group.

"I have a young daughter," he replied, "whom I love very much. If there is a war, and she looks at me as the bombs are falling and asks me, 'Daddy, why didn't you stop it?' I want to be able to say to her that I did everything I could."

If the problem is that we measure ourselves by our work in the world, is the solution to have no means of measurement? Are we on this earth simply to be like a rock or a tree? Is the only alternative to compulsive work in the world escape from it? Does spirituality require this kind of passivity?

If such is our spiritual vision, we haven't gained much by acquiring it. Rather, we need to find some way to creatively and lovingly take part in the world, a third alternative between a destructive public identity and a quiescent spiritual one, between "making something of ourselves" and letting ourselves be as nothing. In this process, spirituality will help guide our presence in the world as well as our private experience.

In fact, spiritual teachers have counseled that our work in the world can be illuminated by a spiritual intention that enables it to avoid the twin evils of a false passivity and a destructive attachment. These various perspectives share the common notion that our essential identity does not depend on some measurable individual accomplishment and yet can also be expressed in active, creative, loving engagement with everything around us. A spirituality of resistance is, in a sense, simply the latest version of a long line of attempts to help us express our true nature in ways that will help other beings to flourish as well. Only now what is at stake is so much more daunting than the corrupt kings and priests assailed by Isaiah, or the vicious racism or colonialism fought by King and Gandhi.

How can we think about who we are? Are we really to be like a rock or a tree? Well, why not? Rocks offer shade from the sun, their undersides are homes to countless crawling, wriggling things, and ever so slowly they decompose and return their mineral wealth to the ecosystems of which they are a part. Trees give us oxygen, detoxify soil and groundwater, offer homes to squirrels, birds, butterflies, and even some tropical ants. Be like a tree or a rock? We could do worse! Give what the system needs, and take what we need in turn. The rock takes space. The tree will go for water, sunlight, CO_2, and minerals from the soil. Likewise, we human beings have been known to search out food and water, shelter and love, tools and a nurturing culture. Perhaps in an age of environmental crisis there is something we can learn from the natural world, some wisdom that will help us heal our wounded hearts and keep us from endlessly wounding each other and the rest of the planet as well.

Two Buddhist monks stood at the top of a hill, surveying the natural world. One of them began to sob, "How horrible," he moaned, "they are all eating each other." "Do not be alarmed," soothed the other, "You do not see quite correctly. Actually, they are feeding each other."

If we are dominated by a compulsion toward individualized accomplishment or consumption, we will never be satisfied. At bottom, what else could such a life be but despair? We need to tell ourselves some other story about who we are, about what is most important, about the meaning of our lives. Suppose that this new story is about living on this earth in a kind of moral kinship with our surroundings. Suppose we try to see ourselves as beings in a natural world, as beings who are all feeding each other. Suppose our participation in these natural processes becomes a central metaphor for how we are to live.

If we saw ourselves in this way, we might begin to learn the absolute value of each of the vastly different kinds of beings that are doing the feeding. For vastly different they certainly are: some, like the bacteria that populate our digestive tracts and are necessary for our survival, exist in the billions and measure their lives in minutes; some, like redwood trees, are few and last for centuries. Some are "keystone" species whom many other members of their ecosystem depend on: the alligators who make water-collecting depressions in dry season Everglade grass and thus enable the survival of a host of other life forms; the bats who pollinate countless flowers and shrubs. Other species, like the gorilla, exist happily at the top of a particular food chain and would not be missed nearly so much by other species.

Some do more, some do less. But is there any one that is not food for another? Any one that doesn't offer some mix of beauty, usefulness, fodder, pollination, waste consumption, food production, habitat maintenance? Doesn't everything have its place?

And if we see ourselves as right alongside all the others, then we also have our place, our value, and our home. We also belong.

As Kierkegaard reminds us: if the task of life is to be famous, to be "world-historical," to achieve, why then most people are going to fail or not feel good enough. If I must stand out to do well, then I must have lots of people around me who are doing badly. If I must belong to the dominant institutions to have a meaningful life, then when those institutions are committing crimes I will have to go along. But if my task in life is to cultivate my own passion, to focus on my own spiritual identity, then no one else can do this for me and no one can do it better than me, for it concerns the uniqueness and infinite value of my own existence.

Or as it was put in an old Hasidic tale: Rabbi Zusya knew that after he died God would not berate him for not being Moses. God would, rather, ask him: "Zusya, why were you not Zusya?"

Can a mosquito be an alligator? An earthworm imitate a redwood? A boring old pigeon pretend to the splendor of an eagle? Yet each has a role, a task, a place in the system of life.

And so nature feeds us not only by providing the stuff to make tossed salads and orange juice, but by providing a model of worth from which we might well learn a good deal. The current social model — hierarchy, elitism, success for a few and mediocrity for the many — is damaging and unecological. Painful when internalized, it wounds to no point or purpose (except the continued power of those few who profit from the system, and even most of them lead lives of quiet desperation). The pain that comes to the mother when a young rabbit is snatched by a hawk is part of the endless, perfect, eating-feeding cycle. The pain of Prozac-masked depression feeds nothing, except the drug companies and pyschopharmacologists. And so we can think of ourselves and our fellows as Thomas à Kempis suggested:

> There is no one living without failings; no person that is so happy as never to give offense; no person without a load of trouble; no person so sufficient as never to need assistance.... Therefore we should think ourselves under the strongest engagements to comfort, and relieve, and instruct, and admonish and bear with one another.

Ecological models of self-understanding and the values that flow from them allow people to feel good about themselves without sinking into narcissism. Feeling at home no longer depends on being special, being number one, rising to the top. I do not have to be "better" at feeding than the next person. Even though he might be an alligator and I merely an intestinal bacterium, we are both part of the Big Show and both have our place in it. This process is not individual. To feed and be fed we need to listen to others and be heard by them, to look carefully and to make ourselves seen. We must connect; we cannot exploit. Solidarity becomes more important than success, being part of a healthy ecosystem (a marsh, a stream, a meadow) more important than being the tallest tree in the forest. Thus the freedom that this model confers is neither the unsustainable freedom of endless consumption nor the self-preoccupied introspection of the cheaper kinds of New Age spirituality. If what it is all about is feeding each other, each in our own particular way (after all, we must, like Zusya, struggle to be ourselves), then we have a spiritual task for a lifetime in finding out just how to do that.

The commitment to feeding and eating will not solve all the difficult questions we face: about whether the distribution of money, power, and property are fair or unfair, useful or exploitative, necessary for efficiency or a rip-off. It will not always tell us when our feeding is wholesome and when diseased or when someone else's munching on us is to be expected or something that should be stopped cold in its tracks. This different way of experiencing our lives will not give us a set of definitive principles or a blueprint for a just society. We probably won't stop driving our cars or heating our homes. We won't automatically become environmental saints as well as spiritual seekers. How this new way of experiencing the self might get translated into social policy or personal choices is a complicated business and might even keep someone awake at night. Yet it is possible we will find in it an alternative to compulsive action and quiet withdrawal.

In my environmental philosophy class all students must keep a "plant journal." They are told to pick some particular "plant," from a blade of grass to a tree, and to sit with that plant three or four times a week, recording their experiences. They are instructed to be with it, talk to it, listen to it, touch it, smell it — to be able to tell the world what would be lost if the plant were to become extinct. Any record of this activity is acceptable, including writing over and over again that they think the assignment is a waste of time and that Gottlieb is an idiot. After years of this practice, I have seen, time and again, the simple "being with" of the practice work its magic. I remember one fellow in particular who for the first two weeks of our seven-week term recorded his disdain for the plant, the plant journal, and his professor. Then he began to notice the details of the small tree he had chosen. By the fifth week he had named the tree "George" and looked forward to visiting it. And his final entry read: "All the other trees have their leaves and George doesn't; I'm really worried about him."

Part II

CHAPTER FOUR

A Sleepless Ethicist and Some of His Acquaintances, Including the Monoculturalist, the Poetic Naturalist, and the Very Famous Biologist

Thankfully, there are many people who have put away avoidance and denial and will not make meaning for themselves by thought-lessly working for the dominant institutions. Their spiritual identities do not contract into self-preoccupation, but expand into a vital concern with all that lives. In this age of environmental crisis, we may think, for example, of those who donate money to the Sierra Club, wear Greenpeace T-shirts, try to save wetlands, and boycott whoever needs to be boycotted the most. Passionate for the cause, they occasionally bore strangers at parties by fulminating against corporate polluters and have been known to give their loved ones bad dreams by compulsively sharing the latest ecological horror story just before bedtime.

Despite our society's escapism, these folks sometimes see their values echoed in the broader culture. In enlightened sermons and at activist Earth Day celebrations, in the ambiance of health food stores and the soothing tones at the end of television nature specials, in Disney movies about succession struggles in lion kingdoms and on the back of politi-cally correct cereal boxes, they are tirelessly reminded that people are but a small part of the great Circle of Life.

Once we have decided that to nourish our truest sense of self we must give to the earth as it gives to us, many of us might want to add our voices to this chorus of environmental responsibility. Unfortunately, however, the attempt to devote ourselves to nature is more difficult than it might seem; and it is hard to maintain spiritual peace in the face of an environmental crisis that often seems to put personal morality out of reach. I have a good friend who is so confused by all this that it keeps him awake nights. His case is interesting, and if we eavesdrop on the contents of his troubled mind, it is just possible we'll learn a bit about our own predicament.

He is a large, bearded, pleasant-looking man, a lot grayer than he used to be, who often has a slightly worried, somewhat abstracted look on his face. Because for some years now he has not slept very well, he often looks tired. This man (call him the Ethicist, for in fact he earns his living teaching ethics, especially ethics in regard to the environment) has listened deeply to the voice of the suffering earth, and he worries about human suffering as well. A decent person, he tries to do his best (in an overly serious way). However, he often does not find it so easy to know what this "best" is; nor is he often convinced that he has done it, even though he has tried. And that is why he doesn't sleep well. He tends to wake very early, face the predawn light with a kind of ethical anxiety, and contemplate some unsettling questions.

Sitting at his desk at 4:47 in the morning, facing bookcases filled with titles like *Planetary Overload, Scorched Earth,* and *Environment under Fire,* he first tries to figure out what is so troubling about his present ethical situation, why the environmental crisis is so different from other moral demands he has faced, and why his spiritual sense of himself is so frequently distressed by an uneasy conscience.

Most people, most of the time, he thinks, want to live rightly. From the biblical prophets to modern social struggles, from the ethics of the Buddha to anti-war movements, our past echoes with reminders to heed the outcry of the oppressed and to remember or discover our better selves. Of course history is also filled with examples of violence and injustice. These dismal occurrences merely reveal how people can succumb to impulses stronger than the attraction to decency and that certain social settings condition people to accept moral offenses like slavery or sexism. But since people generally want to think of themselves as good, even those we see as most evil typically feel compelled to produce elaborate rationalizations. ("I was doing it for my family," says the Godfather; "I was doing it for the Fatherland," says the Nazi.)

As social life changes, our Ethicist knows, so do the moral demands we place on ourselves. For example, in his own lifetime he has seen a new demand — that women be treated as equals to men — go from tiny fringe groups to an international movement that has challenged governments, religions, English departments, and large, bearded men in living rooms. The spread of democracy and the increased number of women with paid jobs weakened the belief in men's natural superiority. Historical changes made what was once taken for granted unacceptable. Out of these changes came a corresponding set of moral demands on men: to give up unjustified male privilege and authority.

The recently emerged demands of feminism may be rigorous, thinks our Ethicist, but a man can respond to them without contradiction. If you are well-intentioned and good-hearted, you can surrender male privilege in your personal relationships: by making yourself emotionally vulnerable, taking responsibility for your actions, and doing your share of the dishes. You can publicly support women's political equality and physical safety and challenge male-biased cultural values. You can resist the sexist locker room jokes, speak out against discrimination in promotions, and make it clear that contempt for women is not part of your particular style of male bonding. Having done all these things, you can then speak with a kind of moral integrity about the evils of sexism. Moral change, moral clarity, and real virtue are possible here.

Now perhaps the principle reason our troubled Ethicist is awake at this ungodly hour is that he senses that the demands of the environmental crisis are very different.

In this crisis we are assaulting virtually all of nature. Spotted owls and children in overcrowded cities, whales and pesticide workers, all have been damaged or are at risk. As recognition of the injustice of sexism provokes the moral demand to end it, so recognition of our ecological disasters provokes a demand for a new ethical responsiveness.

And it is just this demand which the Ethicist, no matter how deeply he feels it, does not always know how to fulfill. This frustrating failure threatens the Ethicist's sleep and weakens his confidence in society's ethical standing. Both our civilization as a whole and the most particular, small-scale details of his own moral, and hence spiritual, life are at stake. He cannot reach a level of spiritual peace while he is so ethically dissatisfied with the way he lives.

Why does he feel so morally feeble?

To begin with, the Ethicist wonders what is happening to a belief that seems essential if we are to have any morality at all, the belief that we are capable of teaching virtue to our children. As adults we assert, directly or tacitly, that we are worthy moral models. We expect children, in turn, to believe that we know what we are talking about. If this is not so, if adults do not know how to be moral, muses the Ethicist, then family life, schools, religions, the legal system, and even political parties are all resting on some pretty flimsy ground.

And that is precisely the case, because adult moral competence is rendered deeply suspect by the toxic waste dumps, thoughtless elimination of other species, and cavalier nuclear testing. How can any of us, he wonders, teach morality to our children or pretend to ethical competence, when breakfast cereal boxes list endangered and extinguished species and kids can ask, as did his seven-year-old daughter: "Daddy, can a time come when there are no more trees?" Who are we to pretend we know what is right when we are living this badly?

The Ethicist knows that since so many people consume in environmentally damaging ways (or would like to) whole populations are now implicated in their own destruction. What then happens to confidence in our right to further develop technological civilization? Might an impartial charitable observer wonder if it is not morality that is lacking, but sanity? Would such charity be very comforting to an adolescent subjected to moral instruction by parents, teachers, and religious leaders — all fully adult members of a society whose morality (or sanity) is doubtful?

In essence, what people have done and continue to do casts doubt on our collective ability to serve as moral models for the next generation. Teaching our children values now seems to require that we turn a blind eye to reality and practice a kind of denial, one that is probably transparent to those we wish to teach. Our Ethicist cogitates: "Don't our children sense what is absent in our moral talk, that we have, for instance, made sunlight dangerous for them, left millions of tons of toxic wastes, destroyed incomparable settings of natural beauty and wonder? When we don't talk about this; or when we do so as if it had no moral implications for us personally, doesn't that further lessen their already limited respect for our integrity and efficacy?"

He thinks of the bitter, cynical, escapist, passive, or techno-addicted young people he knows — and wonders how much of their collective temperament stems from the simple fact that they cannot forgive the moral avoidances and failures of the adult world. He remembers his own childhood, lived partly in awareness and fear of nuclear war. (The teacher's instructions to put his head under his desk in case there was a nuclear attack; the dreams of seeing mushroom clouds over New York City, twenty miles from his house.) He speculates that his own sense of the evils of society may have begun in his perplexity over grown-ups who had put everything on the edge of destruction and were content to live on that edge year after year.

The environmental crisis, while less dramatic than a nuclear war, is already underway. "What," he wonders, having in mind the children who grow up amid all this, "what must they think of us, in those secret places where children hide from a confusing, often crazy, adult world? As they learn what we've done, how much trust can be left?"

"As I lay in a hospital bed for almost two years recovering from the blast," a survivor of the Nagasaki atomic bomb tells us, "I began to hate my parents, and parents everywhere. All who had not opposed the war."

"What the children think of us; and what we think of ourselves," the Ethicist muses. "Both are at issue. We feel, and we want to believe in, our devotion as parents, teachers, examples for the young. Yet how," he asks himself, "can we profess love for our children and simultaneously poison the groundwater? How can we teach them to love their neighbors when energy use in the first world may cause a global warming that will raise the sea level and wipe out island nations? Having tampered with the climate and the protective features of the atmosphere, having dangerously overloaded our planet's carrying capacity, how can we pretend to be experts in morality? We ask our kids 'How would it feel if someone did that to you?' We try to teach them to empathize, to respond to others' needs or pains. And then we continue on, seemingly blind or uncaring. What kind of spiritual integrity can we possess when we live like this?"

Sleep recedes further as the Ethicist reflects that all too often those of us who would resist environmental destruction can offer our children only examples of moral exclusion and impotence. As we seek to disassociate ourselves from the collective agencies that are wreaking havoc on the earth, we must also admit that most of the time we cannot stop them. We may avoid the subject and thus leave our children thinking we are hypocrites. Or we may admit the truth and confess to how little we can do to protect them or the earth. The Ethicist thinks bleakly: "Our heirs can see us as morally corrupt, collectively insane, or impotent. What a legacy for the next generation!"

This moral pall, the Ethicist knows, is cast over all attempts to model virtues like taking responsibility for one's acts, restraint in consumption, or care for others. If we are not to appear obvious hypocrites, our moral instruction to our children should include direct admissions of our own failings. In this regard, our collective complicity in the environmental crisis dramatically reverses the usual constraints on moral instruction. We typically believe that the practicing murderer, thief, or profligate cannot teach others about the virtues of nonviolence, respect for others' property, or chastity. In the case of the morality of our relations to non-human nature (the Ethicist notes with no little irony), such a constraint would leave us with no one to teach anything at all!

Yet it is not only society in general that is causing the environmental crisis. Our daily lives make us individual accomplices to the catastrophe.

The Ethicist, who has some standing as an environmental thinker, wonders at his own situation. He knows, better than most, the dreadful effects of how he lives. But it always seems that there isn't much he can do personally to change, unless he so dramatically alters his life that (like the Unabomber?) he virtually leaves society. He tries to ride his bike when he can, to recycle, and to eat organic vegetarian style. But for the most part, his energy, food, medical treatment, tax payments, clothes, travel, housing, and work continue to involve him in the very form of life he abhors. (And sometimes, though he wouldn't like others to know, he takes the Damaging Shortcut: he uses plastic sandwich bags and tosses them after one day, leaves lights on unnecessarily, skips over the organic produce because it's too pricey.) Thus, it is not just our dominant institutions whose moral status is threatened, but that of self-aware individuals as well. The Ethicist has to admit that virtually all of us (including his environmentally like-minded comrades) participate in and thus tacitly support destructive patterns of consumption and production. "I know," he thinks, "that we protest global warming. But we drive individual cars to the demonstration! We write environmental manifestos and use endless paper for rough drafts." As he prepares his own passionate and sincere speeches, the Ethicist plugs his computer into the same power grid that the well-organized anti-environmentalist Wise Use boys do. Seeking to be part of the solution, he knows that he is simultaneously part of the problem. When he looks, with a kind of depressed fatalism, at the sheer quantity of stuff he has accumulated in his attic, when he goes to the supermarket and sees the endless boxes and bags and knows that they are multiplied daily by (at least) ten thousand in the vast sweep of American consumerism, when he fills up his car at the gas station once again, he knows that the environmental crisis is not just a matter of what others do, but of what he does himself. His own moral and spiritual quest, his attempt to join outer concern and inner seeking, seems hopeless.

Besides feeling guilty over the unchosen consequences of the way he lives, our Ethicist is also pulled in conflicting directions by the moral demands of family, work, social responsibility, and care for the earth. The sheer effort to fulfill any other moral obligation seems to leave him unable to do what he should in regard to the environment.

He thinks of a good friend of his, a Professor of Philosophy. This man lives in Boston and for the academic year commutes to work in Worcester: a hundred round-trip miles four times a week, thirty-five weeks a year. An expert on the religious and political aspects of the environmental crisis, the Professor nevertheless makes his own little contribution to global warming. When questioned, he explains his contradictory behavior by talking about his younger daughter's serious special needs: that her school in Boston is far better than what he could find elsewhere, that her needs for a sensitive, loving, integrated learning environment take precedence over all else. (He himself would much rather live in the country, closer to work.) Of course he could take the bus from Boston to Worcester, but that would double the time of the two-hour daily commute and cripple his ability to fulfill his other responsibilities: as father of two children, husband, teacher, colleague, and environmental writer.

Yet what will happen to his personal credibility when he teaches Bill McKibben's disturbing study of global warming in his environmental philosophy class? Who is he to fume against Exxon or General Motors when he too pours unnecessary carbon dioxide into the atmosphere? How can he generate the necessary self-righteous indignation and model for his students the proper ecological outrage? What is he to do when one of his students asks (as they always do), "But Professor, don't you commute here from Boston?"

Like the Ethicist, the Professor of Philosophy feels a nagging sense of unease about his life. As distinct from the Sincere, Feminist man, who can without contradiction respond to the calls of feminism, these guys feel a little hypocritical, a little guilty, and (even worse) at times a little resentful at how hard the whole business feels. "All of us heartfelt environmentalists," he muses, "want to think that we are on the 'right side.' How is it then, that we do things that we know are not right?"

He sees that since conversations about environmental ethics and spirituality are typically carried out by people who play their own part in what they criticize, the moral issues have become painfully complex. At the very least, our response, while passionate, had better be free of any taint of self-righteousness. Over and over he stresses to himself: "This is not like talking about racism or sexism. We cannot shake our fingers in people's faces and berate them for their failings. For we too, in too many ways, are part of it."

Along with guilt over his own shortcomings, the Ethicist also feels a great deal of anger at the people who are most responsible. He doesn't believe that knowledge of his own foibles should obstruct his awareness that although almost all of us take part in the collective ecological madness, we don't do so equally. He refuses to lose sight of the broader social structures that condition and limit his own individual choices. In those structures some people have much more power and are much more responsible than others.

He knows, for example, that he could compare the farmworkers who handle pesticides in the fields with the people who own the corporations that make them. The pesticides are a global health problem. They cause increased risk of cancer, immune deficiencies, respiratory illness, birth defects, and reproductive problems. These dangers affect us all. Yet besides these long-term effects, there are also approximately two hundred thousand deaths a year from direct exposure to high concentrations of pesticides, mainly among the populations of people who handle them. In other words, the ones who suffer the most from this environmental calamity are the fieldworkers and poor farmers. The ones who profit the most are furthest away from it.

Because of his personal participation in the violence of ecological destruction the Ethicist knows he must be humble. Simultaneously, because he sees the social forces at work, he knows that moral judgment and collective resistance are called for as well. Spiritual awareness and humility can coexist with the forthrightness to call a spade a spade, a peaceful heart with justified anger. After all, not everyone had equal power to continue manufacturing CFCs even after their effects on the ozone layer were known, or to gut funding for public transportation in support of the auto industry, or to export banned chemicals to third world countries. Economic, political, and military elites, usually unconstrained by the rest of the population, shape the world's social life. Ecocide, our Ethicist senses, is their stock in trade.

For this man, apparently, a concern with spirituality leads to ethics, and then, almost without pause, to politics: to the realm of mass institutions, social power, the distribution of wealth, and the governmental use of violence. As we open our eyes to the things that frighten us the most, as we start to question the effects of our work, we necessarily confront the basic organization of society. The more we open our eyes to this reality, he thinks, the more we see how much of it needs changing.

Our Ethicist wonders: "How can I pursue my spiritual life without so much guilt and what is the alternative to a world run by a destructive elite? Can we envision a society in which the environmental crisis is solved and human beings are respected, in which both kestrels and children are cared for?" Feeling a little lightheaded now from lack of sleep, his first thought is: "I haven't the faintest idea, and neither does any one else!" Yet ethicists rarely stop at the first thought, and this one is no exception. "As a start," he thinks, "it is clear that we don't want to have to choose between human well-being and that of the natural world. We'd like to live in such a way, as it were, that everyone is feeding everyone else, and we don't always feel pulled by conflicting obligations."

He begins by thinking about a particular wildlife conservation program in Africa: a 1980s campaign to "save the elephants" by boycotting the ivory trade and trying to arrest (or shoot) poachers. Where the boycott didn't work, it simply raised the price of ivory, drove the trade underground, and led to increased slaughter. Where it did work, the boycott supported a substantial increase in elephants. This, he found out, was not so wonderful for the neighboring farmers whose meager vegetable gardens or fruit trees were destroyed by the large and wonderful objects of foreign (read white European and American) concern. (The Ethicist could not help imagining what would have happened if a few large elephants had been strategically placed next to the cars or vacation condos of the well-off Westerners who supported the World Wildlife Fund's boycott efforts. A few stomped BMWs and Save the Elephants might have gone right down the tubes!)

A better idea, actually tried in a few places, was to attempt a mutually beneficial coexistence between the elephants and the people who lived next to them. Projects diverted ecotourism dollars from foreign companies to the locals, who also got jobs in wildlife refuges. The general lesson was that to save either, we have to care as much for the people as we do for the animals. Rather than forcing a foreign concern for one at the expense of the other, the goal was to repair the connection.

Next, the Ethicist thinks about the Philippines, and how the environmental destruction of this place is enough to make a grown man cry. Something as simple as clear-cutting a forest to export wood for Japanese furniture manufacturers leads to eroding hillsides, silted up rivers, and the destruction of offshore coral reefs at the mouths of the rivers. In congested cities fleets of old American cars without pollution control devices poison the air and ruin children's lungs. Brand-new Mega-Mega Mining operations replace the small traditional "pocket" mines and leave mountains of poisonous residue. Here "nature" is not some abstraction separated from the social life of ordinary people. Like the African elephants and their farmer neighbors, the lives of people and their immediate surroundings cannot be separated.

"And who," the Ethicist muses further, "decided to clear cut the hillsides or open the Mega-Mega Mine? Probably not the people who live next to them. Perhaps if we really want to preserve an ecosystem, we might start by looking at who lives in it, or near to it, and think about what we have to do to preserve them as well. Or, even better, let's ask them what they think they need. It's rare that they will opt for the presence of an Enormous Economic Power from Very Far Way, especially one with no past or future ties to the land. Concern with 'nature' in the Philippines — and everywhere else — is going to be simultaneously concern with getting some democratic access to natural resources and having some real input into decisions concerning the path of economic development."

And so the Ethicist envisions a utopia in which care for the earth and care for people go hand in hand, in which ecojustice and a deep ecological respect for all beings are in harmony. This vision can shape his sense of his own proper place on this earth and help him see how he should — and should not — work. Within this vision, impossible moral conflicts and a continual sense of ethical failure would no longer mar his spiritual journey. He'd get some sleep because the way we lived would fit what he felt in his heart.

Yet as inspiring as this vision may be, deep down the Ethicist must admit that his mental leaps from his own sense of personal inadequacy, to reflections on the ills of society, to visions of Perfect Harmony, are a little quick. It is one thing to mouth generalities about justice for the native and justice for the animals. And sometimes these things will indeed be compatible. However, what about the tough cases where limited resources, limited time, and limited care don't seem to make for such perfection?

Consider, the Ethicist thinks, the kestrel from the island of Mauritius, near Africa. This spectacular, cliff-dwelling little falcon had been about as far down the road to extinction as you can get. The usual suspects of reduced habitat, pesticides in the food chain, foreign predators, and forest alteration by exotic plants left us with about six birds. And this even after the International Council for Bird Preservation spent four years trying to do something. Then Carl Jones, the man assigned to terminate the ICBP project and consign the kestrel to oblivion, committed himself to one last try. With the help of biologists, ecologists, and wildlife specialists, Jones brought the kestrel back. Some birds were bred in captivity; wild birds were induced to accept supplemental food; eggs were taken from nests to promote higher rates of egg production; artificial insemination raised the incidence of reproduction; hatchlings were fed minced quail. And so on. Intense and fulfilling work — because after fifteen years of it there are now hundreds of kestrels in old and new sites in Mauritius. The Ethicist was moved to admiration and hope when he heard the story. As Jones himself said: "If you can save the Mauritius kestrel, you can save virtually anything."

And yet ... and yet. ... The extensive labor, the comparatively small but still substantial hundreds of thousands of dollars required — all these, the Ethicist thinks, might be seen in a different light by people starving to death, caring for crack babies, or lacking reliable water supplies and medicine. The truth is that the kestrel is not one of the parts of nature that we "need" very much. It is very unlike the mythical cancer cures that we'll never get if we burn all the rainforest. We could have used the money to help people, let the birds die, and never really noticed very much. Personally, the Ethicist is damn happy the bird is still around, even though he probably will never see one. But he is not starving, and can get all the water, food, and medicine he needs. How would he feel about the wonderful kestrel project if he were one of the folks in need?

"Yet why," the Ethicist pushes on angrily, "are these the choices that must be made? In a world of immense and unfairly distributed wealth, where umpteen billions of dollars are spent for arms, why think of dropping the kestrel project when people are starving? Couldn't we simply not build a few nuclear submarines? Or delay the introduction of the next generation of computer chips by six months? Cut by 20 percent the amount spent on vacation homes? Wouldn't that be enough to save the kestrels and a few people as well? And what would we lose?"

The Ethicist wonders: Is there a simple way to describe what is wrong with the way we live? He is of course familiar with a number of different ways of putting it. People talk of anthropocentrism — the belief that only people, and nothing else of nature, really matter. The Marxists see it as commodification — or the turning of the whole world into something to be bought, sold, and profited from. Great Thinkers — much greater than our insomniac moralist — have shown that consumerism has replaced participation in public or political life. The Big Questions are left to the Experts, while the rest of us get 1.2 cars per family and a K-Mart credit card. At the same time, people's ties to communities get thinner and thinner and instead of trying to sustain the life of the group they . . . shop. Finally, for Patriarchal Masculinity — otherwise known as Boys will be Boys — manhood means dominating women and other living things.

There is, however, another idea that has captured him: "monoculture." Consider, thinks the Ethicist, a living forest, which contains a variety of trees, shrubs, and plants and provides game animals, herbs for medicine, fodder for livestock, sacred groves for religious rites, wild fruits and berries, and protection for the watershed. To make way for Progress and Big Bucks, this forest can be replaced by endless rows of a single type of tree whose worth is measured solely by dollars per board foot of lumber. In this way, we achieve a monoculture. Or think of how a particular local agriculture produces a variety of types of food for local consumption, for animals, and for exchange. It is managed and sustained by local resources and local knowledge. It supports an integrated system of ethnic communities and social roles. After monoculture strikes, we end up with a highly technologized agriculture based on a single crop. Traditional methods and a wide genetic variety of seeds are replaced by chemical pesticides and fertilizers and bioengineered seeds that require huge loans administered by a central government, that is, by Expertise and Power from Afar. Distinct but traditionally interdependent ethnic communities become competing special interest groups — or fanatically warring sects — driven by their need to get government aid and sell their produce to a world market. The resulting conflicts (in the Punjab, for instance) look like simple ethnic antagonism, when in fact they are created by the forced monoculture.

The Ethicist knows that monoculture thrives on centralized control. The local, the small, and the traditional are to be replaced by the international, the huge, the national government, and the Newer than New. Knowledge held by local communities is dismissed; and Experts from Afar are consulted on how to make the place More Efficient. An interesting example, the Ethicist remembers, is the attack on Thailand's traditional irrigation system (*muang phai*). In muang phai small-scale dams and simple technology control the water. Unlike large modern dams, muang phai dams allow a continual flow of water, silt, and sediment, keeping channels from becoming full. Even more importantly, each muang phai dam has a local user committee, with members responsible for maintenance and collective assignment of work. This highly efficient, egalitarian system was assaulted by the central Thai government with aid from the World Bank. Searching for a monoculture of water control, large dams and centralized irrigation projects were imposed. The costs were immense (while muang phai depended on voluntary contributions from those using the water) and therefore massive loans and foreign exchange were required to pay for the ever-expanding price of a "modernized" irrigation and water control system. And this system did not work nearly as well as the old one. Eventually, a good deal of it had to be dismantled.

The Monoculturalist is often deeply ignorant of the setting he is destroying, thinks the Ethicist, remembering a recent trip to the South American rainforest. There was one particularly instructive encounter when his guide, a Tirio Indian from Surinam, pointed out a few problems with the agricultural technique of the peasants who had come to settle on Indian land.

White man *dumb!*...Look at that garden...I've seen better-looking agriculture inside a leafcutter ant's nest!...Look at that manioc! It is planted too far apart. You saw how we put ours close together; the leaves form a canopy like the forest's, which keeps the sun and rain from directly hitting the soil. And they have only one kind, whereas in our gardens we have more than twenty. That plantation is an invitation for the bugs to move in.... Look at the [absence of] weeds.... In our gardens we always leave some behind because it binds the soil in the rainy season.... You look at that plantation and you know the man doesn't understand the forest. A well-planned garden should look like a hole in the forest opened up when a giant tree falls over. Small openings in the forest are filled in by fast-growing weedy plants that attract game animals. When you cut down too much forest, the little plants can't seed in from the surrounding jungle and you don't have any birds or peccaries coming in that you can hunt.... Besides, this man put up fences at the edge of his garden. What a bad idea! Sometimes a peccary will come out of the forest to steal a green banana or a bit of manioc from my plantation. When that happens, my children eat peccary meat for a week!

The failings of this little plot are multiplied a million-fold in large-scale monocultured agriculture, mineral extraction, and fishing. The destruction of resources, the overconsumption of stocks, and the endless drive to do just one thing and do it for the highest short-term gain wastes the world.

One larger setting where the Ethicist saw this happen was the Newfoundland cod-fishing industry, which was completely destroyed by high-powered trawlers. Unlike generations of local fisherfolk who did not fish for considerable periods of time each year, these enormous fish factories strip-mined the sea all year round. As in the Indian's judgment of the peasant's garden, the local small-scale fisherfolk knew the mega-trawlers were destroying the stocks. Their complaints were ignored until virtually nothing was left.

All these situations, the Ethicist knows, are shaped by the way people treat each other as well as by the way they treat nature. The particular peasant family mocked by his Indian guide, for instance, had been lured from their previous homes to another part of the rainforest by broken promises of governmental support. After the support never materialized, they were swindled out of the little land they had cleared and forced to move on by hired thugs in the service of the local large landowner.

They next went to a jungle area not yet controlled by the land barons. In this new and alien setting the peasants were struggling with an eco-system which they barely understood, and — with racist overtones — they deeply resented the unfriendly Indians who surrounded them.

The collapse of fishing in Newfoundland was also based in an un-equal struggle: between local fishing communities and a few enormous corporations (supported by the Canadian government) with overcapi-talized trawlers. For generations, the fishery was seasonal and fisherman didn't fish on spawning grounds. The technology and power of mono-culture led past these old limits toward a virtual culture of extinction. As a result, forty thousand people lost their livelihoods, while corporate capital moved on. Similar attempts to rip the heart out of the ocean have depleted 70 percent of the world's fishing grounds: New Zealand's orange roughy, the Gulf of Mexico's red snapper, Atlantic bluefin tuna and swordfish, North Sea herring — all these face a dismal future. As an out-of-work fisherman said to the Ethicist: "There's no difference between timber companies felling the last big trees and trawling com-panies catching the last cod. . . . It all boils down to corporate greed and government mismanagement."

These monocultures, our Ethicist believes, are profoundly evil and often grotesquely inefficient. He knows that moral humility compelled by his own many failings had better not get in the way of his ethical obligation to name them for what they are and struggle against them.

But even here, things will not be simple. Once again, the scope of the environmental problem makes it difficult to fulfill our other obligations at the same time as we are resisting it.

The Ethicist thinks of a Mexican-American activist named Domingo Gonzalez. Gonzalez struggles against the *maquiladoras*, or assembly plants, that have sprung up along Mexican-U.S. border. Virtually un-regulated industry has created a vast arena of environmental poison. In one town alone there are an estimated twenty-three locations as bad as superfund sites in the U.S. When he visited Gonzalez's own community of Matamoros (near Brownsville, Texas) he was shown the "Mallory" children (so named for the company that had operated there): fre-quently retarded and facially deformed youths whose mothers worked with solvents and PCBs in the 1960s and '70s. Later, on a casual stroll near train tracks, he saw kids playing beneath railroad cars carrying hydrofluoric acid.

Gonzalez is well known as an organizer and a local source for American reporters who do stories on the environmental effects of NAFTA. He is trying to do something — anything — about the leaking chemicals, explosions, gases in the air, and uncovered toxic waste sites. In response, local industry leaders asked to have him "investigated." Meanwhile, representatives of the parent U.S. chemical company say its Matamoros plant complies with environmental safeguards and has never contaminated the surrounding residences. A spokesman told the Ethicist, "We've made the place much safer. I would live [there] and not have any worries about my health." Trying to soften its image, the company gave some books and a soccer field to the town and had a dance at the plant. "We had hamburgers, sodas. It was quite a nice thing. . . . I think we're changing minds." The Ethicist is glad that minds are changing — but of course cannot help wondering about the lives of the people who have been crippled by that man's chemical company. He thinks, for instance, of just one family Gonzalez took him to: the oldest daughter born with a shriveled leg, another with vision problems, and a little boy born with withered legs and a tumor at the base of his spine.

But while the Ethicist has infinite respect for Gonzalez, he knows the man's devotion to the cause hasn't been easy on his family. Serving nature and other people made him a frequently absent father. His marriage ended in divorce.

> When I would go home . . . eventually it would come time for me to leave, and my youngest son would throw himself in front of the door and scream, "Daddy, don't go, Daddy, don't go."

Our predawn Ethicist suspects that the only escape from these dilemmas is the realization that certain kinds of moral demands cannot be fulfilled by individuals and that a spiritually peaceful heart requires that our social connections, and not only our individual lives or hearts, be transformed. Morality is social not only in the familiar sense of having to do with benefits for others but in the fact that the moral agent is the group as much as it is the individual. "Being moral" — and hence being spiritual — is not something we can do by ourselves, any more than we marry, teach, or play in string quartets "by ourselves." That is why there are such close ties among spirituality, ethics, and politics. For it is in political life that we organize — and change — our social relationships.

The Ethicist realizes that he will never feel fully at home on earth if his collective relationships are toxic. Spiritual development, in some ways so intensely personal, is for him also a group endeavor. In fact, one way to understand the disasters of monoculture is to see them as outgrowths of a form of life in which authentic relationships are impossible because the "other" has been eliminated. Under monoculture, every Other — whether a seed, a culture, a variety of tree in a forest — gets reduced to the Same. Environmentally, the complexity of the living forest becomes the straight lines of the tree farms or the barrenness of a clear-cut hillside. Socially, the last tribes of the rainforest are transformed into a strange species of Christian who wear Nike windbreakers and despise the old Shamans. In his disgruntled insomnia the Ethicist sees an entire globe afflicted with Attention Deficit Disorder as differences of tastes, communal life, and identity formation get flattened out into a series of rapidly changing but endlessly repetitive basketball shoes, pop CDs, and nylon jackets.

Given the weakness of individuals and the power of those who rule the monocultures, the Ethicist wonders, is there any chance of change? The extensive culture of anthropocentrism, the dominating global marketplace, totalitarian or bureaucratic political arrangements — all these block movement toward sanity, hope, or peace.

Yet perhaps (and this is the first happy thought of the night) all these harmful social structures have been rendered suspect by the environmental crisis itself.

It is just possible that our collective life could shift, the Ethicist believes, because global ecological interdependence now reveals (at least to some) personal and collective moral interdependence. The most mundane activities of our daily lives can affect the well-being of people throughout the world. This simple, powerful fact reawakens our awareness of the moral messages of the great prophets, messages now rendered distressingly concrete by the far-flung effects of industrial production and mass consumption. We might have laughed up our sleeves when Jesus told us to love our neighbors, when Isaiah clamored for justice, when Gandhi called for universal compassion, or when Marx hoped that we would give "according to our abilities" and take only what we needed. But when someone else's smokestacks kill our forests or our use of gasoline threatens another's agriculture, the smiles get wiped off our faces.

Simultaneously, as we extinguish or pollute more and more of our surroundings, we begin to realize that their loss is also our own. The growing absence of the natural prompts a great loneliness. Our sorrows over the devastation reveal that personal identity does not stop at our individual or social boundaries, but includes the nonhuman as well. As we reflect on our losses, we sense that our physical bodies, senses, emotions, and even our language evolved by interaction with the nonhuman. That is why the more our world is humanized, civilized, and paved over, the more lonely, frightened, and addicted to distractions we become.

Because of the depths of these connections, the Ethicist is a little hesitant to talk about the "rights" of nature — as if trees could vote or otters required freedom of speech. Rather, our Ethicist's hopeful sense of a new environmental ethics grows out of something else. It is a shared sense that the burning of the rainforest, the pollution of a river, or the elimination of a species is a hurt not to an Other, but to Our Very Selves, or at least to an Other with whom we share the deepest of connections and whose loss irrevocably damages us. The Ethicist doesn't care for his daughter or his mother, his friends or his golden retriever, because of their "rights." Similarly, his love of, and loneliness for, nonhuman nature flourishes through the depth of his kinship with it rather than through abstract principles.

It might just be possible, the Ethicist muses, that the very losses we have suffered could prompt a kind of wisdom. Though a source of great pain, the environmental crisis is thus also an opportunity to transform the world into something a lot better than it is now; and perhaps even to realize a vision of spiritual connection.

But connect to what? and how?

Why . . . to nature of course . . . and . . . naturally! How else?

A perpetually troubled person, the Ethicist must admit to himself that he is not at all sure what this means anymore. While his leanings toward a spirituality of resistance move him in the direction of ethics and politics, he is not at all clear about how to think about this earth that he wants to protect. He recalls, for instance, another acquaintance, a widely respected Poetic Naturalist. One of the man's books focuses on travels to an uninhabited island off the northwest coast, to which he sails over rough Pacific seas and where he then spends time camping and exploring. The Ethicist was particularly struck by two passages in this book. The first describes the end of a long day's adventures.

Toward evening we start a campfire, set up driftwood benches, and look out over the shore. Diminishing surf breaks along the point and against a small bare island across from camp. The tide has risen thirteen feet in the last six hours, submerging the maze of reefs and tide pools so the cove now lies open to the Pacific. Adrift on its own reflection, the skiff looks tiny and vulnerable. Above the silhouette of Ocean Point, snowcapped mountains rise to the fading beams of sunset, and a wilderness of coast dwindles into the distance. The only signs of human presence are this flickering fire and the light of fishing boats anchored in the far coves of Roller Bay. Through my whole adult life, I've sought to experience unaltered, unbridled nature in wild places such as this. I've focused my work around it, chosen my home because of it, given up economic assurance to pursue it, made it a centering point of my existence.

Our Ethicist, whose family ties keep him in the city, envies his friend's adventures and is moved by the lonely beauty evoked in the smooth prose. Yet our Ethicist is also moved to an ironic sadness — or a sad irony — when he rereads a passage that appeared only four pages earlier:

We haven't come unprepared. The engine is in excellent condition, and we have a smaller spare in case this one fails. We also carry plenty of fuel, and the boat is well stocked for emergencies: fire extinguisher, flares, waterproof matches, hand-held radio, the unsinkable Styrofoam punt, and sealed container of emergency gear, plus sleeping bags, tools, flashlights, tent, food, and additional camping equipment. We're wearing coveralls designed for survival in cold water and have wetsuits and surfboards along.

The source of our Ethicist's irony is obvious: just how "unbridled" is "nature" when to approach it we have to schlepp along so many trappings of civilization? And how can his sincere, articulate, but perhaps not always self-conscious friend fail to see the contradiction between those two passages? In a larger and more uncomfortable way, he wonders how any of us can be spiritually and morally "at home on the earth" when we hardly know what the earth is anymore.

Even the most ardent of today's nature seekers is helpless without a vast array of plastic, metal, and Gore-Tex. Even the most devoted emerge from and return to the same old sources of environmental destruction. We have all become like a second generation of refugees, people who cannot approach their ancestral culture without simplified translations into their new "native" tongue or without a guidebook to the major holidays and central myths of the now barely remembered tradition.

Who knows when this began? Some believe, broods the Ethicist, that it started with the triumph of the sky gods over the worship of the Great Earth Mother or with the transition from finding berries to growing large crops. Some see modernity — modern science, modern capitalism, modern sex roles — turning the world into a collection of objects to be counted and controlled. Some imagine an earlier time when speech was closely coded by natural sounds and believe that we became cut off by the replacement of letters which mimic the natural world to a set of letters which only have meaning in the closed world of human speech. As the letters on the page have no intimate relation to our physical surroundings — are not shaped like a leaf, pond, or wolf — our language, ideas, and sense of who we are become exiled to a sterile void detached from breath, fluids, and the pulse of life. Then we forget where we came from. Then we can imagine ourselves Different from All the Rest.

It is paradoxical, the Ethicist knows, that while we are desperately lonely for "nature," it seems we can only approach and comprehend it in human terms. As a Very Famous Biologist and intrepid rainforest researcher put it:

> If I ever seriously thought of confronting nature without the conveniences of civilization, reality soon regained my whole attention. The living sea is full of miniature horrors designed to reduce visiting biologists to their constituent amino acids in quick time. . . . Evolution has devised a hundred ways to macerate livers and turn blood into a parasite's broth. So the romantic voyager swallows chloraquin, gratefully accepts gamma globulin shots, sleeps under mosquito netting. . . . He hopes that enough fuel was put into the Land Rover that morning, and he hurries back to camp in time for a hot meal at dusk.

Perhaps, our Ethicist ruminates, our plight is but an extension of the first uses of sticks and stones. Perhaps it is another facet of McKibben's melancholy notion that as we alter the global climate and atmosphere, "nature" has ceased to exist. This reflection leaves the Ethicist sad and frightened.

And, also, somewhat confused. Like his friend the Poetic Naturalist, the Ethicist would like to encounter "unbridled, unaltered nature." But where would he go to do so? It is not just a matter of what we take with us when we go, but of what we find when we get there. McKibben's "end of nature" comes from an overall climate alteration. But it is also true of countless local settings. The Ethicist knows, for example, that many of the "wild" lands of American national parks, supposedly dedicated to preservation of wilderness at its most pristine, have already been significantly altered by the importation of exotic species of plants and animals. In Hawaii, for example, nonnative mosquitoes, bunchgrass, pigs, and mongooses brought in by white settlers have decimated countless local types of insects, animals, birds, and plants, and even constitute a large part of the park's biomass. Quite often the new species, though "natural," have escaped their "natural" enemies and proliferate with little restraint. The result can approach a spontaneous, a "natural," monoculture. It has gotten so bad that miconia, a plant brought in by gardeners and landscapers, has (according to the governor) the potential "to devastate our islands, forest watersheds, native species and windward farmlands." Without native competition from its native South America, it grows to great heights and creates perpetual darkness on the forest floor. Local species die, and birds, soil, and animals are seriously affected.

Our poor Ethicist's head begins to swirl when he further remembers that it is not simply the recent white settlers who have impinged on "unaltered" nature in Hawaii. As much as he would like to lay the blame solely on technological civilization, he has learned that when the original Polynesian settlers came to Hawaii over a thousand years ago, they brought with them twenty-five species of plants as well as dogs, pigs, and rats. As a result, "The large native Hawaiian birds appear to have been hunted to extinction by the new arrivals." In another example, he has found that large areas of the American forests were managed and altered by controlled burning initiated by Native Americans. And that at times they would stampede herds of buffalo over cliffs and take only the tongues and the humps. (A far cry, thinks the Ethicist, from *Dances with Wolves!*)

Looking at all this, the Ethicist sees that the human effect on nature does not simply depend on what people do to animals, plants, and rivers. As when a world power messes around in local ethnic conflicts, what we do destabilizes relations among nonhuman species, favoring some and fatally weakening others. For an example, the Ethicist thinks of the American songbirds, whose vulnerability was treated in Rachel Carson's classic *Silent Spring*. As larger tracts of forest are developed or broken up into smaller pieces, the young of many songbirds are liable to destruction. Especially, nests are parasitized by cowbirds, who lay eggs in the nests of other birds, and whose larger, more demanding progeny displace the other birds' own offspring. The cowbirds, feeding on insects stirred up by agriculture and cows, flourish in areas where agriculture and construction displace forest and field. We find then a kind of "natural" monoculture of cowbirds! Thus while part of the songbirds' fate is a result of direct human action (e.g., habitat loss, pollution by pesticides), it also occurs when human destabilization simply favors one species over another.

The Ethicist remembers a trip of his own to Sanibel, a small island off Florida's west coast. To escape the ubiquitous hotels and condos, upscale little malls and elegant yet casual restaurants, he had taken a stroll through the local wildlife refuge. Birdcalls delighted his ears, and he saw white ibyx, red-billed moorhens, and softly-chirping black cummingtons. A water snake rippled through a pond and an alligator floated lazily in a shallow, slow-moving river. At the close of his restful stroll the Ethicist found a sign describing the "natural" history of the area. To his dismay he discovered that not only had the entire island been altered by major dredging and waterway construction to eliminate mosquitoes, but a nonnative decorative shrub which had taken over large areas of Sanibel had been attacked with herbicides and bulldozers so that the native marsh grasses could return. This bit of nature, so lovely an oasis amid the desert of civilized holiday development, was in its own way no more "natural" than the grass and ornamental flowers of the nearby golf course.

The Ethicist remembers a time when he taught a class on these matters. A bright, scientifically knowledgeable and somewhat caustic student questioned him closely: "Why should we care about how people are changing the world? Isn't nature always changing anyway? There was a time when the earth had no atmosphere, no oceans. The dinosaurs came and went. Eventually the sun will explode and we will all go along with it. So why make a big deal out of leaks from a nuclear plant or ozone depletion?"

The Ethicist had been stunned by the simple power of the question. And he had to think deeply before he replied: "What you're saying is logical. But can you really maintain it? Imagine (God forbid) that you have just found out that your mother has lung cancer. And one of the causes is the second-hand smoke from *your* cigarettes. Would you say: 'Oh, well, the world will end in six billion years. Who cares?' Or would you be struck with guilt and sorrow? And be willing to do anything to help save her? Experienced, felt, understood — the present set of ecosystems and species of our earth is like that mother. We want her to live, don't we? And to be healthy? (Although we might want her to make a few minor changes: even a mother isn't perfect.) But our love for her is not based in her unchangingness, or the fact that somehow she exists without us. It is based on who she is for us — and who we are with her."

The students were properly awed by the Ethicist's reply. He thought, with just a hint of pompous self-satisfaction, "That time, at least, I moved them." Later that night, driving home, the incident came back to him. And then, underneath the glow of self-satisfaction, a Gnawing Little Voice, in a mocking little tone, began to make him a little less self-satisfied.

"Of course you shut him up. But what if he had been a little more persistent? or had a little more chutzpah? What if he had given it right back to you, like this?

"'Oh, come on, Professor, you think nature is a "mother" because you live in a big supermarket, a safe, easy, centrally heated world. Try having a plague of locusts destroy in two hours the food you've been growing for four months — and then wondering what your family will eat for the next year. Try playing around with bacteria when you have no antibiotics or catching fish in the open ocean from something that looks like a large canoe. Try having a 30 percent childbirth mortality rate. You treat the world like a Sweet Mommy just because the Big Daddy of Technology, with regrettable effects to be sure, lets you look at the world as a religious and aesthetic experience and not a threat. How beautiful the sunset is! How spiritual the waterfall and the call of the loon! And then you drive home, your HMO card that guarantees you technologized medicine safely tucked in your wallet, your pension in place, with several credit cards to make sure you have access to the oil industry, the plastic industry, and (in case you don't actually stare at trees for three hours every night) the TV-CD-Movie-Radio industry. Most people in the developed countries do not need to fear flood, famine, heat, or cold. Such things may be annoying at times, or occasionally seriously hurt a tiny percentage of the population. But because we've tamed it, limited it, and made it do our bidding, nature is not a daily problem. Does this offend you? Then try living like the people who have to depend on their limited wits, without sterile bandages, dependable water supplies, or houses that are warm in the winter. Or at least, at the very least, tell me just exactly what it is you are willing to give up.'"

"Well, well, well," thought the Ethicist, stunned once again. But as much as the Voice troubled him, he wanted to be in dialogue with it. So after a few minutes he replied:

"Perhaps it is true that all the achievements of science and technology have shaped my view of Nature. Maybe I see what I see because of the many triumphs of Physics and Chemistry and Mechanical Engineering, because bridges give us a nice view of raging rivers, and certain skin creams can keep the mosquitoes at bay.

"But that does not mean the view is false. It just means that our sense of the world is going to be determined by where we are. Did you expect something else? We can no more make moral judgments uncontaminated by our historical situation than we can have a sense of what the world looks like that is not based on the kind of eyesight we have. Yet the fact that our views are historically conditioned does not mean that we have to love, admire, or stomach everything that history has produced. The fact that I use a telephone doesn't mean I have to accept fifteen hundred legal food additives, 80 percent of which have never been tested to see if they cause cancer. The fact that I live in a heated house doesn't mean I have to accept centralized nuclear power plants, hundreds of millions of pounds of toxic waste produced each year, or a thoughtless global warming which is making nature a pretty big problem once again. The successes of modern agriculture don't require that we ruin the topsoil. And keep in mind that a lot of our wealth and ease in the developed world depends on the trashing of nature and people elsewhere.

"If nature can be understood, and altered, and made more like a Mother and less like an implacable Enemy, why can't we do the same thing with our social surroundings? Are you telling me that nature can be mastered but society has to remain out of control? That the threat of locusts *has* to be replaced by the threat of ever-bigger holes in the ozone layer? That economies based on horrible levels of exploitation or the creation of polluting military machines are the only way people can live?"

Growing a little heated, the Ethicist then mounted an imaginary soapbox.

"It is precisely from my own life — from our own lives — that we can speak the truth. And the truth is that what we have now is unacceptable."

The Ethicist remembers that the Gnawing Little Voice was properly awed by the Ethicist's Mounting Moral Force, and fell silent. (At least for the moment.) Calmer now that he can remember a victory, if only over a voice in his own head, the Ethicist returns to present reflections on ethical life.

He knows our spiritual and moral sensibilities, open to the realities that surround us in this dark time, have led us to want to honor something we call "nature." But what does this mean? Are we looking for some realm that is untouched by people, completely spontaneous, unplanned? Our Ethicist too would like to honor and defend such a "nature" — if only he could find it! The untouched, after all, is by now hard to come across; and in any case our access to it depends on just those technological powers that are destroying it. Really, it seems to him, talk about the love of "nature" tells us more about the depths of encounters with particular places or beings than they do about some vast abstraction. One man he knew looked into the eyes of a dying wolf that he himself had shot — and saw there a "fierce green fire" that forever altered his sense of humanity's relative importance in the scheme of things. Another saw a polluted river and felt loss that was immense without having to do with his own job or desire for a boat ride. The Ethicist himself recalls entering one of the last remaining groves of redwood trees. He began to weep, thinking of nothing so much as survivors of the Holocaust. All these encounters were precise, personal, particular.

If it is not the unreadable abstraction of "nature," he asks himself, then to what are we connected? It is too late in the night (too early in the morning?) to be comprehensive about it, so he makes a short list: We are dependent for food, water, air, and resources. Through the billions of microorganisms that live in our bodies we interpenetrate with this Other. We feel an empathic kinship with many animals and learn to think, to talk, and to understand moral qualities and physical truths by observing and experiencing the nonhuman realm. We are enthralled by the beauty of ocean or field or mountain. Spiritually, we may sometimes feel so enraptured by our nonhuman surrounding that our isolated egos give way to an identification with a larger, more complete, whole. At such times nature seems to be God or the face of God or evidence of God. Our surroundings are a source of knowledge, and an arena for the pursuit of knowledge. Not unlike our connections to cultural traditions, our surroundings also give us a sense of continuity, a sense of participation in what endures before or after our own brief lives. As we might treasure our heritage as Jews or Mexicans, so we can value our connection to a long-lived river or forest. Natural items are also mediators in our relations with other people. We affect future generations and people in distant lands by the way we treat nature. Finally, our surroundings hold images that reveal our own worth and character. When we look at a well-tilled garden, a clean river, a leaking landfill, or the return of wolves to Yellowstone, we see testimonies to the meaning of our lives.

The Ethicist chooses (for the moment) to ignore all the difficulties bound up in understanding each of these relationships. What he sees instead is that what we call "nature" is really a series of connections each with its own inner life, its possibilities for fulfillment or failure. To nourish these relationships, we must simply (though not easily) attend to the demands of each one. It is the attention to the details of what we are doing that is crucial, for all action — and all healing — flows from awareness.

If we depend on our surroundings, do we want to poison them? Or weaken (e.g., through overused antibiotics) the essential internal organisms in our own bodies? Can we without deep loss torture, poison, or eliminate the species that we love or which give us solace, beauty, and spiritual inspiration? Don't we need to examine the effects of our actions on others? And don't we want to think twice about hurting people through our actions toward nature? Killing strangers or family through pollution? Killing descendants through pollution? Don't we feel bad about ourselves when we look at the world and see what a mess we've made of it!

When we consider our surroundings, do we want them to be more "real," more "natural," in the sense of being more impressive, more deeply connected to other very concrete settings, better sources of information? If so, then we had better be careful — take a close look at the consequences — when we replace living trees with plastic ones, or warm-blooded dolphins by Disney animatronic Flippers. To call the originals more "natural" may just be to say that as aesthetic objects and subjects of empathy, as sources of information about the larger world and as supports of our own existence, they tend to be much better than their replacements.

"Of course," the Ethicist goes on, knowing that even here he must be honest, "sometimes we will opt for comfort and safety over information or spiritual value: we will replace weeds with tomato plants, kill the bacteria in the cut finger and try to keep the sharks away from the beach. There is no one rule of how we will act. Life is too complicated; we face too many competing moral demands; we are connected in too many different ways. But none of this means we can't do infinitely better than we have been doing."

Since everyone's knowledge and experience are limited, all this inquiry into the details, into our own motivations and into the consequences of what we do, must be done collectively as well as individually. Experts can give us information and theories we can't get by ourselves. But the "experts" dismantled muang phai and neglected to ask what would happen to CFCs above forty thousand feet. The environmental crisis demands, we might say, a Democratic Solution: the widespread application of attention, criticism, argument, discussion, and downright yapping about these precious aspects of our lives. If we are all implicated in these relations to our surroundings, as we surely are, then depending on others to know "the" truth would be like having other people live your marriage, your parenting, or your friendships. Since we are all in relation to Nature, we had all better pay attention, put in our two cents, and get to work. (As a friend of his, who went from working-class housewife to a national leader in the fight against toxic waste, said, "I still believe in the system, only now I believe that democracy is of the people and by the people, that people have to move it, it ain't gonna move by itself.")

"Let us then," he thinks, "inquire into the effects of our actions on other human communities and on nonhuman communities. Let us listen to what indigenous peoples say about what is happening to the places in which they live; let us look, quite closely, at the coral reefs dying from warming oceans; let us examine in great detail the lungs of inner-city kids stunted by air pollution, or the water birds so grossly affected by toxins in the Great Lakes that they are born with organs outside their bodies."

Once we have this kind of knowledge, the Ethicist realizes, a host of new questions will be raised. Personally, and as communities, why are we doing what we do? Why is this animal being killed, or that species made extinct? What is at stake when we introduce a new antibiotic and help breed ever more powerful bacteria? Why does the Ethicist's friend the Philosophy Professor need to commute four hundred miles a week? Why aren't there more schools that can handle special needs kids in a creative, loving way? Why can't he get a different schedule to allow him to commute less often? When this particular wetland is paved over, are we meeting a need of substance, or simply offering one more temporary fix to a form of life that will take more and more and more until nothing is left? (The Ethicist remembers the vacuum-cleaner-like man at the bottom of the sea in *Yellow Submarine:* he sucked up everything in sight until the whole world went down his tunnel-like snout. The world was saved only when he sucked up himself.) If spirituality is, as Gandhi said, an inquiry into the truth, these are some of the truths that need to be known.

At this point the Ethicist is clearer about what needs to be done, but the man still can't sleep! For he knows that there are often deep flaws in his own capacity to really pay attention to all these relationships and to get answers to all these questions. The endless busyness of daily life, the sheer scope of the world's suffering, the need to focus on family, work, nearby community: all these can lead him (though not when he is lecturing others!) to ignore far-off rainforests, nonhuman species, or future generations. Thus after all his philosophical reflections about examining our relationships with our surroundings he finds himself drawn back to the nagging theme of his own imperfections.

The Ethicist has to admit that an ethical and spiritual sense of our deep connections to other species and entire ecosystems does not erase the fact that in the ordinary course of our existence human beings necessarily use and displace other life forms. In particular he remembers a Long Sad Tale of animal extinctions in the Americas. One after another: the buffalo, the carrier pigeon, the red fox. It was a drawn-out litany of loss, typically from overconsumption, the turning of animals into objects for sale, or the careless importation of nonnative species.

As he read this tale, the Ethicist noticed with some surprise and even discomfort the wide range of his own responses. First — most obvious and while painful also easy: "This is just horrible. All the beautiful passenger pigeons (etc.) lost. All the immense flocks, herds (etc.) described by the explorers never to be seen again." Second — more philosophical, more reflective: "Is this not a crime against 'nature,' against 'Mother Earth' against 'Gaia' (etc.)." A wave of guilt, rage, and shame follows. Third — perhaps more honestly, or at least with more of a sense of the fullness of what goes on in the human heart: "Who cares, really? I am alive. And I want mine. If I could get a lot of money by doing something like this, wouldn't I at least be tempted? And if I needed what those animals had, really needed it, I might not even think twice."

(He remembers the late spring morning a few weeks ago when he looked out of his bedroom window and saw a fat, sassy crow dive-bombing his garden. The crow swooped down toward the broccoli plants and tore off the largest leaf. This was the broccoli that the Ethicist had nursed from seedlings through the trauma of transplanting and a mysterious malady which made half their leaves turn brown and fall off. That broccoli was now flourishing — but a few more crow attacks and the Ethicist could forget the whole thing. He had run downstairs in his pajamas, bellowing imprecations at the heedless bird, with quick thoughts of "pesticide, electric fences, scarecrows, shotguns" running through his brain. No acknowledgment of the sacredness of life was given at that particular moment — just, "Damn you bird, leave my stuff alone!")

Fourth, and finally, with his unending desire to figure this out: "Yes, it's terrible to kill all the buffalo, but why not exterminate rats in the ghetto, the AIDS virus, or the black flies that cause blindness along the rivers of Africa? Where is the line?"

"After all," the Ethicist responds to yet another imaginary interlocutor, "just like every other animal, we need to consume and alter our environment. We must eat and warm ourselves; and if we are to sustain social life, culture, and politics we are going to use plenty of natural resources. When our goals are threatened, we will strike back. A new-found love of life will not extend to dangerous viruses; and our wariness at tampering with the sacred character of nature will probably be suspended when it comes to genetic engineering to cure cystic fibrosis. When we speak of all life being sacred, does that really include the strep bacteria in our kid's throat?"

In particular, the Ethicist thinks of the freshwater dinoflaggelates recently responsible for the death of ten to fifteen million fish in a North Carolina river. Sneaky little one-celled buggers, they lie in wait at the bottom of the river until the times are right. Then they metamorphose into a dramatically different shape and begin to attack the fish, causing lethal sores on the skin or anus. These "fishkillers" affect people as well: fisherman reported strange, hard-to-heal wounds on their arms and legs; tourists who swam in the waters developed immune system problems. The first scientists who studied them in closed labs suffered asthma, memory loss, and neurological symptoms of decreased mental functioning. The organism is now classified as a level 3 biohazard, just under AIDS and Ebola viruses. While the fishkiller might prompt some justified respect (for they are so tough that submerged in sulfuric acid 20 percent survive), they also inspire fear and a desire to kill. The Ethicist has no desire to coexist in a sacred web of life with these guys.

And so, once again, he realizes that personal spiritual and ethical growth cannot eliminate the hard choices we face: about how much to take for ourselves and how much to leave for others; how much to exercise the control we increase day by day and how much to surrender; when to make fundamental changes in the earth to make things better for ourselves and when to put up with annoyances, aggravations, and even some dangers for the sake of the whole.

(And when the fishkillers wake up, and river posts are covered with crabs frantically trying to escape, who really is the enemy? These organisms, our Ethicist knows, emerge from their torpor when the waters around them become "nutrient rich" from runoffs of pesticides, fertilizer, and organic wastes from industrialized chicken and hog farms. How many times, he wonders, have we created our own worst enemies — and then gone in for the kill, all the while claiming self-defense?)

What can we hope for?

In his own lifetime the Ethicist has seen a worldwide movement improve the condition of women throughout the world. He knows that his individual actions are a miniscule part of a similarly vast effort to reorient society toward environmental sanity. He hopes that as this effort unfolds it will lead us to be more unassuming both in our self-assessment as a species and our desires for a "better life" — even though achieving this self-assessment might require a difficult and contentious social transformation. We may learn that a truly "higher standard of living" cannot be achieved until we curtail our current environmental aggression, and that no amount of toys will cure our loneliness for both natural and human community. We might learn that false expertise should not be trusted, that a monocultured earth is very lonely; and that to love either people or the earth we need to love both. It is only by dwelling on these several prospects and his desire to make his own contribution to them that the Ethicist manages to get a few moments of sleep before his overfilled day begins.

Yet what will happen when he tries to sleep tomorrow night? Ethical humility, political critique, examining and bettering our relations with the human and nonhuman alike, the constraints of personal and social limitations — all these will run through the brain of our troubled Ethicist once more. Is he forever condemned to moral insomnia?

It is true that our Ethicist often finds it nearly impossible to escape his own sense of inadequacy. How little he can do! How little he can change his own life! Perhaps this psychic self-torture stems from illusory models of male omnipotence, and he thinks that he alone must save the world. Possibly his brain is still addled by images of his childhood TV cowboy heroes, tough guys who ride into troubled towns and set things right before the last commercial.

Again, it may be that these ruminations on his own failings merely obscure (usefully, in the short run at least) the depths of his own grief. Better to blame himself than to admit how hopeless it all seems.

Whatever the origins or psychic role, it is a sad business: because our Ethicist is a decent person and deserves to be at peace with himself. ("Even a poor Ethicist," we might paraphrase, "deserves some happiness!")

Can there be another possibility for our Ethicist? Well, there is no way he can fully elude his grief for what we have done, the troubling paradoxes of his own contradictory behavior, or his rage against the perfunctory cruelties of modern societies. But alongside those painful narratives another may well be possible. Not as a replacement, but as a solace; not as ultimately more true, but as equally true.

In this narrative self-consciousness, passion, humility, and doubt coexist with a deepened sense of communion with the mysteries of Nature, and the peace initially promised by spiritual teachings becomes accessible once again. Encircling rather than erasing the legitimate strenuousness and angst of modern moral subjects — who feel the weight of the world on their shoulders — is a more encompassing and calming vision. While our love for Others does motivate anger, self-criticism, and grief, it can also at times soothe our troubled ethical selves — if, that is, we recognize such selfhood as not bounded by our own troubled egos, but in dancing partnership with other people, with maple trees and rivers, kestrels and (yes) dinoflaggelates. The tender devotion that animates us is not only a burden of duty, but also a wonderfully freeing force that wells up from the depths of our utter bond with all that surrounds us. In his celebration of this profound kinship, our Ethicist is able to suspend his hopeless guilt and hopeless rage. He will realize that he can only do his best and then, like an autumn leaf, drift down to the forest floor to prepare the way for other growing things. Just as the sun itself, all any of us can do is shine until the light which God or Goddess gave us is darkened by the soft embrace of time, an embrace which, in the end, will claim all beings.

We can tell a bitter tale, or one of delight. Probably the best we can hope for is that we will end up telling both. The Ethicist need not suppress his fears for tomorrow or his regrets for yesterday. But he may also welcome the peace that comes from his own at once joyous, sorrowful, and exuberant participation in eternity.

CHAPTER FIVE

Finding a Peaceful Heart and Protecting the Earth

Perhaps some day someone will explain how, on the level of man, Auschwitz was possible; but on the level of God, it will forever remain the most disturbing of mysteries. — ELIE WIESEL

Humanity is outraged in me and with me. We must not dissimulate nor try to forget this indignation, which is one of the most passionate forms of love. — GEORGE SAND

At the center of the spiritual journey is the search for a peaceful heart. My own search began as I child, when I sometimes found peace by listening to passionate classical music or while lying in front of a fire on a winter night, staring at rushing sparks and glowing coals. It might take me by surprise on a brilliant spring afternoon when I would walk home from elementary school instead of taking the bus. Every tree, flowering bush, and blade of grass of this well-kept suburban setting seemed wonderfully, almost painfully, alive. And that almost but not quite pain mixed with enough joy to float my little body back to my slightly anxious mother, home wondering where I was.

As I got older the passion for music and the embrace of nature were joined by experiences of sex and grown-up love. I explored Mediterranean islands, hung out in tiny tribal settlements in northern Pakistan, and trekked through the Himalayas. Living as a young man with no responsibilities, far from the industrial madness that seemed to be driving everyone crazy, I discovered an ever deeper experience of serenity: that same wonderful, almost painful, sense of being alive; a simple joy in every leaf, in the glow of stars and moon, in the touch of my lover's hand. I was also helped by psychedelic chemicals that were conducive to deep feelings of peace, belonging, and openness. Under their influence, my heart opened not just to this or that leaf or river, but to the entire cosmos.

So I have known these moments, treasured them, and thanked the spirits for them. Yet at the same time there has almost always been a little voice that came in somewhere during the experience and started to ask painful questions: "Of course, this all feels wonderful. The world is beautiful: that tree, this piece of music, your lover's breast. But what about the Others? What about the people who aren't having such a great time?"

My awareness of the Others has taken many forms. It began, I suppose, on my trips to New York from my home in White Plains. We had family in the city, my father's business was there for many years, and we often took the train instead of the car. For the last few miles, before the cavernous confusion of Grand Central Station, the track ran through the middle of Harlem, then as now a black ghetto. The blocks of tenements, through which the train always moved quite slowly, riveted me. I peered at shabbiness, dirt, laundry drying on back porches, peeled paint, tired old cars, junk-filled yards. And the people glimpsed casually from the train window against which my boy's nose was pushed seemed tired, old at any age, and beaten down.

It all made such a contrast to the brilliant green lawns on my street, to my friends' immaculate split-levels. Looking back, I wonder if I felt vaguely guilty about the differences, because I couldn't see any reason why my family, the other kids at school, and my relatives who had homes in Long Island or Scarsdale should be so much better off. As I passed through Harlem for those fleeting moments, I wondered if it was right to enjoy what I had while these other people had so much less.

Although I was intellectually precocious, this whole train of thought wasn't an argument, a preadolescent theology, or a moral judgment. It was a puzzlement, a mildly gnawing confusion. There was no one with whom I could talk about it, so I typically went on to New York and enjoyed a show, a meal out, a museum, a concert. Returning at night it would be too dark to notice and I would probably be reading or, when young, asleep.

Was it really guilt I felt? I'm not sure, because I certainly didn't feel particularly responsible for my good fortune. Nor was I really aware of racism as a social force. It just seemed obvious that these people, crammed into these ugly buildings, lacking so much that I had, didn't deserve their fate. And it was simultaneously clear that I, my parents, and my friends didn't really deserve what we had either. At any rate, not nearly so much of it, and not while these other people had so much less.

I couldn't figure out what I felt about a world that was set up this way, and I didn't know how to be thoroughly at home here, full of unmixed joy at all the goodies I enjoyed, when I couldn't help but see how different it was for other people.

It reminded me of the people who, having been spared in a car crash which killed four, would say, "It's a miracle that I wasn't killed."

"Some miracle," I'd think. "You weren't taken and all the Others are dead. What kind of miracle is that?"

We have feelings of peace or joy. These feelings, we want to say, prove how beautiful, how holy, the universe is. Or perhaps the feelings call up images of a more personal sense of the divine: of God the compassionate Father/Mother, of Jesus the Savior, of the Grace of Allah. The feelings then become signs of God's perfection and love, of the deep protectiveness with which a Guiding Force holds us.

For me, in between these feelings of love or serenity and the assertion of perfection and God's love there lies an often uncrossable gap: all I know about the pain, cruelty, and injustice that permeates this life, all the suffering for which I can find no justification, rationale, or excuse.

I am concerned that to achieve spiritual peace I will have to accept what should not be accepted: that I will be told to concentrate on myself and forget about others, or that I will be reassured that all this pain is encompassed by Forces and Realities that somehow make up for it. I cannot respond in any of these ways. I seek to live on *this* earth, without having to rely on promises of aid and comfort from Cosmic Forces. And I cannot forget the Others, or the threats to myself and my children. I don't see how I can accept the world, or approve of it, when these other realities are as genuine as any experiences of mystical delight or tranquility. To find a peaceful heart I need a spirituality in which the world's unjustified pain is not denied, avoided, or forgotten. For me, the spiritual challenge is to combine moral and political commitments that direct us to respond to injustice and needless suffering with spiritual teachings about serenity and wisdom. In the act of resistance, I believe, an answer to this challenge can be found.

Many years ago, during a long trip through Asia, I lived in a village in the Indian Himalayas. It was 1970, and I was moving through the East in search of exotic adventures and cheap pleasures. One evening, I was invited to share some food and (of course) a joint or two with a black American hippie who'd been out here for a couple of years. The man was entranced with India, as I was, and had adopted (as I hadn't) what he thought was a basically Hindu view of life. "Everything's getting better for me, man," he assured me. "I just see things more and more clearly every second, and I get freer and freer all the time. And you know what, it's happening all over the world. Everyone's getting better and better! Don't you feel it?"

I looked at him and thought carefully. Should I just go along for the ride or tell him what I really think?

"Well," I started slowly, "I know I'm having a pretty good time." I was thinking of my comfortable home, the cupboard always filled with chips and cookies, the summer camps, the simple fact that I had always lived in the top 5 percent of the world's population in regard to housing, education, and toys. I thought of my college career and this trip which, even though I was doing it on a shoestring budget, allowed me to travel for fifteen months without working. "And," I continued, "I love India. It's beautiful and the people are incredibly interesting.

"But," I slowly went on, "what about everyone else in the world? The ones I saw starving in Calcutta and the ones getting bombed in Cambodia and Vietnam? You really think everything's getting better and better for them?"

My companion stepped back. His eyes widened in a stare that said, "This guy is crazy, or dangerous!" He went his way and I mine, but it was clear to me that what seemed crazy or dangerous to him was my spiritual second nature.

What is "spirituality"?

When we thought our sleepless Ethicist might relax his tortured grip on responsibility and allow himself to merge with the nature he so loves, we might have said, "Ahh...he has found a spiritual resolution to his psychological and ethical dilemmas." We would mean, I think, that the Ethicist had a vision of his fundamental connection to the cosmos, a vision that replaced or soothed his limited view of himself as a separate individual. This vision removed the despondency and insomnia. He had found a peaceful heart at last.

To take a more mundane example: when my disabled daughter broke her arm during summer camp, she not only experienced a lot of pain but also was kept from swimming. Initially saddened, she then brightened and said: "Oh, this is great. It means I can hang out at the barn and not miss snack!" She took, we might say, a spiritual attitude toward her disappointment. By that we would mean that she oriented herself toward finding the good in her situation rather than holding on to what she had wanted, had expected, but could no longer have.

"Take a spiritual view," we say, and mean:

- Look on the bright side.

- Appreciate what you have.

- Give love in a dark time, when everything seems hopeless.

- Open your heart to the pain of the world, without fear or judgment.

- Stand for what you believe in, and respond to injustice without hatred (and here we might think of Gandhi or Martin Luther King, Jr.).

- Do not expect that power, money, or sensual enjoyment will give any more than a fleeting pleasure. Only a deep acceptance, a fundamental gratitude, will give lasting happiness.

- Learn to trust in God, who oversees and protects.

- Follow God's will for your life, and not your own.

These pathways to peace carry centuries of wisdom about how to deal with the human condition. Yet I get apprehensive when they are interpreted as suggesting that we might achieve equanimity at the cost of forgetting, even for a moment, just how much pain there is. For me, a spiritual view will be authentic only if it can celebrate its peacefulness not only despite personal disappointment, but also as it faces the full range of the world's moral horrors.

When I want a fat book contract and get something much less grand instead, making myself miserable over my "failure" is a folly that only leads to self-generated depression. When I am away for my month-long summer vacation in Vermont and my daughter gets sick for a week and needs my care, I had better treasure the brief walks that don't measure up to the six-hour bike rides I'd planned. It's far better to accept what life has offered me, take joy in what I have, and leave the rest to God.

At times this approach has worked well for me. After my first child died at the age of two months, I went through a period of shrinking from the sight of children. Yet I liked kids and didn't want to go through life feeling envious whenever I encountered them. I asked myself what I could do. "It's simple," I realized. "When I see a child and start to feel that gnawing bitterness, I will thank God that I have eyesight to see them. Some people, after all, are blind." This was a spiritual approach: it made me a better person and made me happier. It took nothing away from anyone else, but instead increased the world's positive resources. And all it required was that I change my attitude. Two leading contemporary American Buddhist teachers put it this way:

> Wisdom replaces ignorance in our minds when we realize that happiness does not lie in the accumulation of more and more pleasant feelings, that gratifying craving does not bring us a feeling of wholeness or completion. It simply leads to more craving and more aversion. When we realize in our own experience that happiness comes not from reaching out but from letting go, not from seeking pleasurable experience but from opening in the moment to what is true, this transformation of understanding then frees the energy of compassion within us. Our minds are no longer bound up in pushing away pain or holding on to pleasure. Compassion becomes the natural response of an open heart.

The question is: what am I letting in and what am I keeping out? I believe there is a difference between letting go of my own desires and letting go of my concern for others. And I fear that too often in spiritual literature these may get confused. Give up my own desires — for fame, higher salary, some free time, more sex — this I understand. But what would it mean to "let go" of my hope that poor people might have a better life? Or to "open my heart" to the realities of abused children or the dolphins suffocating in the two-mile-long fishing nets? What might we have to screen out — and what might we have to add in on top — to let go of them?

The well-known American spiritual teacher Ram Dass once said that for him the essential task of spiritual life, regardless of circumstances, is to "quiet my mind, open my heart, and relieve the suffering that I see around me."

> Somehow I have faith in the universe — I'm not sure where it comes from — even with all the horror and the torture and so on. This is hard to say because it's morally reprehensible to even think that the people who died in the Holocaust are, from a soul point of view, on an evolutionary path in which that experience was functional. That sounds too horrible to consider. But that's the part that isn't humanistic about the spiritual path. I have such a deep conviction about that, and it's part of what allows me to be in the presence of suffering. If somebody is suffering, even though I will do my best to relieve them, there's another part of me that trusts that the suffering is in the greater good and if I could see, I could understand.... Certain things are not reversible — like what we're doing to the forests and species, which will disappear.

Supported by his belief that the universe is to be trusted, that it is worth our "faith," Ram Dass acts to end suffering while remaining unattached to the outcome of his actions. Yet this belief takes us far beyond the reality of the earth, and in the last quoted comment about the irreversibility of ecological damage it's clear that even Ram Dass's own metaphysical view cannot accommodate the slaughter of nonhuman innocents. The human-centered view that sees the entire universe as a learning ground for people is a little hard to apply to species made extinct and whole ecosystems poisoned.

What is more poignant is that this extremely intelligent and generous man admits quite candidly that the core of his teaching — the necessity to open the heart to the world's pain — depends on his belief that we (humans, anyway) are all on a cosmic trip of spiritual evolution.

The pain is real, but for the "greater good."

What would have happened, I wonder, if he had lost that faith? Would he still have opened to what was going on around him? Is it truly openness if to sustain it we have to believe that the pain is somehow justified? That like the irritability of the teething infant or the distress of childbirth it is intimately connected to a Greater Good? It is not as if Ram Dass didn't know a good deal about pain. He set up foundations to help the blind and sat in rooms with dying AIDS patients. But when we believe suffering is "all to the good," then the suffering is damped down — as we might do to a fire burning too fast when we toss some water on it and reduce the air flow — by a metaphysics which puts it all In Perspective.

And what, you might ask, is so wrong with that? Isn't the task of all spiritual philosophies to help us find a peaceful heart no matter what? Isn't it appropriate to believe that despite all the apparent suffering, there is an unseen plan? Or in the words of a character in eighteenth-century English philosopher David Hume's *Dialogues Concerning Natural Religion:*

> This world is but a point in comparison of the universe; this life but a moment in comparison of eternity. The present evil phenomena, therefore, are rectified in other regions, and in some future period of existence. And the eyes of men, being then opened to larger views of things, see the whole connection of general laws, and trace with adoration, the benevolence and rectitude of the Deity through all the mazes and intricacies of his providence.

From a contemporary Jewish source, based in part on a traditional voice of eight centuries ago, comes a similar point:

> Ramban (Nachmanides) teaches us that "no man has any portion in the Torah of Moses, our teacher, until he understands that *every one of our words and encounters,* both in private and in public, are miracles and cannot be attributed merely to some natural capricious order of the universe...." And so words, actions, feelings, lives, and history have come from something and are destined to go to something. Coming forth from a shared seed of the past. Setting out for a common fulfillment in the future.

Such faith may work for some, but it doesn't for me. I cannot accept a perspective in which the earth becomes somehow less than real. The promise of bliss in heaven, the guarantee that we are all "learning" something that after countless incarnations we will get the hang of, the trust in a cosmic, miraculous origin to every word and deed — such views cast a veil over the pain that is right before my eyes or that, in this Age of Information, I can witness via my TV, radio, newspaper, magazine, or Internet hookup. How am I supposed to see the latest oil spill as leading to a "common fulfillment in the future"? Where is the "miracle" in the spread of dangerous chemicals through air and water? Acts of kindness, connection, and love may be miracles, even the daily workings of the body are spectacular (the child's first steps, the brilliance of vision, the unstopping heart muscle). But what about the daily greed that poisons a watershed, the fortunes made selling weapons to dictators, the rash of birth defects in the *maquiladoros?* I worry that acceptance of a universe in which these things are our daily fare can be maintained only at the cost of closing (at least) one eye to the full reality of what is around us.

That is why it doesn't help me very much to have the earth turned into a staging ground for some much larger, much more "real," cosmic drama, a main event which will take place Far Away from Here. Nor am I comforted by the assurance that Someone is In Charge. All of this sounds too much like an attempt to cover up the same fear and grief that I feel.

Besides and perhaps most important: my first love is *to the earth:* to the people, the plants, the spotted owls and the unemployed loggers, the geological formations and the way all of these hang together. I cannot accept a point of view in which the rainforest is some spiritually two-dimensional scenery for my cosmic evolution.

I want to know what to say to my daughter when she asks me if there could come a time when there are no more trees. I would like to be able to say to her that yes, this earth is a fine old place, even though the forests are dying. But without being a hypocrite, or someone whose memory is very, very selective, I'm not sure how.

If you believe in a "personal" God — a God to whom you can pray and who cares about whether you act morally — then the presence of suffering in the world emerges as the "problem of evil." The problem is simple, but often intractable: If God is all-powerful and all-good, why is there undeserved suffering? Why does the enormous pain visited on the innocent take place?

There are many attempted solutions to this problem. The most popular one claims that free will, which is essential to our having any moral identity at all, is the source of the undeserved suffering. It is not God who causes the evil; nor could God eliminate it without taking away the very characteristics that make us human: our capacity to choose between right and wrong. Since we can choose, we often will make the wrong choice. As a consequence, we get the misery that bothers us so much. But to end that misery, we would have to give up the prospect of being moral at all. (Automatons programmed to act rightly, sort of robot Boy Scouts, have no moral identity at all; they are just very useful!)

This solution to the problem of evil will work for us depending on how much suffering we actually witness, how much we hope or expect it to diminish, and what kind of "good" we see as coming out of it. There will always be a delicate balance between our expectation that things will ultimately work out, and thus that the pain of the past will in some way be redeemed, and our opposing tendency to see a world filled with pain and little else.

At times, however, particular events can unfold which shake our sense that having a moral identity compensates for all the undeserved suffering that comes from our precious free will. We might stand at a concentration camp or among the kids who live on garbage in Rio and decide that having fully free human beings is not worth the trouble they cause. The babies slaughtered in wars, the fifty million laboratory animals killed each year in trivial experiments, the endless rainforest burned to make hamburgers are just too much. Then we might well turn against God, not out of lack of faith, but out of rage. Our prayers might be filled with anger and little else. Or we might say, as did Dostoyevsky's character Ivan Karamazov after recounting horrible stories about children beaten, humiliated, abandoned: "I accept God, but not His world."

Of course it takes a certain kind of deep strength to accept *that* the world is the way it is. At least to the extent of being able to take in what is going on. Denials, avoidance, hysteria, numbness to the pain, we might say, are ways of not accepting the facts, that is, of not having the emotional courage to be with the dark truths of our time. But acceptance that something is going on is very different from accepting the thing itself, approving of it, or feeling that a universe in which it takes place deserves our blessing. "I accept the universe," said Margaret Fuller. "By Gad, you'd better," replied Ralph Waldo Emerson. But why should we accept it? Just to make ourselves feel more at home? To finally achieve that elusive inner peace? And how are we to accept it without forgetting all the horrible details?

There is an old philosophical brainteaser which goes like this: You are offered a pill that will kill you in about an hour of "real" time. Subjectively, experientially, however, you would have the experience of a long and fulfilling life. Family, career, travel, excitement, ups and downs, plenty of good sex, and things breaking your way when they seem in doubt. Would you take the pill? Is "reality" worth so much that to keep it you would forgo a life that is indistinguishable from the real but is not, and that guarantees you happiness?

Let's change the terms slightly. Suppose I could take a pill that would keep me from ever being deeply upset by the pain caused by injustice. Should I take that pill (a sort of moral Prozac) in order to be happy? I wouldn't become a psychopath or a heartless center of selfishness. I'd still give to charity, love my neighbor, and perhaps work to make the world a better place. What would be gone would be that critical, cutting edge that says to the universe: "I do not accept this. I am not satisfied. I cannot feel peaceful and at home while these things continue."

Like the Ethicist, I hear voices, voices not always thrilled by my ruminations — especially when those ruminations might be verging on the pretentious. These voices like to tease me a bit, and pose some tough questions.

"What good does it do for you to feel miserable because other people are suffering? You want to do something useful? Then work for justice, dry the tears of those in pain, comfort the afflicted and afflict the comfortable. But don't bore yourself (and all of us) with your grandiose interior rebellion. It doesn't change anything or make anything better. You are just like a child who holds his breath until he turns blue, hoping that this will make Mommy alter a disagreeable world. But in a truly spiritual response we find peacefulness in the pain, love for the world even in the face of evil. We are able to care for others without clutching at the pain they are in."

"You are so right," I would like to reply. "I know this distress I feel doesn't help myself or anyone else. I know that the universe, God, or the Great Spirit, if they notice me at all, probably laugh at my childish petulance. I know I should take those rare moments of peace when they are offered and forget about the Others. I know that I'm not a better person just because I'm in pain. And I know that sometimes these bitter, angry feelings just make me depressed and self-absorbed. But I also feel that I need to hold on to the anguish to keep myself in touch with everything around me. Sometimes it feels like all I can give. There must be something else, but often I don't know what it is. Maybe I should take that pill, after all."

And perhaps the conversation would end there. Or perhaps it would go on, and I would ask, in as admiring a tone as possible: "Tell me how you do it. When you sense God's grace or the indwelling of Spirit, how can you can put the Others out of your mind? Tell me the secret of forgetting, or of feeling at home here while you remember. How can you really know the truth and still hold peace in your heart?"

Our emotional lives depend on our relationships with family, lovers, and friends. Our intellectual sense of the world grows out of a heritage of knowledge and reflection. Our religious ideas and practices depend on the insights of others and long-standing traditions. We cannot live without the numberless human and nonhuman beings who support us. In all these ways we simply do not exist by ourselves. As we live in connection to others, so our sense of how fitting, perfect, or divine this universe is can only be legitimately known by considering how everyone else is doing. If I fail to honor these connections, I am evading my own reality; and this does not bode well for spiritual development.

Every religious or spiritual tradition has struggled with this problem. But when the undeserved suffering we grapple with includes nature as well as people, our dilemma becomes even more difficult. Because the natural world has been a source of spiritual inspiration in its own right, the widespread destruction it has undergone darkens our sense of how things are.

Speaking of the need to cultivate a sense of wonder in relation to the natural world and why she took her nephew down to an ocean beach as a birthday present, Rachel Carson wrote:

> There is symbolic as well as an actual beauty in the migration of the birds, the ebb and flow of the tides, the folded bud ready for the spring. There is something infinitely healing in the repeated refrains of nature — the assurance that dawn comes after night, and spring after the winter.

The powers of nature, suggested Ralph Waldo Emerson, lie in offering a

> delightful suggestion of an occult relation between man and the vegetable. I am not alone and unacknowledged. They nod to me, and I to them. The waving of the boughs in the storm, is new to me and old. It takes me by surprise, and yet is not unknown. Its effect is like that of a higher thought or a better emotion.

Or as Anne Frank wrote in her diary:

> The best remedy for those who are afraid, lonely, or unhappy is to go outside, somewhere where they can be quite alone with the heavens, nature, and God. Because only then does one feel that all is as it should be and that God wishes to see people happy, amidst the simple beauty of nature. As long as this exists, and it certainly always will, I know that then there will always be comfort for every storm.

Yet what would have happened to Carson's birthday present if she had noticed raw sewage and used syringes washing up on the beach? Or if Emerson's stroll across the landscape had been disturbed by the noise of nearby strip-mining operations? Suppose Anne Frank had gone outside and found a beautiful, tree-lined brook — and then (true story from a lovely tourist town in western Massachusetts) saw signs warning "not under any conditions!" to eat fish from the stream because of toxic chemical pollution?

As the Raji people, forest dwellers facing extreme deforestation on the Nepal-India border, put it: "Before, we knew where the gods were. They were in the trees. Now there are no more trees."

As we have seen, there is no escape. Even as simple an injunction as the Buddhist lesson to "breathe in and out, watch your breath..." is rendered somewhat suspect on those urban summer days when polluted air makes this simple spiritual practice problematic.

Well, someone might reply, the only resort is to go to that nonmaterial, truly individual, interior space of love, nirvana, or no-self. This Heart of Truth (whatever particular theology it is attached to) is inaccessible to the physical world and cannot be touched by pollution. Here is a pure sanctuary in a toxic world. Here is a source of peace and acceptance that is unconditioned. Here is a way to lasting happiness despite the Pains of Existence.

I believe, however, that the inside is always the inside of an outside. A meditative bliss, a formless consciousness, a mystical encounter with the Divine — all these have their value and importance, but cannot exist by themselves. We may go to them for insight and wisdom, for renewal and relaxation. But as long as we are alive our visits are temporary. No matter how far we travel "inside," we always come Home for Dinner. And we are always dependent on all those beings on the outside that make our interior experience possible. Their fate is part of our own.

How strange is the Jewish marriage ritual. When the elaborate ceremony is completed, at the moment of greatest joy, a wineglass is crushed under the foot of the groom. The point: to remember, precisely at this moment of greatest joy, the terrible loss of the Great Temple which had been the center of Jewish life two thousand years ago.

During the Passover Seder, Jews celebrate their escape from Egypt and God's triumph over the earthly powers of the kingly Pharaoh. How extraordinary that we take drops of wine out of the ceremonial cups to symbolically lessen our pleasure. We do so in memory of the sufferings the Egyptians underwent when the plagues rained down from the sky-god and, in the end, their first born had to die.

How is it that our greatest joy requires that we remember our deepest loss?

Many years ago, when people did all sorts of odd things in graduate school, I took a "Social Psychology" course at Brandeis University that was actually an extended study of Eastern spiritual practices. The professor, trained in highly technical academic sociology, had flipped his wig and spent the course teaching us yoga postures, Buddhist meditation, extreme forms of fasting, and what sugar, coffee, and alcohol do to your chakras. He was a sincere, intelligent man, who after being denied tenure eventually became a leading teacher of Buddhist meditation in the Boston area.

One day, after concluding our period of meditation (I'll call him) Larry asked for questions. A student inquired: "I live in a dorm room and it's incredibly noisy. Loud stereos, people shouting and goofing around. How am I supposed to concentrate with all that going on?"

Larry smiled. "Well, I don't live in dorms anymore. But I do live on a pretty noisy street in Cambridge. There are times when the ambulance or police sirens come one after another. It could be unbearable. But that noise, you see, it's just another form of energy. So if there is a loud siren, I just take that energy in instead of resisting it. I focus it at the base of my spine and bring it straight up to my third eye in the middle of my forehead. I let the noise help."

Not a bad idea, I thought at the time. But later I started to wonder, and then I wasn't so sure. What rolled around my mind was a very concrete image: scenes from the movie that had been made of *The Diary of Anne Frank*. Throughout the film there was the periodic sound of the sirens of the police vans that collected Jews from hiding places. Until the last scene the sirens always passed Anne by. But in the last moment, as she is about to embrace the teenage boy whom she loves, the siren comes on louder and louder until they, and the audience, realize that they have been found.

At the beginning of our next class I raised my hand. "Larry," I began, "remember what you said in our last class about using the energy of the siren, taking it up your spine to help you in the meditation? Well, that's great if it's some fire truck going across town or an ambulance taking a heart attack patient to the hospital. But what if it's the police rounding up Jews?"

Larry was a decent man and a good teacher. He didn't laughingly point out that there weren't too many police vans rounding up Jews in Cambridge that year. Or that if there were, there might not be too much he or I could do about it, meditating or not. He understood that my question was beyond the scope of his earlier response, beyond anything he had thought of as part of the course at all.

"Well," he said, "we do have to be discriminating in our understanding of what is going on around us."

Or, to paraphrase King Solomon: there is a time to take the siren noise up your spine and a time to do something about the noise, even if doing something costs you your peace of mind.

When I was a boy one of my favorite books was a well-known collection of photographs and brief quotations from classic writers called *The Family of Man*. Dozens of photographers worldwide had contributed wonderful images of childbirth, marriage, work, play, children, families, lovers, and old people. I leafed through that book again and again. Here a newborn baby was still attached to its mother by the magically spiraled umbilical cord. Here two lovers kissed underneath a Paris bridge. Here jet-black, rigidly muscled arms grasped the oars of an African fishing boat. And here a young Japanese bride-to-be arranged her ceremonial costume.

And the quotes, the wonderful quotes: from Shakespeare and Albert Einstein and Plato and the Bible and the Bagavat Gita. Beautifully wise sayings about the dignity of work and the importance of nature and the magic of love.

In its last pages *The Family of Man* had pictures of war, with appropriate statements condemning the waste and horror of mass violence.

There was one image and one saying to which I returned over and over again. Beneath a smoke-darkened sky, surrounded by burning buildings, a small group of raggedly dressed, shell-shocked people walk down a city street with their hands in the air. Near them march a few soldiers carrying weapons. It is the final days of the Warsaw Ghetto, and these are the few survivors of the Jewish uprising against the Nazis. In the front row of the group a young girl stares into space, her hand raised to cover her mouth. How, I always wondered, could she have survived that long — after years of starvation, deportations, and random shootings? And could there be any doubt that in a few days she would in fact be dead, since the destination of all Jews from Warsaw was Franz Stangl's Treblinka death camp?

But this image, compelling as it was, might have taken its place alongside countless other Holocaust pictures I studied as a child. I was riveted by the quotation beneath the picture. "Humanity is outraged in me and with me. We must not dissimulate nor try to forget this indignation, which is one of the most passionate forms of love."

Anger as a kind of love, like the anger in the prayer that began this book — how can such a fleeting emotion, as powerful as it is when I feel it, carry me toward a full sense of spiritual life? We can approach an answer if we look, once more, to the Holocaust.

I am suggesting that to be legitimate, any spiritual celebration of life, of the world, of the cosmos, of God or Goddess has to take place with Auschwitz in mind. Just as that hippie who wanted me to agree that "everything was getting better for everybody" was forgetting the mass slaughter in Southeast Asia, so any vision of the perfection of existence or the glory of God which does not include the concentration camps is leaving something out.

If we want to measure our faith and hope against the darkest moments of reality, the Holocaust is a good place to start. Of course, others could be chosen: child sexual abuse, genocide against Native Americans, the burning of women accused of witchcraft, Stalin's terror campaigns. But I know the Holocaust best, and in many ways it seems the most extreme version of all this. So in order to illuminate our central question, to warm us up as it were, before we continue to tackle the more diffuse case of ecocide, let us ask again: what is spirituality in the face of Auschwitz?

Can we "make peace" with the murder of a million innocent children? Or, because the abstractions of large numbers may not touch us, we might consider how certain Nazi officers befriended the newly arrived Jewish children at the camps, offered them sweets, joked with them, and then personally drove them to the gas chambers. And then:

> Six hundred children were pushed savagely and cruelly to their death in the gas chamber. Some pleaded with the Sonder-kommando prisoners to save them. Others appealed to the SS men who instead of replying shoved them even more forcefully into the bunker. The screams and sobbing of the children were deafening until death silenced them, at which moment an expression of satisfaction slipped over the faces of their tormentors.

If there is a God who created and who still orders our world, I do not know how to worship that God, having these "facts" before my mind. If not God but the character of the universe and our place in it are at stake, then I don't know how to feel really at home here, to take the moments of peace or grace I do experience and transform them into an outlook which fully makes sense of being here.

This problem can be further explained by reference to a particular piece of traditional Jewish theology. In preparation for the observance of Yom Kippur, the most sacred day of the year, Jews are enjoined to engage in *tshuvah,* or repentance. This term signifies a "turning": toward God and away from the mistakes of our too often thoughtless, unaware life. Central to Jewish life, *tshuvah* is both a religious obligation and a spiritual model of how we may reorient ourselves to be in harmony with the Ruler of the universe.

My spiritual dilemma is that during those times when I am most conscious of the horrors of the world, I have no desire, and I think it may itself be a sin, for me to turn toward God — toward peace, acceptance, and praise. This dilemma is powerfully expressed in Elie Wiesel's memory of the struggle to observe Yom Kippur in a death camp. A fellow inmate, an observant Jew who had previously directed a rabbinical school, refuses to fast on Yom Kippur. It is not, the man says, because of physical weakness. Rather:

> Until now, I've accepted everything. Without bitterness, without reservation. I have told myself: "God knows what he is doing." I have submitted to his will. Now I have had enough. I have reached my limit. If he knows what he is doing, then it is serious; and it is not any less serious if he does not. Therefore, I have decided to tell him: "It is enough."

Later, during the traditional Yom Kippur prayers in which Jews proclaim their collective sins and ask for forgiveness, Wiesel himself rebels.

> Why did we take responsibility for sins and offenses which not one of us could ever have had the desire or the possibility of committing?...It was in order not to provoke an open war between God and his people that we had chosen to spare him, and we cried out: "You are our God, blessed be your name. You smite us without pity, you shed our blood, we give thanks to you for it...." I admit to having joined my voice to the others and implored the heavens to grant me mercy and forgiveness. At variance with everything my lips were saying, I indicted myself only to turn everything into derision, into farce. Any moment I expected the Master of the universe to strike me dumb and to say: "That is enough — you have gone too far." And I like to think I would have replied: "you, also, blessed be your name, you also."

In the end Wiesel's friend does fast. Why?

> Not out of obedience, but out of defiance. Before the war, you see, some Jews rebelled against the divine will by going to restaurants on the Day of Atonement; here, it is by observing the fast that we

can make our indignation heard.... Here and now, the only way to accuse God is by praising him.

We may praise God, but our praise is colored by a dark irony. We pray out of habit, but behind that habit is now a despair in which God is the object not of love — but of wrath.

Jewish and Christian versions of this anger will necessarily arise in the context of a personal, transcendent, creator Deity. For spiritual traditions that are not so centered, the dilemma takes a different form. In these settings — Buddhism perhaps, or varieties of witchcraft in which spiritual energy comes from the Earth — there is no personal God at whom to be angry. Here spirituality takes the form of connection to and oneness with the basic (and basically impersonal) energies or Truth of the universe. We do not turn toward God, but celebrate our relations with the larger whole; we do not pray to Another but find ourselves At Home in a world whose deepest powers hold and comfort us; or we possess a state of mind marked by patience, compassion, and acceptance.

What appeared as the Problem of Evil in Judaism or Christianity then reappears as the question: How can I feel at home here? How can peace, acceptance, or a feeling of the deep holiness of the universe arise while I am facing the truth about what the universe contains?

I might be walking across a mountain meadow, filled with simple joy at being alive. The clear air, the sound of birds, the wildflowers' riot of color, the distant sound of a stream. All these seem to be perfection itself. I feel the grace of belonging and sense the perfection of the world's deepest energies. I have found spiritual fulfillment. And then I turn a corner and I see that a truck has driven up along the old logging road and is dumping something into the stream: what is dumped hisses as it hits the water. The vapor stings my eyes and makes me cough. Some dead fish float to the surface and some water plants begin to wither, as if they had been exposed to flames.

Do I still feel "at home" on this mountainside? Do I still celebrate the world's beauty and perfection?

For those who find the whole notion of spirituality to be obscure, I can perhaps put the point in secular terms. It was expressed best by Herbert Marcuse, at the end of *Eros and Civilization,* a book in which he tried to provide a model of a truly liberated society. After describing a world in which toil and exploitation are replaced by sensual freedom and playful creativity, he concludes with these words: "But even the ultimate advent of freedom cannot redeem those who died in pain. It is the remembrance of them, and the accumulated guilt of mankind against its victims, that darken the prospect of a civilization without repression."

Or to quote a considerably less exalted source, we may remember Woody Allen's casual self-description in *Annie Hall:* "I'm the kind of person, if someone is starving somewhere, it ruins my whole evening."

Is it a kind of sacrilege to be fully happy with the world? To accept God when this world is the way it is?

A story, from the Hasidic tradition:

Rabbi Levi Yitschak of Berdichev asked an illiterate tailor what he did on Yom Kippur since he could not read the prescribed prayers.

The Jew reluctantly replied: "I spoke to God and told Him that the sins for which I am expected to repent are minor ones. I also said to Him: 'My sins are inconsequential; I may have kept leftover cloth or occasionally forgotten to recite some prayers. But You have committed really grave sins. You have removed mothers from their children and children from their mothers. So let's reach an agreement. If You'll pardon me, I'm ready to pardon You.'"

The Berdichev rabbi angrily rebuked the unlettered Jew: "You are not only illiterate but also foolish. You were too lenient with God. You should have insisted He bring redemption to the entire Jewish people."

We have the right, that is, not to let God off the hook! We can demand as well as supplicate, stand back and let the universe know we want some answers (which we probably won't get) as well as feel at one with it all. The anger does not interrupt the prayer, but is at times essential to it.

But the anger with God or the deep unease we feel about the universe as a whole does not end the story. Strangely, even magically, there is something more. Once again the Holocaust has a lesson for us. Consider the following statement by concentration camp survivor Sara Selver-Urbach, remembering her teenage years in the Lodz ghetto during the Holocaust:

Sometimes I was seized with shame because I felt happy. Happiness! How could it have entered my heart? From where came this tiny seed which longed to burst into ringing laughter, this urge in my soul and in my hands and in my arms to love, to embrace.... Today, when I think back to my long-lost youth in the Lodz ghetto, I must note that no matter how utterly illogical it seems, those were indeed the best and most beautiful years of my life. Neither before nor since have I been able to penetrate so deeply into the meaning of my existence, never again have I been capable of such profound and sincere faith, of such perfect unity with the universe, and this despite the daily deportations and relentless death that surrounded us.

What can be made of this wonderful and puzzling recollection? Completely aware of the bitter truth, she nevertheless experiences the "best years" of her life. In reality and in memory, "the daily deportations and relentless death" are with her just as much as happiness. She knew at the time that her reaction was strange, or else she would not have remembered the "shame" she felt for her happiness. Somehow, when least expected, when it makes no sense, the full beauty of life is felt. (I recall, in the months immediately after our son's death, my wife saying that despite the grief she felt sometimes the wonder of life filled her with joy. "I feel a little ashamed of it. How can anyone understand that I love him and miss him and my heart is broken — and yet I feel so happy?")

Has Selver-Urbach offered us a different model of spiritual growth and fulfillment? We might not call it peace, but perhaps it is a kind of communion. She lived in "perfect unity" with a universe that was out to destroy her, ready to embrace in a world that sought nothing so much as to degrade her capacity to love and her will to live. She was aware, at all times, of the forces arrayed against her — forces that day by day claimed the lives of friends, family, and community, forces that threatened the entire world and seemed invincible. This spiritual communion has none of the comforting guarantees of cosmic order that soothed Ram Dass. It flowered without a confident belief in an unseen future and an unfelt power.

Could it be that the very source of Selver-Urbach's joy lies in the knowledge that she must resist, and that she is resisting, the forces that would destroy her? Could it be that the source of her love is her pure knowledge of just what is at stake and her clear understanding of the

sacred goal of survival against all that is arrayed against her? Could it
be that a fierce will to live, to love, and to embrace provides its own
pure happiness?

We have found here the beginning of a spirituality of resistance, a
spirituality in which evil is not avoided, wished away, or neutralized by
a metaphysics that promises that it will be All Right in the End. In
this spiritual realm we can fully experience the deepest of joys because
we engage directly with unjust suffering by opposing it. In the act of
resistance, our acceptance of cruelty, injustice, and unnecessary death
is made complete: we embrace them by seeking their end.

A Zen Master was once asked: "How do you show compassion — that
universal Buddhist value — to Hitler?"

"Compassion for Hitler," he answered, "is simple. You kill him."

The Warsaw Ghetto revolt, which began April 19, 1943, was the longest
sustained localized military resistance to German forces throughout the
war. Although over 80 percent of Warsaw's Jews had been deported to
death camps, the remaining inhabitants of the ghetto mounted an uprising. Weakened by four years of merciless occupation, starvation, and
disease, facing a trained army and air force, the resisters were armed
with a pathetic handful of pistols, ancient rifles, and Molotov cock-
tails. Nevertheless, the Germans sustained serious losses and it took
them longer to conquer the Jews of Warsaw than it took them to defeat
Czechoslovakia or Poland. They triumphed only when the German air
force leveled all the buildings with bombs, and poison gas was pumped
into the sewers, where the last of the resistance fighters had taken
refuge.

The leader of the revolt was Mordechai Anieliwicz, a twenty-three-
year-old Socialist-Zionist. Shortly after the uprising began, he sent word
to a comrade hidden outside the ghetto. "Greetings to you who are
outside. I hope that we shall see each other again. But I doubt it. The
last wish of my life has been fulfilled. I am happy to have been one of
the first fighters in the ghetto."

Anieliwicz's happiness is not one he would have chosen for himself.
No twenty-three-year-old wants to see his community slaughtered and
know with almost complete certainty that he will be dead before long.

It was, rather, the happiness that can come from the full embrace of what God has given us. The fear of death, which had constrained a subject population, was thrown off. A world shaped by oppression could be accepted just because the oppressors were being completely resisted.

This acceptance, however, was not that usually described in spiritual literature. For one thing, it does not have even the slightest hint of passivity about it. What makes it peaceful is that by the act of resistance all the psychic energy that had been trapped by denial, avoidance, hopeless despair, untrammeled grief, or submissive waiting was liberated. The full reality of what the Nazis were could be squarely faced: they had to be opposed, even if that meant a fight with no hope of success. The signal of happiness was not quiescence but action, not calm but a fierce resistance.

Why is resistance so powerful? Because in the act of resistance we fully engage that which frightens and depresses us the most. What we would avoid, deny, submit to, or go along with is brought into full reality. We no longer have to feel that it is too much, that we cannot tolerate a world in which this exists, or that we have to let it command our obedience. We can open our hearts in full acceptance of the world, but not by telling others or ourselves that there is some cosmic meaning for all this pain.

Instead, we find that the only way to fully take in what surrounds us, to be fully at peace, is to resist. And in resistance there is not only acceptance, but also happiness.

Mordechai Anieliwicz says, "I am happy. . . . " Happy! Have we really heard him? "Happiness," says Selver-Urbach, "how could it be possible?" Because at last we are fully open to what is, an opening which takes the form not only of a flower opening in the morning sunlight but of a fighter in the ghetto.

We may well take inspiration from the Jewish resistance, which occurred not only in Warsaw but also (in a story seldom told) in every ghetto and every death camp, and throughout partisan groups in all of occupied Europe. We can find a similar inspiration in the living stories of ecological resistance. From Chico Mendes, perhaps the best known of local people who fought the mad burning of the Brazilian rainforest, to Ken Saro-Wiwa, who resisted the oil industry's poisoning of tribal lands in Nigeria. Each gave everything he had; and both were murdered for what they did.

Yet for most of "us" — the author and the audience of this particular book — the situation is considerably less dramatic. In the immediate sense, we do not face a kill-or-be-killed situation. Rather, we exist somewhere on what might be called a spectrum of assault. At one end of that spectrum are the poor and often Afro-American, Hispanic, or Native American communities victimized by environmental racism. Toxic waste dumps, incinerators, polluting mining operations, and so forth are disproportionately located in their communities. At the other end of the spectrum lie the privileged and protected, whose immediate surroundings are much less polluted. Yet all of us, regardless of where we reside on this spectrum, face certain universal problems: increased vulnerability to sunlight from holes in the ozone layer, air quality problems which frequently permeate an entire region, the shared loss of biodiversity and wilderness, a vulnerability to global warming, the widespread toxins in water and food. All these conditions are a threat. Collectively they constitute the many facets of an environmental crisis.

What is the spiritual meaning of resistance to this crisis? We might begin by remembering the statements by Sara Selver-Urbach or Mordechai Anieliwicz and realize that there can be great joy and feelings of tremendous liberation in confronting that which fills us with so much dread. Yet a simple acknowledgment will not be enough, because it is likely that the psychic stress of denial will then be replaced by overwhelming despair, grief, and rage. As we study texts like *The Last Forest, Scorched Earth,* and *Planetary Overload,* face the corporate polluters' high-priced lawyers, and watch the colonels burn the rainforest, the scope of the crisis appears so overwhelming, the odds against us so unequal, and the temporary victories so limited.

It is then that a turn of the mind and a turn of one's life — a real *tshuvah* — become necessary and possible. In this turning we can once again derive inspiration from the Holocaust. I believe that our sense of the spiritual meaning of that dreadful time is profoundly changed when we think of it not solely as the history of how the Jews were slaughtered but of how they fought back. The reality of the event is not wished away, but transformed. The images of victimization remain but are joined by images of Selver-Urbach, Anieliwicz, and countless others. Along with the piles of dead bodies we see images of resistance fighters. Auschwitz becomes identified not only with the millions who were gassed, but also with the organized network of inmates who blew up one of the crematoria. Poring over the historical record, we see that the Jews not only died by the millions, but sang songs to celebrate their survival, smuggled forbidden food into the ghettos, blew up Nazi troop trains, and at times expended superhuman courage and determination just to stay alive. When we think of the Holocaust we can remember all those moments of resistance alongside all the murders.

In the same way the despair engendered by the wholesale destruction of the environment can be redeemed by our knowledge of the people throughout the world who are resisting that destruction; and our own spiritual life can reach its most profound point when we join our energies to theirs. Our sense of the ultimate meaning of the environmental crisis may change if we see it as a time of joyful resistance, a time when we can, as Selver-Urbach did, deeply penetrate the meaning of our existence.

What is that meaning? It is, simply, to be here and to be fully a part of what we have been given. Yet being a part does not mean smiling with detached cosmic patience when we see that the rivers of Poland are so polluted they can't be used even by industry, or beaming with serene confidence that God has it all under control when we see that in the little town of Casmalia, California (home to a 250-acre liquid toxic waste dump), nearly 80 percent of the town's schoolchildren suffer from chronic respiratory illness. In such cases to be fully connected, open, and at one means to sense how wrong such things are.

What has fighting back got to do with spirituality?

Perhaps, at least at some times, they will not be connected at all. We can turn the institutions of resistance into (yet another) occasion of ego-gratification: trying to get the credit for the successes, avoiding any blame for mistakes, and above all looking to get power in our group. We can fight back with desperation, bitterness, or guilt that we are not fighting back hard enough. Since there is never a guarantee that a spiritual practice won't be used wrongly, these possibilities do not distinguish resistance from any other spiritual practice. Meditation can lead to selfish self-absorption, prayer can produce self-righteousness, and yoga can support arrogance about how fit and attractive we are. Even reading the Bible too much has been known to cause eyestrain and unjustified theological smugness.

Resistance, while often a lot more socially useful than other spiritual practices, is no exception. We can find countless examples of political activity that combined an overtone of resistance to oppression with an unpleasant undertone of self-interest, violence, and power seeking. We might think of revolutionary groups who fought for themselves and thought little of other oppressed communities. For example, women's interests were sacrificed in the attempt to get Afro-Americans the vote, white feminists initially took little note of the specific concerns of black women, liberal environmental groups ignored the "environment" of the inner city, and male radicals wanted their women to take orders and make the coffee. We can think of how Lenin, whenever his fellow leaders disagreed with him on important policy decisions, threatened to quit the group or have his opponents expelled.

Yet there are also examples in which the struggle to resist evil embodies a real spiritual grace. We can contrast Lenin to Gandhi, who typically counseled dissenting comrades to obey their own deepest sense of what was right rather than side with him out of a mistaken sense of loyalty. We can think of Cesar Chavez, who devoted his life to using nonviolent social action to better the life of farmworkers, trying to protect them from poverty and pesticides alike. We can think of numberless ordinary activists who reached out to form a union, resist apartheid, open a battered women's shelter. We can see efforts to remake a painful world stemming (at least in part) from compassion rather than hate, from a loving indignation which is not seeking to replace the old oppressors with new ones, or from an authentic anger that is a necessary stepping-stone to authentic self-respect and compassion.

In this effort, perhaps surprisingly, some of the spiritual attitudes and practices that are essential to the search for a more personal peace can be quite helpful. And this aid is necessary, just because politics, along with its insistence on collective liberation, has too often been the scene of highly individual competition, greed, and violence, or a setting for some particular group to try to advance its social position over that of other groups. Further, even the most principled of political settings can be the scene of desperation, burnout, and an egotistical attachment to one's own position.

There is, unfortunately, little that can be done "spiritually" about people who are not committed to a moral pursuit of political change. However, for those people who are so committed, and who would like to do it better, spiritual resources can provide some real assistance. Consider prayer. Authentic prayer need not, in my view, require a belief in God — though such a belief can help! Rather, prayer is a way of focusing moral intention — articulating to ourselves and the cosmos our commitment to selfless love, concern for the world, and longing for positive self-transformation. We pray for good things, it is true, but good things that make ourselves *and* others happier, ourselves and others better people. (The simplest Mahayana Buddhist prayer is: "May all beings be at peace; may all beings be happy.") We don't legitimately pray for vengeance or to win the lottery — because each of those requires that others suffer or go without. But we can pray for a peaceful heart, for an increase in compassion, for the ability to listen openly to criticism. Political settings are necessarily places of struggle, fear, anger, and aggression — all so inevitable in the contexts of oppression and resistance. Those of us who function in them would do well to pray for an openness, for patience, for the ability to get along with people who irritate us, for humility when we don't get much applause and acceptance when we get voted out of office. If our efforts at resistance are supported by a quiet sense of devotion as well as our outrage at God and the universe and the polluters, we are more likely to stay sane while we struggle to produce love rather than violence.

Or consider the Jewish concept of Sabbath — understood as a time of rest when we are to accept the world as it is. Of course the moral dimension of such acceptance is problematic, and we need not understand it as including an embrace of oppression and unjust suffering. But, as Michael Lerner suggests, we *can* see the Sabbath as a regular period of time when we will not work to make money (for our employers or ourselves) and during which we "celebrate the grandeur and mystery of the universe and recall and honor the struggles for liberation of past generations." This notion of Sabbath, derived from an ancient spiritual tradition, would do wonders for the personal lives of those involved in political resistance. It would also broaden the typical discussion of "rights" and "equality" to include a gentle appreciation for the simple and wondrous fact of being alive.

At times, resistance may be the only way to make meaning out of the pain that surrounds our lives. In classic spiritual terms, it can be a "dying of the self." But what is dying is not simply possessiveness toward objects or some obsessively sought after social position. What we renounce is our blanking out, our inauthentic erasure of what we should not forget. The horror remains horrible. It is not transformed into something else. We recognize that this universe holds the ghosts of concentration

camps, the spread of environmentally caused cancers, local famines created by the commodification of agriculture, and local ecosystems trashed
for the flimsiest of reasons. And we know that we can never really be
a part of it or experience our deepest connection to its ultimate nature
unless we oppose those parts that are evil. As with any other spiritual
orientation or practice, we cannot be sure how this type of spiritual
journey will turn out. Resistance does not guarantee bliss or spiritual
advancement, but it does, in this dark time, make them possible.

All religions have taught that we must respond to the suffering around
us, even if only, as in Theravada Buddhism, by being models of how to
overcome the ignorance that creates suffering. The Torah tells us to care
for the "widow, the stranger, and the orphan." Christianity asks us to
help the downtrodden. Islam makes giving alms to the poor an essential
part of daily religious life. However, these traditions also include the
belief that the universe is ultimately sympathetic to our moral concerns.
God is not only the Source of our morality, but a Power who envelops
our pain, promising that however bad things seem here, there is some
compensating realm.

I am not able to share that faith, and for me a spirituality of resistance unfolds without it. My commitment is to the earth. I do not
believe in guardian angels for this realm, nor that they are needed. And
after the Holocaust, I do not trust in any saving Grace. Whatever the
powers of God, I do not believe they will be used to stop human madness. The healing powers of nature, our own human ability to see the
moral truth and act on it, these will — or will not — be enough.

For me God could be at best an inspiring partner in the healing of
the world, one whose dominion is clearly so much less than infinite. At
times God is simply an image of my hope that this universe is sympathetic to our collective struggles for wholeness, peace, and justice. To
believe in God is to imagine ourselves, if only for a time, less lonely —
and thus for a moment or two to be less lonely. At the least, a belief in
God signifies that our lives — that all of life — matters. When I do pray
to "God," then, I am seeking to remind myself of what is most important in life, to reorient myself to what I have learned (often kicking and
screaming) about how I should live if I want to be truly happy (and not
merely "successful") and truly good.

Further, all religious traditions, no matter how profound, are limited by the particular view they take of the social reality in which suffering unfolds. The Sermon on the Mount, for instance, aims to give rise to respect and concern for the poor and meek, who deserve some sympathy, care, and help in their poverty. The compassion that is so strong an element in Mahayana Buddhism offers an image of numberless beings creating their own misery through various kinds of ignorance and delusion. This image applies with equal force to everyone who has ever existed, whatever their social position. From the Buddhist perspective, all of us — rich or poor, powerful or downtrodden — create our own misery by our attachment to our desires.

Over the ages, these teachings have been essential in correcting the self-centered, doctrinaire, and socially passive tendencies of mainstream religions and eclectic spiritual traditions alike. Yet they are not fully adequate to a time of Holocaust and ecocide. Here we might be much more likely to have recourse to the ideas of liberation theology, in which Christian moral teachings were adapted to the social struggle between the oligarchs who ruled Latin American dictatorships and the poor peasants and workers who were exploited and controlled by them. For liberation theology, the poor and meek deserve not just charity and care, but a fundamentally different kind of social order. We can also reach back to the ideas of the prophets of the Hebrew Bible. When the prophets call for justice — "Let justice roll down like water, and righteousness like a mighty stream," cried Amos (5:24) — they are not just telling individuals to act rightly, but are driven by a sense that the unjust are actually running the show. A spirituality of resistance cannot rest with the ideas of compassion, charity, or care, unless those ideas are embodied in a social vision that includes some sense of how human suffering is the result of a relentless, highly organized, and immensely powerful social system. A spirituality of resistance, we might say, marries traditional religious ideas of moral concern with social awareness. In an ecocidal age, that awareness will see the suffering not just of my neighbor, but of the whole world, and will extend itself to the nonhuman as well as the human.

Just what is resistance?

To begin with, to resist is to oppose superior and threatening powers, in a context of injustice, oppression, or violence. When we resist we cannot be neutral or tolerantly accept that everyone's viewpoint is equally valid. When we fight back against rape, or concentration camps, or environmental ruin, the lines are drawn.

Nevertheless, while resistance means we take a stand in the face of a painful reality, it is not always clear exactly what should be done. Nor does it mean that the people we oppose are unredeemably evil (though they sometimes are). People may take part in unredeemably evil activities, even though they are more frightened, numb, or weak than they are outright ethical monsters. What this does mean is that in answer to the question my students sometimes ask — "But who is to judge what is right or wrong?" — my answer is, "We are, each and every one of us." We make the judgment, even though the situation may be (as the Ethicist found) terribly complex. We oppose the evil, even as we try to have compassion for the evildoers.

To resist is to act with the aim of lessening the collective injustice, oppression, and violence we face. We are not resisting if all we are trying to do is get the pain shifted somewhere else. Working to have the toxins stored in the next town over, building the smokestacks higher so that the acid rain forms over someone else's forests, buying a lot of sunblock for my kids when the thinning ozone makes the sunlight dangerous — these things might be prudential, or good for my health, or clever. But they do not really count as resistance to the massive forces of environmental destruction. Individual self-protection poses no threat to the powers-that-be, but seeks to accommodate those forces, to coexist with them.

Because the engines of environmental destruction are strong, entrenched, and often mighty rich, and because, as we saw in the Ethicist's case, we carry conflicting obligations, time pressures, and simple fatigue, it often seems easier or safer not to resist. Thus if we are to act, we will need to overcome the temptations of fear or laziness, of complacency and habit. These temptations, as I know very well from my own life, are continual. Unless we are in the throes of some extreme situation — the Oil Company at the gates of our little village, as it were — or unless we are heroes, or just plain tirelessly devoted, we will give in to those temptations.

But that is not what we always do. For while the dominant social forces make it ever so easy to go along with business as usual, a realization may arise that these same forces are controlling, constraining, and limiting us. To "oppress," in this context, is related to the word "press" — as in to press down, to keep under control. To resist is to break out from under that pressure, to liberate some energy previously restrained. "I will resist" is a cry of freedom.

Since resistance involves throwing off limits, there can be an element of gladness, even joy, when we engage in it. Instead of conforming to the ways things are, living day to day with the gnawing feeling that something is not right, we refuse to go along. We attempt to halt or slow, if only in the most minuscule ways, the machinery of ruin. And when we do so we often experience the rush of feeling which comes from liberating the energy long buried by our suppressed awareness that we have been part of something we know to be wrong. In this light, the deep satisfaction recorded by Holocaust resisters makes perfect sense. They had chosen to resist — and to just that extent, no matter what the forces arrayed against them, they had become free. Their actions teach us that despite all the pain inflicted by violent oppression, freedom is always possible. Not freedom from the situation, but freedom within it.

With that freedom comes a unique and pure happiness. It may last for only a short while before it once again gets clouded by regrets for losses, confusion over strategy, and fear for the future. But for a precious time we are at one both with ourselves and the world. Life, usually so flawed, has become perfect. Feeding the world as it has fed us, we are at that moment like a bee pollinating an apple tree, like the salmon struggling upstream against the rapids to lay its eggs, like the hawk bringing back fresh kill for its chicks, like a maple tree offering soft red buds to the warming April sunshine.

Resistance takes many forms. In any given situation, we can see that there are choices to be made: between living in denial and living in the truth, between accepting the way things are and saying "no" to them. We can speak up, act up, share our concerns with others, give money, teach our children the truth, confront political candidates, write letters to the editor, join groups to keep indigenous peoples from being slaughtered, hug trees to protect forests from bulldozers, shut down the local polluter, nationalize the oil industry, and overthrow the government. For a start.

We can take a good look at what we know and try to defend it. Consider, for example, Loorie Otto of Madison, Wisconsin, who waged her own small war against monoculture. Otto discovered that the wondrous blossoms that adorned the fields and woods of her youth were becoming extinct. The flowers were dying from lost habitat and assaults by nonnative species and herbicides. It would have been easiest just to forget, to mourn the loss and move on, or to plant other, perhaps equally beautiful but less threatened flowers. But Otto refused to do any of those things. She began, instead, by letting a corner of her yard grow wild, and watching it fill with native perennials that had lain dormant in the soil. She had to fight off the city government's attempt to make all the lawns neatly trimmed grass monocultures and to make them pay damages when they cut the wild growth while she was away one weekend. Picking up steam by instructing anyone who would listen about the history and uses of these threatened plants, she got her son's school to plant native species, spread the news through cable TV and lectures, and combed backwoods areas finding — and then replanting — threatened species. She is now considered a pioneer of the natural gardening movement and tells us: "You feel so much better when you are in an area where the plants, birds and insects match up. . . . I think when people come to Wisconsin they ought to be able to look around and tell by the trees and flowers that this is Wisconsin."

In my own community of Jamaica Plain, a racially and economically mixed section on Boston's southern edge, people banded together to protect our treasured Jamaica Pond: an actual lake — one and one-half miles around — within the city limits! The pond is bordered by a thin belt of trees and graced by sea gulls, Canadian geese, ducks, exotic looking cormorants, snapping turtles, and imported swans. Its marvelously clear water attracts joggers, strollers, baby carriages, dog-walkers, drummers on hot summer nights, old Chinese ladies doing Tai Chi, and couples of various sexual persuasions dreamily holding hands. On brilliant weekends in July or sweltering August afternoons, city-owned rowboats and sailboats allow the city-dwellers to feel like they've gone away to summer estates.

When you stand at the little boathouse where popsicles and popcorn are sold, you can look across the water and see the sun set over wooded hills. These hills, which border the park but are not actually part of it, have been sold to a builder who wants to replace the old trees with luxury condos — so that proud owners can enjoy the vista of the pond while the rest of us can view the sun setting over expensive apartments.

A local social worker spearheaded the opposition, collecting four thousand signatures demanding that the local development board forbid the project and the city or state acquire the land. On the coldest night of the winter of 1998, 350 people jammed a local church to make their voices heard, to say that this spot was not only lovely, but sacred. Each of us at the meeting could have found something else to do that evening, could have left the effort to others, could have felt, "Oh, well, you can't fight the developers." But we didn't, and in the end the project was stopped.

Even as we care for what we know, it is good to be open to the unexpected. Film producer Kenny Ausubel came to New Mexico to make a film about the little-known network of "seed savers," people building a botanical ark against the rising tide of plant extinction, trying to save something of genetic variety against the giant seed companies who sell limited numbers of hybrid varieties of food crops. It would have been easier to continue with his work as planned, to leave the seed work to someone else. After all, he made films. Seeds were (weren't they?) someone else's department. Instead, he put his filmmaking aside and founded a company to unify this loose network into an international company to market organic, open-pollinated seeds. His company provides some alternative to the dominant multinationals who sell a limited range of species, typically precoated with pesticide, that require large amounts of agricultural chemicals. Greater variety means less dependence on chemicals and greater resistance to the pests or diseases that can be devastating if the range of food species grown is limited. It means a response to the fact that we've lost between 80 and 95 percent of the seed varieties we had as recently as 1900. It means an alternative to monoculture.

As we resist, we look for allies, and sometimes find them in unlikely places. Melody Chavis, a writer and community activist in Berkeley, faced a neighborhood increasingly dominated by the drug trade. She watched local kids grow up to be pushers, junkies, and gang members, and offered them something better. She connected them to a local organic gardening center, where they learned to work the land with their own hands and take deep pride in the ecological quality of what they were growing. For a number of kids the healthy connection to the soil meant a viable alternative to the polluted options that surrounded them.

Our allies can be from the neighborhood, or from very far away. As the Ethicist realized, in an ecological age "Love your neighbor" includes the whole world. Consider, for instance, the way international activity has been mobilized in response to the Narmada River Valley project in

India. Called by critics the "world's greatest planned environmental disaster," the project envisaged 30 major, 135 medium, and 3000 minor dams throughout central India. If completed as planned, it would displace close to four hundred thousand people, destroy wildlife habitat, and flood some of the last remaining tropical forest in India. As early as 1977 local opposition formed when people realized that there was in fact no land available for the local people who were to be displaced, that they would simply join the millions of other "refugees from development." During the next decade and a half opposition grew and took a variety of forms: road blockades, hunger fasts, demonstrations at state capitals, and massive gatherings at sites which were to be flooded. What is crucial here is the way a ring of international solidarity has formed around resistance to the Narmada valley project. Japanese environmentalists persuaded their government not to advance money to it, while American activists pressured the World Bank. In 1992, facing reports that the entire project was colored by fraud and incompetence, legislators in Finland, Sweden, and the U.S. asked the World Bank not to lend any more money. The International Rivers Project, located in San Francisco, organizes financial and technical aid to the continuing struggle.

Even though ozone depletion and acid rain make everyone "neighbors," we should remember that if the dam goes through, the writer and the readers of this book will not be displaced, but people in India will. We are not all affected equally by everything that takes place in the world. Martin Luther King's claim that we are bound by an "inescapable network of mutuality, tied in a single garment of destiny" must be read in the most general of ways, or else we will paper over the differences between the drowned and the saved. Yet it is also true, I believe, that similar forces are at work in crazy dam projects, unnecessary condo building, and the decimation of our seed resources. Monoculture, Big Money, blind indifference, and shortsighted thoughtlessness carry their weight everywhere. For that reason, resistance to one is resistance to all.

At times acts of resistance will demand everything we have. Domingo Gonzalez, the environmental activist who lost his family over his environmental involvement; Lois Gibbs, who went from housewife to overworked national coordinator of the national toxics movement; Chico Mendes, who was murdered for defending the rainforest and the people who live there — these and countless unknown others have put their time, money, energy, and even their lives on the line.

However, some acts of resistance will involve doing just a little more than we are doing already. We can make one extra phone call, toss a few more dollars toward the organization that is doing good work, not buy the chemicalized food, take the trouble to ask the office manager to use the organic bathroom cleanser, teach a different book in the Introduction to Philosophy course. Returns on such actions won't be as grand or dramatic as those times when we manifest a greater devotion. Still, they can be essential parts both of a worldwide environmental movement and our own, most personal, spiritual life. Like a short but heart-felt prayer, a daily ten minutes of meditation, a brief reading from the Psalms, each act of resistance can be a small but loving acknowledgment of our yearning to join the best within us to the best for others.

Finally, in resistance we can keep up our hope. Optimism of the will is not always easy to hold on to, especially as we become more and more knowledgeable about what is really going on. But our knowledge should include successes as well as failures, our moments of grace as a species and culture as well as our moments of degradation. We can read of Gaviotas, a tiny Colombian village that reclaimed seemingly barren land with sustainable agriculture, democratic decision making, and an inclusive economic structure. Its windmills convert mild breezes into energy, its solar collectors work in the rain, and children's seesaws power its water pumps. In the shelter of the Caribbean pines planted as a renewable crop, an ancient rainforest is regenerating. We can marvel at the growth of the organic food industry, the resurgent forests of the American northeast, the refusal of Australian longshoremen to unload nuclear materials, the return of the wolves to Yellowstone. We can look at the World Bank and see that it has to some extent changed its policies toward development projects, very much because people all over the world researched and publicized the truth, shared their resources, supported one another, and protested. We can marvel at the growth, in about a decade, of an environmental justice movement that includes groups from Texas to Massachusetts, from California to Georgia. All these examples of resistance can inspire our own. They are precious opportunities to know, as deeply as we know anything, that the environmental crisis is a time of great courage as well as great loss.

The question of violence arises, as it always does when politics is discussed in a spiritual context. How far are we entitled to go to protect the earth, and ourselves? There is little question that the knowing pollution of the environment is a kind of slow, anonymous violence and murder (as well as suicide). And there is no question that in some particular struggles — over the rainforest, which led to the killing of Chico Mendes, over oil, which led to the execution of Ken Saro-Wiwa — those resisting the ecological devastation have been intentionally killed.

Is violence ever justified in response to these threats?

An extended answer, which does full justice to this question, is not possible here. But I can make one small point.

I believe it is a mistake to think that "violence" is everywhere and always one thing and that we therefore can say that it is, or is not, without exception justified or unjustified. There is the violence of war, mass public slaughter initiated by impersonal governments. There are the quiet killings that are part of covert operations. There are back-alley muggings. There is domestic violence, brutality covered by a cloak of family life. There is the daily violence of racism, sexism, and homophobia. And there are all the different ways in which we can be assaulted by poisons in the environment.

Given this range (and surely many more examples could be offered), we can also think of all the different contexts in which resistance arises. There are nonviolent demonstrations against war, pacifist refusals to serve in armies, boycotts of chemicalized foods. And there are individual women who strike back against abusive husbands or indigenous tribes who try to protect themselves from hired thugs. We have the shining examples of Gandhi and King, and also the shining examples of Jews who killed guards in concentration camps and blew up Nazi troop trains.

The meaning, effect, and value of "violence" may be rather different in these different settings. And therefore I believe we must examine each one very carefully before we say, with anything like moral assurance: "This kind of resistance is justified, and this isn't."

Is this talk of resistance an invitation to anger or hatred? Am I advocating an "us vs. them" attitude that is at odds with spiritual life? Like violence, anger and hatred have also been thought to be irreconcilable with true spirituality. Whatever our actions, we are often told, they should be motivated by love and compassion, not rage. We may well want to be open to our grief for the world, but we should also maintain a kind of equanimity about those who commit even the worst crimes. Forgiveness, not hatred, is what we need. Anger will get us nowhere.

In particular, there seem to be two main reasons why hatred and anger are spiritually suspect.

First, as Thich Nhat Hanh put it, hatred of evildoers is hard to maintain if we realize that any of us, raised under certain conditions, might behave similarly. We are not so different from those "others" we condemn so harshly. Speaking of the sea pirates who rape and murder refugees from Vietnam, he says: "In my meditation I saw that if I had been born in the village of the pirate and raised in the same conditions as he was, I am now the pirate. . . . I cannot condemn myself so easily."

There is a rich sense of compassion here, but his response does not fully satisfy me. It leaves too many of my questions unanswered. While we may well want to give up our hatred, do we not owe our world the willingness to make moral judgments? Why is it necessarily true, for instance, that "as the pirate" he cannot condemn himself? If he is a pirate, does he not deserve condemnation? Wouldn't it be a mark of moral development, of real growth, for the pirate to condemn himself? Do we really want to write off the pirate as someone who could never see that what he has done is terribly wrong? Is it really respectful to the pirate to say: "Obviously, you couldn't help yourself"? Haven't there been people — from the Schindler of *Schindler's List* to the CIA operative Daniel Ellsberg who leaked the Pentagon papers, to anonymous violent criminals of all types — who have looked at their lives and repented? Isn't the whole idea of repentance based on the possibility that we are capable of the most basic kinds of moral change — and that we *should* change? Ethically, spiritually, do we want to adopt a point of view for which repentance makes little sense?

To say "I would be the pirate" is to exchange moral responsibility for a kind of fatalism. Put me there, Thich Nhat Hanh is saying, and I would behave as badly. But are people, after all, just the products of their environment? I do not believe so. In every social setting, no matter how twisted, we can find people who stood against evil. From Nazi Germany to the slaveowning South, from societies overrun by militarism to the destructive march of economic "development," some spirits have always cried "no." This is partly because human beings are free, and also because our social environment is itself not just one thing. Social settings contain a variety of messages. To be sure, some are trumpeted and some whispered. But we always have some choice as to which ones we will heed. Every society provides examples of honor or compassion from which we can learn. Even under the most brutal dictatorships, some people manifest love and care, which can then be extended to those the regime would dismiss as less than human.

Of course, from one point of view — that of the social planner or the policy maker — we do have to treat people like products of their environment. Knowing how people generally react to what is around them enables us to make decisions about educational programs, offer guidelines for parents, and criticize violence in the media. But when as individuals we face painful moral decisions, try to do the right thing, or justify our actions to others, such "I'm just a product" thinking radically weakens moral life. Praise and blame, taking responsibility when we must and offering explanations if they are valid, these are all part of ethical existence. (My daughter used to justify her misbehavior by pleading, "But, Dad, that's just what kids do." My reply, which understandably didn't please her, was "Well, maybe so. And I'm going to take away some of your privileges. That's just what parents do.")

Thus although hatred may be a mistake, moral judgment is not. If we cannot condemn what the pirate has done, then we are in for some real trouble, because then we will not be able to stand for something morally or to teach our children: "Here is a good person, and here is a bad one." This does not mean that we cannot have some compassion for the path that brought him to his ways or that we must seek to punish the bad man after we have stopped him. And it does not mean we have to carry ourselves with moral arrogance. It simply means that we are moral beings, and being moral includes making real judgments, taking real actions, and committing ourselves to one type of life over others. A morality that sees no difference between the generous and the cruel, between Gandhi and Hitler, between the sea pirate and Thich Nhat Hanh, would not be very useful.

A spirituality of resistance does not command us to hate those responsible for evil, though surely feelings of hatred will arise at times if we acquaint ourselves with the truth of the world's evil. Nor does it demand that we constantly feed our anger — as long as we can continue to act without it, and as long as we are not avoiding the truth to keep ourselves from getting too perturbed. It is about resistance, the refusal to accept the world's evil, the commitment to act against it. To do so we must name that which we resist, be able to say what it is and why we resist it. Can we resist compassionately, without hatred? We will need to try. Here is where the traditional teachings about the psychic effects of hatred have an important place. Because hatred indicates a sense of powerlessness and upsets our own inner balance, we will do better to get past it. The key issue, however, is to act. We can keep in mind that, as Gandhi said, it is better to act with hatred than not to act at all, and that a period of hatred, supplanting one of passive fear, may well be a necessary step toward a greater ability to be compassionate.

In a related way, we are often taught that the emotional energy of anger is self-destructive. It poisons the person who carries it, twists the soul, and robs one of any chance of serenity. (As the Dalai Lama said, when asked if he was angry at the Chinese for the genocidal treatment of his people: "They have taken everything we have; I will not give them my peace of mind as well.")

Such a view of anger is, I think, too simple. Like violence, anger is not always one thing — always destructive, always toxic. Depending on how we integrate it into our lives, it can be as worthy an emotion as joy or love. Anger is, we might say, a kind of wake-up call. It demands that attention be paid. In the first place, anger can teach us about the quality of our most important relationships, about what is lacking, and about what needs to be done. When there is a violation of trust, safety, or rights, the feeling of anger is appropriate. Also, a passionate concern with the sorrows of the world indicates a precious willingness to keep our minds and hearts open to others. Such anger can be a loving gift — as, for instance, when it is directed at war's waste of life. However, the twisted resentful anger we might feel because someone else got the promotion we thought was ours is a different story, as is the sexist rage sometimes directed at women who speak up for themselves. In short, the emotion itself is neither good nor bad, loving nor toxic. Like all the details of relationships the Ethicist had to examine, the spiritual value of anger can be assessed only if we discern what it tells us about the world and ourselves. We can enter into anger, see what it has to teach us, without immediately acting it out. We won't discover anger's lessons, however, if we are unable to tolerate it, if we seek to banish it the moment it appears, or if we simply try to detach ourselves from what provokes it. It is the inability to be in the presence of our anger, not anger itself, which so often provokes uncontrolled violence, bitter revenge, or the loss of peace of mind.

And what of forgiveness? Isn't that the proper "spiritual" response to evildoers? I am not so sure. Consider Simon Wiesenthal's haunting story

The Sunflower, in which a dying Nazi soldier, responsible for the deaths of innocent Jews, asks a Jewish survivor for forgiveness. The story ends as the soldier describes what he has done. The Jew is silent, refusing to respond. Perhaps, some commentators suggest, he did not have the right to speak for the others and to forgive. Perhaps he wanted to and couldn't.

And as we now face the poisoned earth, do we have the right to forgive? And if we cannot forgive — either the people who have done all this or the Great Cosmic Spirit in which or in front of whom it un-folds — then what chance have we to realize in our hearts the spiritual states of stillness, serenity, and compassion?

Let us imagine Mordechai Anieliwicz at the moment of his death. His rebellion has been crushed; his friends and family are gone. Is there anything that would allow him to forgive the murderers? Would he be a more spiritual person if he did? What would it mean, in the end, to forgive them? When we talk about the virtues of forgiveness, such extreme situations — which admittedly few of us face — paint these questions in bold relief.

To begin with, it seems to me that for us to authentically forgive someone, we must have, at the least, some sense of rough equality with him or her. The powerless do not truly forgive the powerful if the latter have all the guns and police on their side and the former have noth-ing but their pain. Only if the downtrodden are able to develop a new sense of themselves — some kind of identity that doesn't depend on social power — can they mobilize the personal strength to forgive. To forgive others, as opposed to merely groveling before them, we must in some sense be as powerful as they are. This sense of power can come, as Nietzsche observed, by imagining an indefinite future (a heaven) in which God reverses the scales of power and success. Similar security can be found in the idea of karma, which asserts that today's sinner will pay tomorrow (or, at least, in the next life).

But if we are seeking to live on this earth and are not banking on Other Realms, then it seems to me that the solid sense of self which is the precondition of forgiveness might be found only in acts of resis-tance. In resistance we fully sense our own strength, value, and ability to act. In resistance we get beyond the hopeless passivity of victimhood. Only then can we honestly see the folly of having our minds dominated by bad feelings toward another. We can then view the guilty with true compassion, since compassion will not be a mask for our own paralysis or impotence. We can forgive the evildoers when they have been rendered powerless — or at least can let go of our hatred because we ourselves have achieved a sense of our own moral and spiritual force. Perhaps this is what Gandhi had in mind when he stressed that civil disobedience is anything but passive. And when he further counseled that it was better to act, even violently, than to be so overcome with fear as to be unable to act.

Without resistance, forgiveness becomes too much like surrender, too much like forgetting all the victims, too much like an evasion of fate.

There is a further significance to the process of resistance, one that helps us confront the dilemmas raised about what work in the world means to us. We have seen that a crucial source of modern, institutionalized, technologized forms of mass destruction is located in an exaggerated and unquestioning attachment to our jobs or careers, to our participation in large and powerful institutions. Lacking the ability to feel that one has a self outside of one's job, profession, social role, or nationality, we get swept up into the madness toward which these institutions are directed.

Now spiritual identity has long been offered as an alternative to social life. The love of God is meant to compensate for the suffering caused by oppression, the riches of heaven for earthly poverty. To me, however, the promise of a future bliss doesn't compensate for the miseries of the present. I see little guarantee that all this suffering has a higher purpose. I only see (as in Ram Dass's case) a desperate wish that it be so.

Once more resistance provides a way out. In fighting back we find a meaning, an identity, a sense of what is of ultimate value about ourselves. This meaning is both spiritual and social, both transcendent and as grittily earthy as can be. All the dissolution of ego praised by the great spiritual teachers occurs; it occurs, however, not as an escape from a social situation that is just too painful to face, but as an embrace of all that surrounds us.

These deepest spiritual connections are active, not passive. They involve hope, risk, and making decisions. As we engage in resistance we must weigh alternatives, face demons in others and ourselves, and truly know what we have lost. All these activities are of a different order from some of the other images of spiritual development with which we may be familiar: the benevolent expression, the comfortable body posture on the meditation cushion, the person rapt in prayer about the state of her soul, the dreamy concentration on the face of God.

It is not that any of these images are in themselves bad or false. We all need a little quiet, a little (or a lot more) peace. There is a time to worry about the condition of our individual souls, to ask for help from the Goddess, to dream of heaven. But for me, these are not the apex of spiritual life. Not now at any rate. For outside the meditation room, the cathedral, the ashram, or the synagogue, too much of life is being maimed and poisoned. Whatever we call that life — fellow children of God, God's body, Mother Earth, God's Beloved Creation, Gaia — it calls to us now. And it is in our willing response that we just might find our highest spiritual vocation.

If we look at the people who are engaged in environmental resistance, we may see some of the essential features of the kind of spirituality I am trying to describe. As one might have studied the lives of biblical prophets, Buddhist sages, or Christian saints, we can discover something in them that will enlighten and inspire.

To begin with, we can discover that in acts of resistance people lose a good number of the conventional forms of self-doubt and insecurity that contribute to their usual powerlessness and victimization. There are countless examples of this in the national toxics movement, most of which was organized from the ground up by housewives with little education, no technical expertise, and social identities based in traditional female roles. Time after time these women, burdened with awareness of the illnesses of their own and their neighbors' children, had to trust their own growing sense that something was deeply wrong. They had to face down government spokespeople who said that the illness in their families came because they "didn't know how to clean their houses" rather than from the toxic slag that came from the nearby lead smelter. They had to resist the engrained sexism that forbade women to speak in public, make demands on legislatures, and challenge engineers and scientists. But these women, resisting the economically and politically sanctioned poisoning of their communities, conquered their fear, shed habits of servitude, and reached new levels of authentic power.

The spiritual lesson here is that resistance can liberate our ability to engage in life to the fullest, that we can go well beyond the imposed limitations of a social order that would keep us in chains of self-doubt and deference to authority. Is not spiritual life in part about shaking off the unnecessary chains of the conventional ego? Resistance can be a key to just that unshackling.

Consider Diana Steck, a housewife from Yukon, Pennsylvania, who confronted the chronic illnesses of her own and many of her friends' children. She saw the relation between their health problems and the liquid dump nearby that contained chromium, cadmium, lead, arsenic, mercury, and dozens of other toxic chemicals. She struggled with government officials who condescended to her, promising an investigation and doing nothing. She faced health "experts" who told her she didn't know what she was talking about. Luckily, she stumbled across Lois Gibbs, who had been through it all before at Love Canal and told her to reach out to her neighbors. She and some others became a group with a name, received training in grass-roots environmental politics, got arrested for sitting-in at a state office, and took over a crucial public meeting when public officials tried to dodge the issue. Like Domingo Gonzalez, all this put a stress on her family. Her husband wondered why his wife had to take on the whole world. Her children would sometimes complain: "You love the dump more than us. Why can't we have a normal life." Friends and relatives were shocked when she was arrested or tried to stop trucks from going to the dump. But Diana had become a different person, one who wouldn't get stopped by her own fears or others' judgments. "All this," she said, referring to countless illnesses in her town, "happened for a reason. Otherwise we'd still be out here, just stupidly working and making money, oblivious to the world around us. We wouldn't be the people we are today. We wouldn't be as complete."

Another characteristic of resistance is a simple joy from knowing that what we are doing is of real value to others. This is not the greedy pleasure of the pursuit of fame, for in this context what sometimes shines through is the impersonal joy of service. This impersonal joy can be found in Anieliwicz's saying that he was "happy" to be one of the first ghetto fighters. He was happy that what he had to give could be offered in the right way at the right time — even if it was his sad fate to do so in the midst of mass murder. Here we realize how we can "feed" the world as it feeds us.

In a contemporary setting, we find the widely read Nigerian author Ken Saro-Wiwa working on behalf of his country's Ogoni tribe. The tribe had been devastated by oil development by Royal Dutch Shell: livestock destroyed, rivers and air poisoned, terrible diseases spreading.

Saro-Wiwa lent his name and skill to the fight, itself an almost classic environmental tale of corporate power, a national government seeking to get rich off destructive economic development, and a local subsistence community ravaged. Saro-Wiwa was imprisoned and tortured for his work and then executed by the Nigerian government in 1995 on trumped up charges. During his last months he wrote to a friend:

> I'm in good spirits.... There's no doubt that my idea will succeed in time, but I'll have to bear the pain of the moment.... The most important thing for me is that I've used my talents as a writer to enable the Ogoni people to confront their tormentors.... My writing did it. And it sure makes me feel good! I'm mentally prepared for the worst, but hopeful for the best, I think I have the moral victory.

One need only think of the familiar ego involvement most of us have with our work: all the problems with conventional public identity, including the desire to stand out, the need to fill an internal psychic emptiness, and an addictive attachment to unending "success." Saro-Wiwa's story contains just the opposite, for he was willing to give up precisely the social identity most of us cling to, in order to resist.

The overcoming of oppressive limitations, a simple joy at giving in a difficult situation — these are some of the fundamental spiritual values that arise in resistance. But there is more: in acts of resistance we can also experience a transcendence of self and feel a deep connection beyond the boundaries of the isolated ego.

The Australian rainforest activist John Seed, engaging in civil disobedience to obstruct the clearing of a major area of forest, realized:

> I was able to embody, to bring to life, my intellectual knowing in interaction with other beings — protesters, loggers, police, and with the trees and other inhabitants of these forests. There and then I was gripped with an intense, profound realization of the depth of the bonds that connect us to the Earth, how deep are our feelings for these connections. I knew then that I was no longer acting on behalf of myself or my human ideas, but on behalf of the Earth... on behalf of my larger self, that I was literally part of the rainforest defending herself.

In this well-known reminiscence we find something surprising and wonderful. The spiritual sense of connection emerges in a concrete piece of political action. Seed is not experiencing this oneness as he hikes in the wilderness, kayaks solo in a bay filled with waterfowl, or visualizes his power animal. It is the activity of resistance that calls forth the jubilant sense that he can be part of something so much larger than his own flesh, so much more enduring than the limited history that began when he was born and will end with his death. Is this not an almost perfect example of spiritual fulfillment?

In my own experience, only with a spirituality of resistance can I know the full joy of loving, and living on, this earth. I can remember political actions during the sixties and seventies that gave me great joy. I knew, as I stepped into a Washington street to stop traffic to protest the Vietnam War or stood in a supermarket parking lot asking shoppers to avoid the nonunion lettuce, that I could be fully at home on the earth. A rich sense of kinship swept over me, pushing aside my obsessive concern with proving myself. I felt the depth of my connections to the Others — and to the best parts of who I was. When I first began to take small acts in defense of the environment, I felt as if a great weight were taken off my shoulders. I could look myself in the eye again without flinching. I was touched by a simple but profound gladness at being alive, at being part of the human and more-than-human worlds.

I am neither a saint nor a hero. I haven't given up everything for the cause. And I have, like most other people in their fifties, experienced enough anguish to make me feel at times that I only want to care about myself and my family. But at least I can give some of my energies to help those in pain and to serve this earth. And I can know that such giving, rather than the quiet times of meditation and prayer, is really at the center of my spiritual quest.

Most of us will not be heroes. Chico Mendes and Mordechai Anieliwicz are sources of inspiration, but few of us are so brave. Like the Ethicist and his friends, we will all have other concerns a good deal of the time. These limits, and the inconsistencies of behavior they lead to, are to be expected. Almost every spiritual life is more like a long (and thus, by definition, troubled) marriage than like some cosmic event that works once and for all. In our relationship to the Divine or Inner Truth we grow closer and further apart; have days, weeks, or even years when we don't get along very well; experience breakthrough moments when everything seems clear and wonderful; enjoy long periods when the relationship works well; and then find ourselves slipping, bit by bit, into distance and frustration. My point is simply that it is precisely the movement of resistance which may signify the times when the relationship is at its best, when we are most at home in this troubled world.

If spirituality means, among other things, moving beyond my isolated ego (and this is, indeed, the way it is frequently portrayed), then resistance is that movement. For in acts of resistance I move beyond my isolation, my self-concern, my very sense of myself as fully separate ("I was part of the rainforest..."). And that sense of moving beyond my ego takes me not only into connection with the suffering Others who are human, but with the more-than-human as well. I can walk over to Jamaica Pond, pat the trunk of a sugar maple tree I pass along the way, and say, only half believing I won't be understood: "You and me, pal, we're in this together. Best of luck to us both." I can know that my kinship with the beings of this earth is essential to who I am and that I will not let them be wantonly destroyed without some defiance.

Perhaps then I can join the Ethicist in getting a good night's sleep. For I will have, if only for a time, entered into a communion with this earth that God has given me — and to which I have been given. The painful struggle for justice; the compassionate action for the suffering of others; the refusal to say, "Let the evil be, I have other things to do and to think about, and besides, it is All in Good Hands" — these moments in which I am at my best serve as the gateway to a full celebration of life. And within that sense of life, joined and fulfilled not only by the easy but also by the difficult, not only by sweetness but also by grief, within that sense and only then, I can let go of what has bound me to the pain. I can put down my burden of selfhood and responsibility, that searing sense that I must make it all better. There will be moments, and the memory of those moments may carry me through the other times, when I realize that I am merely a brief flower of mind and feeling in this vast meadow of existence. At my best I will try to be a true flower and not some plastic rose that doesn't bloom and will not wither for a hundred years. I will have offered myself to all the other flowers, to the life and health and blossoming of the rest of this garden we call the earth. Having done so I will then be able to feel the full sweetness of the springtime sun, the evening rain, and even the approach of the chill winter morning of my own natural, fitting, and joyous death.

Afterword

"That's all quite moving, if a little overwrought," said Harry, as he took another sip of decaf latte from the garish extra large mug he always brought to the Farbucks coffee shop. (Harry never used the thick, disposable cups: "Waste of paper, and of the resources used to produce them, and of landfill space when they're garbage," he'd say, leaving out any mention of the resources it took for him to drive to Farbucks, or to import his favorite coffee from Senegal to the unnamed North American city he lived in.) "But it's so, I don't know, *individualistic*, so narcissistic. Here is the environmental crisis, the world is in desperate shape. Here's this virtual juggernaut of globalization making resistance to pesticides or genetically engineered foods or toxic additives to gasoline something democratically elected governments can be sued over, for God's sake. And here this guy Gottlieb seems most concerned with the state of his own precious soul. It seems to me that thinking about environmental problems in terms of some weird idea of spirituality is just a distraction. This is not about 'feeling at home on the earth'; it's about power. The big global corporations have the armies, and most of the governments, and the money boys (the World Bank, the International Monetary Fund, the NAFTA regulators) on their side. What have the rest of us got?

"I'll give you one example: Enron spreads a little money around some state government in India, and as a result, that government commits to buying power from Enron-built plants. Enron's plants produce electricity that's three times as expensive as Indian plants, and the U.S. government applies the screws when the locals try to change the deal. And, surprise, surprise, America's assistant ambassador to India gets a fat job at Enron when he leaves the state department. The end result is billions of dollars going from some poor area of India to a U.S. corporation. I could tell you endless stories like that.

"If we don't build an international movement of the masses, a movement that's willing to be just as tough as the big boys we're fighting, we're all screwed. Resistance isn't about one person just looking around his neighborhood; it's about building an international movement for real economic democracy. For most of the people in the world, all this stuff about 'finding a peaceful heart' is just an impossible luxury. They are worried about eating, about having any work at all, about pollution from some plant killing their kids."

"Calm down Harry," laughed Sarah, blowing on her gingermint tea to cool it. "You'll give yourself a headache. I don't think you're saying anything Gottlieb isn't aware of, but look who he's writing for. You think the people losing their villages in the rainforest or trying to breathe the coal dust-polluted air from China's brave new industrialization need this book to tell them there's an environmental crisis? The great tragedy is that many of the people directly or indirectly responsible for the world environmental crisis are the people most shielded from what's actually going on. Here in the middle and upper classes of the United States, or in northern Europe or Japan, we face global warming and pollution, sure. But a lot of it is displaced or hidden away. If our water or air get dirty, we buy spring water and air purifiers. If our kids get asthma from the pollution we certainly don't like it, but those of us with health care can see a specialist and get the latest steroids and inhalers. We don't have to watch our kids coughing and wheezing themselves to death.

"Yet it is our government and the giant corporations we work for or invest in (or our pension plans invest in) that are at work. And we're the ones who have the luxury to worry about our peace of mind. I think that's why Gottlieb's simple message is important: No political awareness, no resistance, no confrontation with the environmental crisis—no peace of mind!"

Leo cleared his throat, swallowing the last bit of cinnamon scone he'd been nibbling on, and the other two glanced at him expectantly. He was their friend, and they all enjoyed gathering at Farbucks to discuss books, the news, and each other's lives. But he tended to get a little nervous around heavy criticisms of "huge corporations" or "capitalism." His father had come to the United States from Poland to escape the violent rhetoric (and reality) so easily employed by communist dictatorships. "Well, capitalism may have its weak points but at least there's freedom to make changes. Just like Gottlieb, you keep harping on the evils of corporations. I'd rather face them than some repressive 'revolutionary' party."

"Who likes repression?" demanded Harry. "But the world has plenty of repressive regimes that never had anything to do with communism. I mean the ones that welcome the polluting industries and shoot any worker or peasant who tries to resist. Besides, except for China and Cuba and North Korea, communism is dead. Seen any great improvements in the world environmental picture now that the Evil Empire has fallen and capitalism rules the roost? I sure haven't."

"Who can even tell?" Leo replied. "There's good stuff and bad stuff. I can't get any sense of the whole picture—the world's just too big. We've got global warming, that's for sure; and mass extinctions of lots of species. But some corporations are trying to be more responsible. Not just Ben and Jerry's or The Body Shop either. Compaq and Toyota and even British Petroleum are trying to be a lot greener in what they do. And look at this: in Bangladesh there's a movement of peasants committed to organic farming. *Nayakrish Andolon*, it's called. They refuse to use chemical fertilizers or pesticides, and they save seed varieties, and they try to use their food for local consumption instead of tying into the world market. And this group is not just a few Westernized types, but 60,000 poor peasants. Think they'd be allowed to decide that under communism? The city of Ciutuba in Brazil combines social services and job training and mass public transportation and beautiful downtown parks. All this not in an isolated village but in a city of close to 2,000,000 people. The spirit behind it came from a lot of folks, but the center was one man: the mayor—who had a kind of spiritual vision of people and the city and the land all coming together."

"Yeah, I read McKibben's book too," said Harry, "so I've heard of Ciutuba. But don't forget his other happy story there: Kerala. That's where people living on less than 400 dollars a year have gotten nearly a hundred percent literacy, a life expectancy in the seventies, and are approaching gender equality. And all of that without polluting industrialization and consumerism. But if you want to know how that happened, don't look for some spiritual visionary. And don't look for benign corporations either. It was the communist party of Kerala that set it in motion.

"And speaking of benign corporations, I'll be impressed when these noble 'green capitalists' devote some advertising dollars to encouraging us all to consume less, not more. Or when they stop making their SUV plants 'greener' and just stop making SUVs! Until that happens, I'll keep harping on the evils of corporate power!"

"What all this means," said Sarah, playing her usual conciliatory role, "is that there is no one single answer. It's not just individual visionaries, or mass movements, or the very poor, or the spiritual types in the Western middle classes. It's all of us. Every environmentalist needs every other environmentalist. Everyone who seeks justice *here* needs everyone who seeks justice *anyplace else!* Whether or not corporate globalization is better or worse than communist dictatorships, one thing is clear: the forces of globalization are very well organized and they do a good job supporting each other. We'd better do the same."

"Well, talking about 'all of us,' brings up something else that bothered me about this book," chimed in Leo. "I mean, this is a book about spirituality, right, but there's practically no mention of God. Everything is 'horizontal'—what I feel, what other people need, the earth, the animals, the trees. There's nothing 'vertical,' nothing transcendent, nothing really holy. I mean . . . there's no God!"

"And that bothers you?" smiled Harry.

"You're darn right!" said Leo. "What's religion without a sense of God? Where else will morality get some real support? We go for the spiritual because it makes us feel good. Well, what if something else makes us feel good? Is it going to be all right to give up on morality then? God created us and has told us what is right and what is wrong. That's what religion is and that's the foundation for even thinking about people having rights or being worthy of respect: that we're all made 'in the image of God.' All this talk of spirituality is really a cover for self-indulgence. It ends up being pretty wishy-washy—if it doesn't start out that way."

"Oh I don't know," said Sarah. "I guess like anything else, there's spirituality and spirituality. When it's people just looking to be more comfortable it's self-indulgent; for some being more peaceful allows them to feel the reality of other people's pain, and to act to lessen it. But you're certainly right that a traditional belief in God seems to have a particular power to motivate. It just seems more forceful than a sense of spirituality which focuses on the self instead."

"Yes, it's forceful all right," interjected Harry, an edge of irritation in his voice. "About as forceful as a large explosion. Do the words '9-11' mean anything to you? Those guys had a very clear handle on what God wanted and what they were supposed to do about it. Religious believers aren't really the greatest place in the world to look for ecological wisdom or social justice, if you know what I mean. The stronger the religious spirit, the more intolerance, fundamentalism, and fanaticism. That's why religion should only be done in private among consenting adults. Bring it into politics and all you get is a big mess. I prefer Gottlieb's brand of spirituality. At least it's innocuous."

"You're not being fair, Harry," chided Sarah. "Or, at least, you're certainly not being particularly accurate. Of course the fundamentalists get the big press. But it is simply not true that they are the only game in town. There are plenty of religious thinkers, and movements, and groups, who have learned how to respect other people's faiths, about the importance of democracy and human rights, and who are hard at work changing traditions of sexism or disrespect for the earth. Why, just the other day on TV, I saw this slick ad about defending the Alaskan National Wildlife Refuge from oil development—and guess what? It was cosponsored by the Sierra Club and the National Council of Churches. This guy Bartholomew, head of the Eastern Orthodox Church (which only has around 150 million members) says straight out that pollution is a sin. Some Evangelicals in the United States are asking everybody, 'What would Jesus drive?' to make them think twice about SUVs. A friend of mine is part of the Interfaith Coalition on Climate Change; they've got chapters in eighteen states and he's working with Buddhists, Jews, Catholics, Moslems, and liberal Protestants and even some Evangelical types to change our stand on global warming. Even though they are 'people of faith' from different religions, they all get along because they are willing to support one another on environmental issues, and they take it for granted that in some general sense the differences in the names of God or rituals aren't really that important."

"Oh well," said Harry, "Maybe when I generalize about 'religion' I'm not really thinking about these kinds of things. But you have to admit, Sarah, that *most* of religion is politically conservative, doesn't give a damn about nature, and is really just after protecting its own institutions and promoting its own narrow view of God and morality."

"No I don't *have* to admit anything," Sarah replied, smiling. "But even if that *is* true, so what? Maybe most religious believers are politically conservative, don't take the environmental crisis seriously, and don't pay attention to things like environmental racism. Of course, you shouldn't forget that it was a research report by the United Church of Christ that helped propel environmental racism to national attention. Somehow the marvelous secular environmental groups hadn't shown much interest until a bunch of black ministers pointed it out!

"But even if a lot of religious people are more part of the problem than the solution, isn't that true of secular folks as well? Religious or secular, most of us are bystanders to the world's evil, whether it's some dramatic terrorist attack or the quiet deaths caused by economic power.

"You know something? This world scares me. And it's not just al-Queda and the Religious Right, but the secular fanatics as well. Around 3,000 people were killed by religious lunatics on 9-11. And we've seen that this sort of thing is going on all over the world. But that's not the only kind of terror there is. When Union Carbide's plant blew up in Bhopal a lot more people were killed. Tribes are wiped out because some oil company devastates their land. Hundreds of thousands, probably millions, of deaths from cancer are caused by polluting industries. Is it really going to help us to argue over whether the religious fanatics or the corporate ones are worse? There has got to be some third choice between religious violence and secular violence. There just has to be."

"So what you're saying," observed Leo, "is that knowing that people are religious or secular doesn't really tell us very much about them."

"That's right," Sarah answered. "It doesn't tell you whether they are environmental or antienvironmental, incredibly violent or deeply committed to peace, into voluntary simplicity or hooked on consumerism. Of course it would be really easy if we could just know that believers are moral and secular people immoral—but even a casual glance at last year's headlines about the sex abuse scandal in the church should end that notion. Likewise, it would be reassuring to know that a good liberal commitment to economic modernization and human rights will take care of all our problems. Unfortunately, even a casual glance at the state of our air, water, and climate show us that individual rights and a free market can be pretty dangerous if they are not surrounded by some kind of commitment to the encompassing communities of both people and nature."

"So . . . have we come full circle?" Leo wondered.

"What do you mean?" Harry asked.

"Confusion, despair, fear, and hopelessness. There's no clear path, no easy certainties. No wonder that guy couldn't get to sleep."

"Oh, I don't think it's as bad as that," Sarah said soothingly, pausing to admire a new moon rising in the crystal clear night sky. "If we really look, we can see a good deal of what's wrong in the world. And even if we don't have some reassuring fable about how God or the masses or progress or technology will save us, we can tell that there are good things going on: real, live resistance that we can be part of. Whether it's Nayakrishi Andolon or the Interfaith Coalition on Climate Change or work against environmental racism or bringing our own mugs to Farbucks," ("Hey, that's me," chortled Harry), "we have enough light to find a path to struggle for the earth and each other. If we are not heroes, (and Gottlieb is right there, few of us are) we can always be a little more moral than we are right now. Every situation has choices—to live worse or live better, to consume more or less, to let things pass or to challenge them. And if we're humble enough as we pursue those choices, we're a little more likely to see when we've made mistakes and correct them."

"Still," said Leo, "there seems to be something missing from all this."

"Isn't there always," murmured Sarah. "But what exactly do you mean?"

"I mean," Leo went on, "that part of religious—or, what the heck, *spiritual*—life that is not about ethics or morals or relating to other people at all. I mean those quiet, precious moments when it's just you and God. Or, to be fair to my Buddhist friends, when it is simply the clarity of breath and awareness, and we no longer have a sense of self. Whether it's dissolving the ego or standing in the light of the Lord, part of religion or spirituality or mysticism takes us out of history and society and everything that we do with other people. Gottlieb's book just doesn't seem to take that sort of thing seriously."

"You're right," said Harry. "Even I, who take all this talk of God and Spirit with a very large grain of salt, can see that his version of spirituality is really a lot of social critique masquerading as something else."

"I don't think so," replied Sarah. "Not at all. I think he really believes that we can find peace, and get over our ego, and serve God. He's just very concerned that all that sort of thing not be a cover for self-indulgence. He believes that if spirituality doesn't look like social critique, it's going to look like selfishness: whether the selfishness of the narrow believer who 'knows' the ultimate truth and will shove it down your throat or the selfishness of someone who thinks a purely personal peacefulness is all that God—or the Spirit—requires of us."

"But why talk about God and Spirit at all?" Harry broke in impatiently. "We've got the world, and other people, and injustices to fight. Why drag in this other stuff? It's unnecessary."

"Is it?" Leo asked. "But then tell me, Harry, why do you bother with that dopey mug of yours? Why do you care if there's a little more pollution or waste?"

"Because, dammit, the world is beautiful and precious and we shouldn't foul it up. People, animals, the forests . . . life should be cherished, all of it."

"And that," said Sarah quietly, "is just the point. When you say that what we have on this earth is precious and beautiful, that we should—no, that we want, that we must!—nurture it instead of tearing it to bits—well, when you say that your political environmentalism itself becomes a kind of spirituality. You're not just interested in your own fate, or that of some limited group. For all your bluster and anger there's a kind of selfless love in what you do and what you seek. And that's why you—who get a headache when someone uses the word 'religion'—can have a common cause with all those who want to 'save the rainforest in Jesus' name' (as the Christian Evangelical group Target Earth wants to do) or who believe that the earth is sacred because it is the Body of God.

"And don't forget one last thing, which Gottlieb seems to. Without some spiritual clarity, some self-awareness and compassion, political action aimed at changing things often gets as violent and unproductive as what it's trying to change. Some kind of spiritual grounding can help all the passionate fighters, even you, Harry! Maybe if you learned to meditate you'd get fewer headaches."

Surprisingly, Harry smiled, "As the saying goes, then, maybe this can be the beginning of a beautiful friendship between the environmentalists and the spiritual types."

"God willing," chimed in Leo, also smiling, "God willing."

"Oh well, it's getting late," said Sarah, "and I have to be at the office early tomorrow morning. I'm talking to my supervisor about redesigning the building so we'll use less energy. I piss him off because I won't let it alone." She laughed a little anxiously, "I hope it won't cost me my job."

"I've got more work tonight," sighed Harry, "so I'll probably drink some more coffee. My group is doing a presentation at the mayor's office this Friday. We've got the hard facts on where toxic waste facilities are located around here. Can you just guess which neighborhoods they are in? Our little report might create a bit of a fuss."

"Good luck on that," said Leo. "As for me . . . I'm going to catch the midnight mass. And maybe I'll talk to the priest about doing something special for Earth Day. He's a nice fellow but simply doesn't know very much about what's going on."

The three said their goodbyes and parted, taking with them the warm glow of friendship and a tiny, if temporary, bit of hope.

Behind the Farbucks counter Maria Dellato, who had come north to the United States after her Central American village had been turned into a coffee plantation and her brother had been killed for trying to protect it, looked after them as she cleaned the large pots. It was hard to tell exactly what expression was in her eyes.

Notes

Chapter 1: Spirituality and Resistance

Page 14. **about how we feel.** These ideas are developed throughout Kierkegaard's writings. See especially *Either/Or* (Princeton, N.J.: Princeton University Press, 1963) and *Concluding Unscientific Postscript* (Princeton, N.J.: Princeton University Press, 1966).

Page 15. **at radioactive waste sites.** There are wonderful exceptions in some of the recent writings of "engaged" Buddhism. See Arnold Kotler, ed., *The Engaged Buddhist Reader* (Berkeley: Parallax Press, 1996).

Page 15. **really we just don't know.** Pema Chodron, *When Things Fall Apart: Heart Advice for Difficult Times* (Boston: Shambala, 1997), 9.

Page 18. **described in very limited ways.** See Kotler for different approaches.

Page 18. **frustrating qualities of normal life.** Sharon Salzberg, *A Heart as Wide as the World: Living with Mindfulness, Wisdom, and Compassion* (Boston: Shambala, 1997).

Page 18. **for mainland, white Americans.** International Physicians for the Prevention of Nuclear War, *Radioactive Heaven and Earth: The Health and Environmental Effects of Nuclear Weapons Tests in, on, and above the Earth* (New York: Apex Press, 1991), 81–84.

Page 19. **to create difficulties everywhere.** Kierkegaard, *Concluding Unscientific Postscript,* 165–66.

Page 20. **peace as the end approached.** Leo Tolstoy, *The Death of Ivan Ilyich;* Elisabeth Kübler-Ross, *On Death and Dying* (New York: Macmillan, 1969).

Page 20. **someone other than it is.** Steven Levine, *Who Dies?* (New York: Doubleday, 1982), 157.

Page 21. **he was robbed of his death.** Elie Wiesel, "The Death of My Father," in *Legends of Our Time* (New York: Henry Holt, 1968).

Page 22. **stems from environmental causes.** Sandra Steingraber, *Living Downstream: An Ecologist Looks at Cancer and the Environment* (Reading, Mass.: Addison-Wesley, 1997).

Page 22. **It's all O.K.** Levine, *Who Dies?* 169, 162.

Page 23. **perceptions of the one existence.** Levine, 171.

Page 24. **kind of material immortality.** See Linda Lear, *Rachel Carson: Witness for Nature* (New York: Holt, 1997), 86; Rachel Carson, *The Sense of Wonder* (New York: Harper & Row, 1965).

Page 25. **relates to other people's suffering.** The account of Buddhist history is based on many sources, including E. Conze, ed., *Buddhist Texts through the Ages* (New York: Philosophical Library, 1954), and E. A. Burtt, ed., *The Teachings of the Compassionate Buddha* (New York: New American Library, 1955).

Page 26. **one's own individual situation.** Other issues were at stake, but for the present discussion, only this one is crucial.

Page 27. **spiritual destinies are incomplete.** For a rich contemporary account of this dimension of Judaism see Michael Lerner's *Jewish Renewal* (New York: Harper, 1994).

Page 30. **will inevitably pull through.** Joanna Macy, *World as Lover, World as Self* (Berkeley: Parallax Press, 1991), 16–17.

Page 32. **most of my energy here.** I have worked at the other direction in a number of places: for instance, the last chapter of *Marxism 1844–1990* (New York: Routledge, 1992); "Heaven on Earth: A Dialogue between a Political Radical and a Spiritual Seeker," in Roger S. Gottlieb, ed., *A New Creation: America's Contemporary Spiritual Voices* (New York: Crossroad, 1990); "Spiritual Deep Ecology and the Left," in Roger S. Gottlieb, ed., *This Sacred Earth: Religion, Nature, Environment* (New York: Routledge, 1996).

Chapter 2: No Place to Hide

Page 34. **the "more-than-human."** This wonderful phrase comes from David Abram's *The Spell of the Sensuous* (New York: Pantheon, 1995).

Page 37. **avoid the threatening news stories.** This line of reasoning is indebted to Jean-Paul Sartre's critique of Freud's theory of the unconscious, in *Being and Nothingness* (New York: Pocket Books, 1966).

Page 38. **consisting in not having any.** Søren Kierkegaard, *Concluding Unscientific Postscript* (Princeton, N.J.: Princeton University Press, 1966).

Page 41. **years in 1995–97.** World Resources Institute, *World Resources 1998–99* (New York: Oxford University Press, 1998), 186.

Page 45. **that mark its history.** John Nance, *What Goes Up: The Global Assault on our Atmosphere* (New York: Morrow, 1991).

Page 47. **write the regulations themselves.** Dan Fagin, Marianne Lavell, and the Center for Public Integrity, *Toxic Deception: How the Chemical Industry Manipulates Science, Bends the Law and Endangers Your Health* (Secaucus, N.J.: Birch Lane Press, 1996).

Page 47. **cancer continued to rise.** Robert Proctor, *Cancer Wars* (New York: Basic Books, 1995), 73.

Page 48. **witness the ruin that had taken place.** Bruce Rich, *Mortgaging the Earth: The World Bank, Environmental Impoverishment, and the Crisis of Development* (Boston: Beacon Press, 1994), 120.

Page 48. **where they can't be easily seen.** Dashka Slater, "Dress Rehearsal for Disaster," *Sierra* (May–June 1994).

Page 48. **adequate news coverage.** Al Gedicks, *The New Resource Wars: Native and Environmental Struggles against Multinational Corporations* (Boston: South End Press, 1993).

Page 48. **where the mine would be located.** Gedicks, *The New Resource Wars*, 43, 62.

Page 48. **lied to the government about the findings.** Proctor, *Cancer Wars*, 80, 179.

Page 48. **like irradiation and genetic engineering.** See "Food Slander Laws in the U.S.: The Criminalization of Dissent," *The Ecologist* 27, no. 6 (December 1997).

Page 49. **can be subpoenaed.** "Researcher Investigating Toxin Becomes Subject of Investigation," *Minneapolis Star Tribune*, May 17, 1998.

Page 50. **not just experience, but imagination, wasn't it.** Gita Sereny, *Into That Darkness: From Mercy Killing to Mass Murder* (New York: McGraw Hill, 1974), 151.

Page 51. **he alone knew the truth.** Elie Wiesel, *Night* (New York: Avon Books, 1958), 16–18.

Page 52. **Clan of One-Breasted Women.** Terry Tempest Williams, *Refuge* (New York: Vintage, 1991), 283.

Page 53. **and other government agencies.** "Lawmakers want to bar talk about global warming," *Boston Globe*, July 7, 1998.

Page 53. **news services and on-line information sources.** See the journals mentioned earlier in this chapter, as well as the wonderful on-line newsletter *Rachel's Environment and Health Weekly* (erf@rachel.org).

Page 54. **this is mine; this is my self.** See, for example, Edward Conze, *Buddhism: Its Essence and Development* (New York: Harper, 1951), and Lucien Stryk, ed., *World of the Buddha* (New York: Anchor, 1969).

Page 54. **they deserve our attention.** The next paragraphs are indebted to Miriam Greenspan's work, especially her forthcoming *Healing through the Dark Emotions.*

Page 54. **terribly needs to be done.** Sandra Steingraber, *Living Downstream: An Ecologist Looks at Cancer and the Environment* (Reading, Mass.: Addison-Wesley, 1997), 232.

Chapter 3: Working Ourselves to Death

Page 61. **out the best in me.** I realize that this is not always the case in political life, which can be marked by self-seeking and violence.

Page 62. **carries on for a lifetime.** Kierkegaard, *Concluding Unscientific Postscript.*

Page 68. **killed myself in 1938.** Gitta Sereny, *Into That Darkness* (New York: Vintage, 1983), 364, 39.

Page 70. **between the two events.** For two comprehensive treatments of the Holocaust which will support this claim, see Raoul Hilberg, *The Destruction of the European Jews* (New York: Harper, 1961); Leni Yahil, *The Holocaust: The Fate of European Jewry* (New York: Oxford, 1990).

Page 71. **the Jews be exterminated.** Richard Breitman, *The Architect of Genocide: Himmler and the Final Solution* (New York: Knopf, 1991), 202–4.

Page 71. **bloodstream as bottle-fed infants.** See Sandra Steingraber, *Living Downstream: An Ecologist Looks at Cancer and the Environment* (Reading, Mass.: Addison-Wesley, 1997), 237–39.

Page 71. **corporate, and governmental enterprises.** I am not saying that this is the major explanation of the Holocaust, only that it may be the one most relevant in helping us explain the environmental crisis. Other causes of the Holocaust included: religious anti-Semitism, pseudo-scientific racism, violent nationalism, historical trauma, militarism, psychological authoritarianism, and class struggle.

Page 72. **dissension from Nazi policies.** See, for instance, M. Geyer and J. Boyer, eds., *Resistance against the Third Reich 1933–1990* (Chicago: University of Chicago Press, 1992); Detlev J. K. Peukert, *Inside Nazi Germany* (New Haven: Yale University Press, 1987).

Page 72. **point of no return.** Christopher R. Browning, "Bureaucracy and Mass Murder: The German Administrator's Comprehension of the Final Solution," in Asher Cohen, Jav Gelver, Charlotte Wardi, eds., *Comprehending the Holocaust: Historical and Literary Research* (Frankfurt: Verlag Peter Lang, 1988), 174.

Page 72. **indifferently or even apathetically.** Hilberg, *The Destruction of the European Jews*, 576.

Page 72. **service of mass murder.** Christopher Browning, *Fateful Months: Essays on the Emergence of the Final Solution, 1941–2* (New York: Holmes and Meier, 1985), 58.

Page 72. **for a job well done.** See Saul Friedlander, "From Anti-Semitism to Extermination," in François Furet, ed., *Unanswered Questions: Nazi Germany and the Genocide of the Jews* (New York: Schocken, 1989); and Daniel Goldhagen, *Hitler's Willing Executioners: Ordinary Germans and the Holocaust* (New York: Knopf, 1996).

Page 72. **save their "favorite Jews."** Breitman, *The Architect of Genocide*, 243–44.

Page 72. **"more humane" forms of murder.** Breitman, *The Architect of Genocide*, 220.

Page 73. **with genocide were seriously punished.** See Daniel Goldhagen, "The Paradigm Challenged," *Tikkun* (May/June 1998).

Page 74. **"private, still moral" self.** See, for instance, Robert Lifton's theory of "doubling," in *The Nazi Doctors: Medical Killing and the Psychology of Genocide* (New York: Basic Books, 1986).

Page 74. **totally different from you and me.** Goldhagen's position, in *Hitler's Willing Executioners.*

Page 76. **scientific study were completed.** Robert N. Proctor, *Cancer Wars: How Politics Shapes What We Know and Don't Know about Cancer* (New York: HarperCollins, 1995), 190.

Page 76. **AEC wanted to pay attention.** Proctor, *Cancer Wars,* 191.

Page 77. **global warming treaty of 1997.** On the industry group, see *New York Times,* April 26, 1998. For a summary of information about global warming, see *Rachel's Environment and Health Weekly* no. 596, April 30, 1998 (*www.monitor.net/rachel/*).

Page 78. **that are destroying the world.** For this "cultural feminist" view, see (among many others), writings by Carol Gilligan, Nancy Chodorow, Jean Baker Miller, and Jan Surrey.

Page 79. **Jews who managed the camp.** Sereny, *Into That Darkness,* 207.

Page 79. **his "hardest time."** Sereny, *Into That Darkness,* 249.

Page 80. **it was irreversible.** Sereny, *Into That Darkness,* 202.

Page 80. **removed from our own lives.** This is the express perspective of Goldhagen, *Hitler's Willing Executioners.*

Page 81. **used against them in court.** Dan Fagin, Marianne Lavell, and the Center for Public Integrity, *Toxic Deception: How the Chemical Industry Manipulates Science, Bends the Law and Endangers Your Health* (Secaucus, N.J.: Birch Lane Press, 1996), 2–6.

Page 82. **the truth about formaldehyde.** Fagin et al., *Toxic Deception,* 5.

Page 82. **working on something interesting.** Hugh Gusterson, *Nuclear Rites: A Weapons Laboratory at the End of the Cold War* (Berkeley: University of California Press, 1996), 54.

Page 87. **he himself was doing his job.** As opposed to Goldhagen's interpretation, which is closed to the possibility that the use of cruelty was careerist as well as sadistic.

Page 91. **he remembers with pride.** Deborah Shapley, *Promise and Power: The Life and Times of Robert McNamara* (Boston: Little, Brown, 1993), 9.

Page 91. **largest number of people.** Shapley, *Promise and Power,* 18.

Page 92. **inefficient way to run a planet.** Shapley, *Promise and Power,* 477.

Page 92. **while discussing a new project.** Shapley, *Promise and Power,* 477.

Page 92. **that he himself was "ordinary."** Shapley, *Promise and Power,* 541.

Page 92. **onto the production line.** Shapley, *Promise and Power,* 520.

Page 93. **an institution to fulfill his dream.** Shapley, *Promise and Power,* 480–81, 492, 504–20.

Page 93. **as abstract industrial inputs.** Bruce Rich, *Mortgaging the Earth: The World Bank, Environmental Impoverishment, and the Crisis of Development* (Boston: Beacon Press, 1993), 40.

Page 94. **water tables in arid regions.** Rich, *Mortgaging the Earth,* 135.

Page 94. **to obscure its failures.** Rich, *Mortgaging the Earth,* 576–77.

Page 94. **declined to virtual extinction.** Rich, *Mortgaging the Earth,* 114–15.

Page 94. **benefited from the Bank's programs.** Rich, *Mortgaging the Earth,* 552.

Page 94. **be part of the action.** Rich, *Mortgaging the Earth,* 537.

Page 95. **numbers to suppress uncertainties.** Rich, *Mortgaging the Earth,* 567.

Page 95. **or a "banality of evil."** For instance: Susan Griffin, *A Chorus of Stones* (New York: Doubleday, 1992), *The Eros of Everyday Life* (New York: Doubleday,

1995); Richard Schmitt, "Murderous Objectivity," in Roger S. Gottlieb, ed., *Thinking the Unthinkable: Meanings of the Holocaust* (Mahwah, N.J.: Paulist Press, 1990); Rich, *Mortgaging the Earth*, 222, 237; Hannah Arendt, *Eichmann in Jerusalem* (New York: Viking, 1964).

Page 96. **as Miriam Greenspan observes.** Miriam Greenspan, "Befriending the Dark Emotions," *Common Boundary* (May 1998).

Page 97. **sustain us in our morality.** This idea derives somewhat from Kierkegaard's notion of the relation between ethics and religion. See *Either/Or*, vol. 2.

Page 98. **I did everything I could.** I don't remember the source of this story. It made the rounds during the years of nuclear terror.

Page 101. **bear with one another.** Quoted in Raghaven Iyer, ed., *The Jewel in the Lotus* (Concord, Mass.: Concord Grove Press, 1983), 323.

Chapter 4: A Sleepless Ethicist

Page 109. **not opposed the war.** Quote taken from *The People's Century: Total War,* a documentary shown on public television.

Page 111. **study of global warming.** *The End of Nature* (New York: Times Books, 1989).

Page 112. **people who handle them.** E. Chivian et al., eds., *Critical Condition: Human Health and the Environment* (Cambridge: MIT Press, 1993).

Page 114. **we do for the animals.** Raymond Bonner, *At the Hands of Man* (New York: Knopf, 1993).

Page 114. **surroundings cannot be separated.** Robin Broad, *Plundering Paradise* (Berkeley: University of California Press, 1993).

Page 114. **future ties to the land.** For an account of a contemporary struggle, see Joe Kane, *Savages* (New York: Knopf, 1995).

Page 115. **can save virtually anything.** David Quamen, "Evitable Fate: Carl Jones and the Mauritius Kestrel," *Orion* (Spring 1996).

Page 116. **in public or political life.** Jürgen Habermas, *Legitimation Crisis* (Boston: Beacon Press, 1978).

Page 116. **we achieve a monoculture.** Vandana Shiva, *Staying Alive: Women, Ecology and Development* (London: Zed Books, 1989).

Page 117. **their produce to a world market.** This analysis comes from Vandana Shiva, *The Violence of the Green Revolution* (London: Zed Books, 1991), and *Monocultures of the Mind* (London: Zed Books, 1993).

Page 118. **peccary meat for a week.** Mark J. Plotkin, *Tales of a Shaman's Apprentice* (New York: Viking, 1993), 194.

Page 119. **virtual culture of extinction.** Susan Pollack, "The Last Fish," *Sierra* (August 1995). See also Dick Russell, "Vacuuming the Seas," *E Magazine* 7, no. 4 (July/August 1996), and Dick Russell, "The Crisis Comes Home," *E Magazine* 7, no. 5 (September–October 1996). The phrase "culture of extinction" comes from Fred Bender.

Page 120. **Daddy, don't go, Daddy, don't go.** This discussion is based on Bruce Selcraig, "Border Patrol," *Sierra* (May–June 1994).

Page 121. **gets reduced to the Same.** For a rather abstract philosophical account of this same-other dynamic, the reader might consult the work of French philosopher Emmanuel Lévinas.

Page 122. **includes the nonhuman as well.** For a survey of this "deep ecological" view, see Roger S. Gottlieb, "Spiritual Deep Ecology and the Left: An Attempt at

Reconciliation," *Capitalism, Nature, Socialism: A Journal of Socialist Ecology* 6, no. 3 (September 1995). Reprinted in Roger S. Gottlieb, ed., *This Sacred Earth: Religion, Nature, Environment* (New York: Routledge, 1996).

Page 122. **interaction with the nonhuman.** David Abram, *The Spell of the Sensuous* (New York: Pantheon, 1996). See also works by Paul Shepard.

Page 123. **centering point of my existence.** Richard Nelson, *The Island Within* (New York: Random House, 1989), 93.

Page 123. **wetsuits and surfboards along.** Nelson, *The Island Within,* 89.

Page 124. **Different from All the Rest.** This is David Abram's thesis in *The Spell of the Sensuous.*

Page 124. **a hot meal at dusk.** E. O. Wilson, *Biophilia* (Cambridge: Harvard University Press, 1984), 12–13.

Page 125. **a spontaneous, a "natural," monoculture.** David M. Graber, "Resolute Biocentrism: The Dilemmas of Wilderness in National Parks," in Michael E. Soule and Gary Lease, eds., *Reinventing Nature? Responses to Postmodern Deconstruction* (Washington, D.C.: Island Press, 1995).

Page 125. **soil and animals are seriously affected.** "Hawaii Declares War on a Plant," *Boston Globe,* April 15, 1996.

Page 125. **extinction by the new arrivals.** Graber, "Resolute Biocentrism," 130.

Page 125. **take only the tongues and the humps.** See Noel Perrin, "Forever Virgin: The American View of America," in Daniel Halpern, ed., *On Nature: Nature, Landscapes and Natural History* (San Francisco: North Point Press, 1987).

Page 126. **displace forest and field.** Also, fragmented forests make many species more liable to predators. There is a further dependence on forests in Latin America: as they are cleared for settlement or agriculture, the wintering grounds of American songbirds are destroyed. Scott K. Robinson, "Nest Gains, Nest Losses," *Natural History* (July 1996).

Page 129. **desire for a boat ride.** References are to Aldo Leopold and J. Baird Calicott.

Page 130. **what a mess we've made of it.** Compare this list to Stephen R. Kellert's account of the nine values which nature has for us: *The Value of Life* (Washington D.C.: Island Press, 1995). Also, one could easily map the different schools of environmentalism (conservationism, social ecology, etc.) onto this list by seeing which of these relationships forms their principal concern.

Page 131. **better sources of information.** Albert Borgman, "The Reality of Nature and the Nature of Reality," in Soule and Lease, eds., *Reinventing Nature?*

Page 131. **ain't gonna move by itself.** Lois Gibbs, quoted in Celene Krauss, "Women of Color on the Front Line," in Robert Bullard, ed., *Unequal Protection: Environmental Justice and Communities of Color* (San Francisco: Sierra Club Books, 1994), 263.

Page 132. **animal extinctions in the Americas.** Clive Ponting, *The Green History of the World* (New York: St. Martins, 1991).

Page 133. **Where is the line?** For an account of black flies, including different attitudes toward them where they are a "nuisance," see Sue Hubbell, *Broadsides from the Other Orders: A Book of Bugs* (New York: Random House, 1993), 74–89.

Page 134. **AIDS and Ebola viruses.** See Robert H. Boyle, "Phantom," *Natural History* 105, no. 3 (March 1996); "Beware the Killer Algae," *E Magazine* 7, no. 2 (March/April 1996); Rodney Barker, *And the Waters Turned to Blood* (New York: Simon and Schuster, 1997).

Chapter 5: Finding a Peaceful Heart and Protecting the Earth

Page 142. **response of an open heart.** Joseph Goldstein and Jack Kornfield, *Seeking the Heart of Wisdom* (Boston: Shambala, 1987), 105.

Page 143. **species, which will disappear.** Ram Dass, in Catherine Ingram, *In the Footsteps of Gandhi: Conversations with Spiritual Social Activists* (Berkeley: Parallax Press, 1990), 194, 192.

Page 144. **intricacies of his providence.** David Hume, *Dialogues Concerning Natural Religions* (New York: Hafner, 1969), 67.

Page 144. **common fulfillment in the future.** Lawrence Kushner, *Honey from the Rock: Ten Gates from Jewish Mysticism* (New York: Harper and Row, 1977), 59; my emphasis.

Page 148. **spring after the winter.** Rachel Carson, *The Sense of Wonder* (New York: Harper and Row, 1965), 89.

Page 149. **higher thought or a better emotion.** Ralph Waldo Emerson, *Nature: Addresses and Lectures.*

Page 149. **there are no more trees.** Eric Valli, "Golden Harvest of the Raji," *National Geographic* (June 1998).

Page 149. **this simple spiritual practice problematic.** A point made in conversation by Miriam Greenspan.

Page 152. **most passionate forms of love.** Quote from Georg Sand, in *The Family of Man*, created by Edward Steichen (New York: Museum of Modern Art, 1955), 167.

Page 153. **the faces of their tormentors.** Nathan Cohen, "Diaries of the Sonderkommando in Auschwitz: Coping with Fate and Reality," *Yad Vashem Studies* 20 (1990): 303; from the diary of Leib Langfus.

Page 155. **to accuse God is by praising him.** Elie Wiesel, "Yom Kippur," from *Legends of Our Time* (New York: Henry Holt, 1968).

Page 156. **a civilization without repression.** Herbert Marcuse, *Eros and Civilization* (New York: Vintage, 1955), 216.

Page 156. **to the entire Jewish people.** This tale appears in many places. Quoted here from Philip Goodman, ed., *The Yom Kippur Anthology* (Philadelphia: Jewish Publication Society, 1971), 118.

Page 157. **relentless death that surrounded us.** "A Brief Spring," in J. and E. Eibishitz, eds., *Women in the Holocaust* (Brooklyn, N.Y.: Remember, 1993), 49. Miriam Greenspan brought this passage to my attention.

Page 158. **the first fighters in the ghetto.** In Ber Mark, "Warsaw Ghetto Uprising," in Yuri Suhl, ed., *They Fought Back* (New York: Schocken, 1975); Leni Yahil, *The Holocaust: The Fate of European Jewry* (New York: Oxford, 1991), 109. For other resources on resistance, see Lucien Steinberg, *Jews against Hitler* (Glasgow: University Press, 1974); 457–98; Hermann Langbein, *Against All Hope: Resistance in the Nazi Concentration Camps 1938–1945* (New York: Paragon House, 1994).

Page 161. **from chronic respiratory illness.** Fred Setterberg and Lonny Shavelson, *Toxic Nation: The Fight to Save Our Communities from Chemical Contamination* (New York: John Wiley, 1993), 31–36.

Page 162. **a mistaken sense of loyalty.** References to Gandhi in this chapter are based on a variety of his writings, but especially Louis Fischer, *The Life of Mahatma Gandhi* (New York: Harper, 1950).

Page 163. **for liberation of past generations.** Michael Lerner, *Jewish Renewal: A Path to Healing and Transformation* (New York: Harper, 1994), 347.

Page 165. **actually running the show.** A well-known liberation theologian applies the position to ecology in Leonardo Boff, *Ecology and Liberation: A New Paradigm*

(Maryknoll, N.Y.: Orbis Books, 1995). On the prophets and justice, see Abraham J. Heschel, *The Prophets: An Introduction* (New York: Harper, 1955), 195–220.

Page 165. **just what is resistance?** I've offered a detailed analysis of this concept in "The Concept of Resistance: Jewish Resistance to the Holocaust," in Roger S. Gott-lieb, ed., *Thinking the Unthinkable: Meanings of the Holocaust* (Mahwah, N.J.: Paulist Press, 1990).

Page 166. **to keep under control.** This understanding is developed beautifully in Marilyn Frye's *The Politics of Reality* (Freedom, Calif.: Crossing Press, 1983).

Page 167. **the machinery of ruin.** I can remember Mario Savio, leader of the Berkeley Free Speech Movement, making this point in a speech at Brandeis in 1965. "Throw yourself," he told us, "on the very gears of the machines that are destroying the world."

Page 167. **but freedom within it.** There is some resonance with the work of Sartre here, especially his play *The Flies.*

Page 168. **that this is Wisconsin.** Steve Lerner, *EcoPioneers: Practical Visionaries Solving Today's Environmental Problems* (Cambridge, Mass.: MIT Press, 1997), 19–26.

Page 169. **an alternative to monoculture.** Lerner, *EcoPioneers*, 309–20.

Page 169. **options that surrounded them.** Melody Ermachild Chavis, *Altars in the Street* (New York: Belltower, 1997).

Page 170. **Narmada River Valley project in India.** See accounts of this in Bruce Rich, *Mortgaging the Earth: Environmental Impoverishment, and the Crisis of Develop-ment* (Boston: Beacon Press, 1993), 251–53; and Madhava Gadgil and Ramachandar Guha, "Ecological Conflicts and the Environmental Movement in India," in Dharam Gahi, ed., *Development and Environment: Sustaining People and Nature* (Oxford and Cambridge: Blackwell, 1994).

Page 170. **single garment of destiny.** "Letter from a Birmingham Jail," in W. Chafe and H. Sitcoff, eds., *In Our Time: Readings on Postwar America* (New York: Oxford University Press, 1995), 183.

Page 171. **courage as well as great loss.** See Alan Weisman, *Gaviotas: A Village to Reinvent the World* (White River Junction, Vt.: Chelsea Green Publishing Co., 1998); Bill McKibben, *Hope Human and Wild* (Boston: Little, Brown, 1995).

Page 173. **condemn myself so easily.** Thich Nhat Hanh, *Being Peace* (Berkeley: Parallax Press, 1983), 62–64.

Page 175. **peace of mind as well.** I heard this many years ago in a TV interview and have no idea how to pin down the source.

Page 175. **always destructive, always toxic.** I am particularly indebted to Miriam Greenspan for this point.

Page 176. **Jewish survivor for forgiveness.** Simon Wiesenthal, *The Sunflower* (New York: Schocken Books, 1975).

Page 178. **the nearby lead smelter.** Ronald Robinson, "West Dallas versus the Lead Smelter," in Robert Bullard, ed., *Unequal Protection: Environmental Justice and Commu-nities of Color* (San Francisco: Sierra Club Books, 1994). This entire book and *Toxic Nation* are excellent resources for this issue.

Page 179. **wouldn't be as complete.** Setterberg and Shavelson, *Toxic Nation*, 41–65.

Page 180. **have the moral victory.** Ken Saro-Wiwa, *A Month and a Day: A Detention Diary* (New York: Penguin, 1995), xiv–xv.

Page 180. **rainforest defending herself.** John Seed, *Thinking Like a Mountain* (Philadelphia: New Society Publishers, 1988), 6.

Afterword

Page 183. **governments can be sued over**. The antiglobalization literature is now huge. For informative recent treatments, see Jerry Mander, "Economic Globalization and the Environment," *Tikkun* (September–October 2001); Mark Weisbrot, "Tricks of Free Trade," *Sierra*, September–October 2001; the International Foundation on Globalization, www.ifg.org; and Global Exchange, www.globalexchange.org.

Page 183. **area of India to a U.S. corporation**. See Arundhati Roy, *Power Politics* (Boston: South End Press, 2002).

Page 185. **greener in what they do**. See Joseph Romm, *Cool Companies: How the Best Businesses Boost Profits and Productivity by Cutting Greenhouse Gas Emissions* (Washington, D.C.: Island Press, 1999).

Page 185. **60,000 poor peasants**. See Farida Akhter, "Resisting 'Technology' and Defending Subsistence in Bangladesh: Naykrishi Andolon and the Movement for a Happy Life," in Veronkika Bennholdt-Thomsen, Nicholas Faraclas, Claudia von Werlhof, eds., *There is an Alternative: Subsistence and Worldwide Resistance to Corporate Globalization* (London: Zed Books, 2001). And the Nayakrishi Andolon website: http://membres.lycos.fr/ubinig/naya/

Page 185. **the land all coming together**. Bill McKibben, *Hope Human and Wild* (St. Paul, Minn.: Ruminator Press, 1997)

Page 186. **I mean . . . there's no God**. See David S. Toolan, "God's Good Earth" (review of *A Spirituality of Resistance*), *America*, October 16, 1999.

Page 186. **in the image of God**. For this position, see Michael Perry, *The Idea of Human Rights* (New York: Oxford University Press, 1998).

Page 186. **focuses on the self instead**. A position argued by Rodney Stark in *One True God* (Princeton, N.J.: Princeton University Press, 2001).

Page 186. **in private among consenting adults**. A position forcefully argued by the leading political philosopher of the last thirty years, John Rawls. See his *Political Liberalism* (New York: Columbia University Press, 1995).

Page 187. **aren't really that important**. For a wide range of sources on religious environmentalism, see Roger S. Gottlieb, ed., *This Sacred Earth: Religion, Nature, Environment, Second Edition* (New York: Routledge, 2003). For an expanded account of the convergence of religion and secular environmentalism, see chapter 7 of Roger S. Gottlieb *Joining Hands: Politics and Religion Together for Social Change* (Cambridge, Mass.: Westview, 2002).

Page 190. **it is the Body of God**. Target Earth is a Christian organization seeking to "love our neighbors as ourselves and to care for the earth," www.targetearth.org; Sallie McFague, *The Body of God: An Ecological Theology* (Minneapolis: Fortress Press, 1993).

Page 190. **even you, Harry**. The full version of this argument is in Gottlieb, *Joining Hands*.

Page 190. **expression was in her eyes**. Extremely helpful comments from Nick Baker, David Barnhill, and Miriam Greenspan improved this afterword.

Index

DATE DUE